RESOURCES FOR YOUTH MINISTRY

Resources
for
Youth Ministry

Edited by
Michael Warren

PAULIST PRESS
New York/Ramsey/Toronto

Library of Congress
Catalog Card Number: 77-14806

ISBN: 0-8091-2083-6

Published by Paulist Press
Editorial Office: 1865 Broadway, New York, N.Y. 10023
Business Office: 545 Island Road, Ramsey, N.J. 07446

Printed and bound in the
United States of America

Contents

vi   *Contents*

PART II

DEVELOPING DIOCESAN PROGRAMS

PART III

DEVELOPING LEADERSHIP

PART IV

SPECIAL ISSUES

Contents vii

Introduction

This book represents a hope born almost five years before its publication. Between 1973 and 1975, as specialist for youth catechesis in the Department of Education at the United States Catholic Conference and charged with assessing the state of youth catechesis in the United States, I was introduced in my travels to many persons doing creative ministry with teens. I had a sense that some of the people were ahead of their time—indeed, were forging a new day for ministry to American Catholic youth.

Most of these persons were relatively unknown, especially outside their immediate area or diocese. Also, most of them did not see themselves as writers and had never considered making available to others written accounts of their projects. Ironically, during that same period, except for the seeking out of writers by Sheila Moriarty O'Fahey and Mary Perkins Ryan, editors of a remarkable catechetical journal called *Pace,* there was relatively little writing done on practical work in youth catechesis or youth ministry. Thus, I determined that part of my role at the national level would be to encourage these persons to put in writing their vision as embodied in their experiments. As nearly as I can remember, almost none of these persons, even after my initial encouragement, ever submitted on her or his own an article for publication.

Last year, with the encouragement of Robert Heyer, editor at Paulist Press, I decided to solicit from these persons accounts of their work. By that time I knew each of them personally. Letters, phone calls, in-person encouragement at various national meetings, were helpful in prying loose some of the excellent material in this book. I am pleased to have here a record in writing of some of the creative efforts at ministry to youth that have characterized a bit of the American Catholic experience in the early to mid-seventies. In addition, I know that several of these writers are pleased to have finally articulated for others their own vision and tactics.

1

Now that the material is assembled, I find it interesting to see certain common elements that surface through many of these articles. One of these is a preoccupation with the relationship of ministry and spirituality. If not at center stage, that concern is there at least in the shadows of almost all these articles. This is a matter that must continually preoccupy those in any ministry, including youth ministry. It shows a sound direction for the future. Another feature of these articles is a concern with calling others to ministry. These practitioners are not interested in a pseudo-ministry of domestication but rather a work of liberation and of summoning others to be sharers in ministry. Is not this feature a mark of any true ministry in the name of the Gospel? A third common feature is the kind of language found in most of these articles. It is a language preoccupied with ministry itself, rather than with instructing and running programs. These writers represent, I think, a growing consciousness of ministry as the dominant focus of efforts on behalf of the Gospel. Such a language and focus are relatively new among Catholics in the United States.

I wish to point out that three-fourths of the articles in this book were written by laywomen and laymen. This fact suggests that pastoral action at the local level is in the active and competent hands of laypersons. These lay ministers are obviously taking their own ministries seriously; it remains for those at higher administrative levels in the Church to encourage these persons to stay in ministry and to make it possible for them to do so.

Finally, hidden in most of these accounts are principles of ministry applicable to other ministries in the Church. Serious attempts to understand the personal and cultural situation of those being served, to meet their real needs, to call them into fellowship in the name of Jesus, and eventually to summon them to ministry characterize most of the accounts in this book. These same attempts should be marks of ministry to any age group in the Church, not just ministry to youth. We can all hope that continued imaginative praxis of ministry to youth will enrich the wider Church for many years to come.

Part I

Developing Parish Programs

Youth Parish Workshop

Richard Costello

Richard Costello's report on his Youth Parish Workshop is an example of innovation and creativity in youth ministry. The concept out of which Costello was working was bold and daring when he attempted it a few years ago and would still be daring today in many parts of the country. As a comember of the catechetical team to which Costello belonged, I can remember the difficulties and even heartaches that eventually became associated with this project. Richard Costello omits for the most part those aspects of his youth parish efforts. I mention them here by way of insisting that difficulties are no criterion of the ultimate value of our efforts to take innovative approaches with youth. For the young people involved in the youth parish project, the entire effort was a major learning experience of the true nature of Church and of the possibilities of its coming to life.

Though merely alluded to in the following report, another aspect of the project, and one that formed a major context for the entire effort, was the matter of prayer and worship. Costello has begun the formation of a community of prayer as a first step toward a "parish." The ambience of the workshop itself was one of close attention to prayer, especially the Eucharist. This ambience is hinted at in the final paragraphs of this report; they should not be overlooked.

Finally, behind this project of Richard Costello, the reader will find a belief in the concept of parish, that is, of groups of Christians bound together in the fellowship of faith in the Father of Jesus. Though some pastors feared this program would subvert youth's affiliation to parish, the program goals were quite the opposite. One of the guiding principles of Costello's ministry to youth was rather that of assembling the community and of summoning youth to be part of the larger parish structure.

"Open your eyes, hey look around you!" proclaims the anthem of the Pepsi Generation. For the current generation of Church leaders and religious educators, however, it may not be such an enticing invitation.

If we open our eyes and look around, especially at Sunday Liturgy, we can't help noticing that most of the faces belong to parishioners who have long since passed the "soda pop" stage.

We are forced to conclude that there just aren't as many young people attending church as there used to be.

But teenagers are not just absenting themselves from church attendance. Enrollment in catechtical programs for grades nine through twelve is also down in most parishes in most dioceses across the country.

Certainly it is one thing to open our eyes and see the problems that confront us; it is quite another matter to provide a vision to deal creatively with the situation.

The Youth Parish Workshop, which is the focus of this article, was one attempt to confront teenage misconceptions about church and to challenge them to take another look at prayer, catechesis, religious education, and church attendance.

It is my hope that this model will serve as a springboard for other youth ministers, catechists, and pastors to creatively design and structure programs for youth. Their efforts will offer the young people they serve a rationale and a sense of belonging to that community of believers we call Church.

Background to the Workshop

In an effort to do something about dwindling Church attendance among teenagers, eight parishes in Flushing, N.Y., decided to plan together to develop a workable youth ministry program.

To this end, the pastors of the eight parishes established a Religious Education Board. The first decision of this newly constituted board was to hire two full-time youth ministers for the area. I was one of the youth ministers hired.

Since there were no existing programs on the parish level in any of the eight parishes, our first task was to simply make contact with the Catholic youth of the area. Outdoor basketball courts, pizza parlors, and public parks became the focus of our search.

During our first six months we spent most of our time listening. We listened to teenagers who told us why the Church had little or no meaning for them, why they had decided to drop out, and in some cases why they continued to "go through the motions."

Most of the teenagers felt that their local church did not need them, did not take them seriously, and did not give them any real responsibility.

We suggested to the pastors and to the Religious Education Board that perhaps one viable way of confronting teenage negativism and irresponsibility was to challenge them to create in detail their own concept of parish. The pastors were open to the possibility, but we had to prove to them that a separate, autonomous, ninth parish, with a membership of young people and interested adults, was necessary.

What we needed was a definite plan of action. Therefore, we designed and presented to the board a weekend we called the Youth Parish Workshop.

Preparation for the Workshop

The thirty workshop participants were chosen from among the street teens whom we had met in the previous six months. All of them were in high school, some in public schools and others in Catholic schools.

In preparation for the weekend, each teenager was required to attend three preliminary meetings. During these sessions we shared with them some basic theology of Church and we drew from them the questions and misconceptions they had regarding Church. An underlying motive for the three preliminary meetings was to insure that they were indeed serious and willing to commit themselves to the task of planning a Youth Parish.

Structure of the Workshop

Our main concern in planning the workshop was to structure it in such a way that most of the responsibility was placed on the participants. Each teenager was assigned to both a committee and a task group. We wanted to give them the opportunity to mix with and get to know as many of the other young people as possible.

Committees

There were three committees functioning during the weekend: liturgy, prayer, and entertainment. When the teenagers arrived on Friday evening they received envelopes containing a description of their responsibilities as members of given committees. The responsibilities for each of the committees were as follows:

Liturgy Committee
(1) To select a chairperson.
(2) To pick a theme for the liturgy (the theme should be consistent with the readings for the Mass).
(3) To choose songs appropriate to the theme.
(4) To write a "prayer of the faithful."
(5) To choose a meditation song or record for after communion.
(6) To select people to bring up the offertory gifts.
(7) To choose a setting where you wish the liturgy to be celebrated.
(8) Any other suggestions that would enhance the communal celebration of the Eucharist.

Prayer Committee
(1) To select a chairperson.
(2) To decide on the place for the prayer service.
(3) To choose a theme.
(4) To design a prayer service about 20 minutes in length. (Resource material including books for readings, records, and slides are available. If anything needs to be printed, a typewriter, stencils and a mimeograph machine are at your disposal.)

Entertainment Committee
(1) To select a chairperson.
(2) To find whatever talent is present in the total group (not just the members of this committee) and recruit them for the show.
(3) To draw up a program for the show.
(4) To choose an M.C. for the evening.
(5) To choose a place and setting.

N.B.

(1) The entertainment should avoid ethnic references.

(2) The program should be about 1 hour in length.

(3) Props and costumes should be kept to a minimum and whatever is used must be returned immediately.

Specific times were scheduled during the workshop so that each of the committees would meet twice for a total of one and one-half hours.

Task Groups

The purpose of the task groups was to challenge the teenagers to think concretely and creatively about the problems that a Youth Parish would encounter. Each teenager was assigned to one of five different task groups. On Saturday morning each participant received an envelope specifying to which task group he or she would belong and what the responsibilities would be.

The Task Group Instructions read as follows:

Today's work will be largely in your small groups and each small group will be on its own. Listed below are the projects that your group must complete by 8:00 this evening. You have about 5 hours working time. Be sure to conserve your time and work as diligently as you can.

Your Projects

I. Opening projects: (approximate time: 45 minutes)
   a. Elect a leader (the leader will be in charge of the group for the rest of the day; he makes assignments, leads the discussion, etc.).
   b. Name your group (be creative).
   c. Devise a creative cheer or song for your group (to be presented later this evening during recreation time).

II. Problem-Solving: (approximate time: 1 hour)
   a. Find the problem in your group's envelope; read it, discuss it, and agree upon a solution to it.
   b. Next, think of a skit that would dramatize the problem and its solution, assign parts and prepare the skit in such a way that each member of your group is involved in acting it out (to be presented to entire group later).

An example of one such problem was as follows:

You are a member of the Teen Club at St. Mary's Parish. Your group has been planning activities for the youth of the parish for the past year. Father Dunn is the priest moderator of the club. He is a nice guy, who is really interested in the youth of the parish. However, he has a tendency to take over the meetings. He does most of the talking and often decides what the group should or should not do.

Many members of the Teen Club are upset with Fr. Dunn. You want to somehow get across to him that he's turning a lot of teens off and yet you don't want to dampen his enthusiasm for the youth of the parish. What do you do about the situation?

(Note: Each of the five groups had a different problem to solve.)

III. Tasks: (approximate time: 3½ hours)

Each group will be given five tasks typed on sheets of paper. One of the tasks is marked "Optional." You are asked to do this task only if you have the time.

a. Read each task, discuss it, and try to come up with a solution to it. (Remember: you will not arrive at final or perfect solutions so don't spend too much time on one task; the prime purpose of the task is to help each person to begin thinking creatively about the problems that a Youth Parish must deal with.) Spend no more than forty minutes on each task, even if you've completed only part of it.

b. You will be given a large white sheet of paper and two magic markers; list the solutions to your tasks in large print on this paper (more paper will be provided if you need it). You will be asked to present your solutions to the larger group this evening.

(There were eight specific tasks, but no group was asked to deal with more than five. The tasks were as follows.)

TASK 1: Government of Youth Parish

Assume your Youth Parish has decided to set up a Parish Council to take care of the operations, activities, and decisions of the parish. You have been appointed as a committee to decide how the Parish Council will be set up. You are asked to come up with answers to the following questions:

1. Who should be on this Parish Council?

   How many?

   How should they be chosen?

   What about adults—should there be a priest and/or other adults on the council? If so, what would their function be?

2. Who would be in charge of the Parish Council? (Example: a chairman, a president, a pastor, a lay advisor, etc.)

How would this person be chosen?
3. Who could attend the meetings of the Youth Parish Council?

TASK 2: Organization of a Youth Parish
  Introduction: In most parishes, as well as in most large corporations, certain organizations exist for the benefit and enjoyment of their members. These organizations serve as outlets for the talents of their members and as ways of pulling people together. You are acquainted with some of these organizations in your local parish, and you are aware that most of these organizations fill the needs of older people but often do not appeal to young people and are not directed to the interests and needs of young people.

Assume you have been asked by the Youth Parish to consider the problem of establishing organizations for the parish. At present, assume the Youth Parish has no clubs, programs, group activities, religious activities, etc. You are asked to do the following:

1. Think of *three* different kinds of organizations that a Youth Parish might establish. BE CREATIVE!
2. Give each of these organizations a creative name.
3. Describe briefly the purpose of each organization.
4. Describe the kind of teenager that would be attracted to each of these three organizations.

TASK 3: Membership
  Assume the group of people making this weekend is the entire Youth Parish. Assume also that they are completely organized and ready to move as a parish. You are a committee appointed to devise a list of rules regarding membership in the parish. Your task is to devise this list of rules with explanations that give your reasons for each rule.

To help you do this, study the examples given on the next page. Notice the kinds of rules that are given. You may wish to construct seven similar rules for Youth Parish membership, or you may wish to add more. The reasons are not given for the rules in the examples; remember to give a short reason for each rule you construct.

TASK 4: Youth Parish Services
  Introduction: Any organization that is alive finds ways of going beyond itself to serve the surrounding community. Even banks sponsor local community action programs, drug education programs, etc. As you know, the Catholic Church for centuries has spread itself and its services through various forms of missionary work. Often a Catholic parish becomes stagnant because it closes its eyes to the needs of the surrounding community and decides to serve only itself—in a word, such a parish becomes

Kind of Rule	Model A (Joe's Bar and Grill)	Model B (Sister Angela's First Grade Class)
1. Permanent Members	Joe, his bartenders, the waitresses, the piano player	Sister Angela
2. Age qualifications for general membership	21 years or older	6 years old
3. Race qualifications for general membership	whites only	all races
4. Religious qualifications for general membership	none	baptized Christians
5. Dues for general membership	none, except that you pay for your drinks	annual tuition
6. Decisions on membership in the case of a question about the rules	Joe makes all	The school administration makes decisions as to who is admitted, who is kicked out, promoted, etc.
7. Limitations on size of membership	125 at a time (because of fire laws)	41 (Sister and 40 students) because there are only 40 desks in the room

cliquish, ingrown, and caught up in nothing but its own petty problems.

One way some parishes have begun to overcome this kind of inbreeding has been by becoming more aware of the real human needs in their area and setting up services to deal with those needs. For example, one black parish in Queens saw a real need among the young children of the parish who came from poor families. Often these children had to go without breakfast because of the lack of food at home. The parish decided to set up a storefront kitchen to offer breakfast to the school children before school each morning.

To avoid the problem of inbreeding, the Youth Parish has asked your group to give consideration to the kind of services the Youth Parish should offer. You are asked to deal with the following three questions:

1. What are some of the real needs you see among the people (of all ages) in Flushing right now? (Make a list of these.)
2. If the members of a Youth Parish were interested in dealing with some of these needs, which do you think they could handle? Be realistic.
3. Be specific now. Spell out, concretely, two particular services that a Youth Parish could offer to help deal in a creative way with two specific problems in Flushing.

TASK 5: Place for Youth Parish
   Introduction: Any group needs a place (or places) where they can come together to meet. The place should be as centrally located as possible.

Assume that the Youth Parish has met to discuss in an open meeting the question of a place. At this open meeting, some suggested that a storefront be rented, others suggested that a portion of an existing parish building be used; still others suggested that there be no permanent place and that the Youth Parish rotate from one existing parish to another for its different activities. The question was not resolved and as a result your group was asked to discuss the question further and try to arrive at a solution. Here are two possible ways for you to deal with the question.

1. Think of the advantages and disadvantages of each of the suggestions given at the large open meeting.
2. After looking at the advantages and disadvantages of each suggestion, which do you see as best? (Note: You may have a fourth suggestion that is either a totally new one, or a combination of those already given.)

TASK 6: Priests for Youth Parish
   Assume you have been appointed as a committee to locate and approach priests for the Youth Parish. You are asked to discuss and then answer the following four quesions:

1. What qualifications (ideally) would you like to see in the priest(s) you are trying to get?

2. In approaching a priest, what would you tell him he would be expected to do? In other words, what would the specifics of this job be?

3. How much time each week would the priest(s) associated with the Youth Parish be asked to give? (Try to be specific—1 hour, 5 hours, full-time, etc.)

4. How would you determine the number of priests your Youth Parish should have?

TASK 7: *Finances for Youth Parish*

Assume you have been designated as a financial committee for the Youth Parish. Assume also that it has been agreed that the Youth Parish needs an initial operating budget of $5,000 and that this money is needed in two months.

1. List as many ways as come to your mind that this money could be obtained by this date given above (stealing not allowed). BE CREATIVE!
2. Decide on which of these ways would be the best and devise a step-by-step plan of how the plan would work (that is, how many people you would need, who would do what, etc.). Remember you have less than 2 months to pull this off.

TASK 8: *Publicity for Youth Parish*

Assume the Youth Parish is organized and ready to move. Your group has been asked to take care of the publicity for the parish. You have two tasks.

1. To date no one knows about the Youth Parish and you would like to advertise it throughout the area. Devise a creative, imaginative plan for getting the word around as quickly as possible, so that people begin to know that it exists. Remember you would like to inform the adults as well as the teens of the area, so your plan may have to have several parts to it. (BE CREATIVE!)
2. Assume the Youth Parish has been underway for several months and it becomes necessary to keep the teenagers of Flushing informed as to its activities, programs, etc. List some ways this might be done; secondly, decide which of those creative ways is best and give a detailed description of how it could be carried out.

Though the participants were spending the majority of their time in small-group work, either in committee meetings or in task groups, there was some opportunity for input from the adult leaders. During the task-group sessions two of the adult leaders went to each of the groups to discuss "Being a Leader" and "Church." These talks were given to each of the five separate task groups to allow each participant an opprotunity to ask questions.

Each participant was given the following schedule notifying him or her of the time for committee meetings, task group sessions, and the two talks in the respective groups.

SATURDAY'S SCHEDULE:

9:15 Workshops: Session #1 begins
               Talk schedule:

Group A:	"Being a Leader"	9:45
Group B:	"Church?"	9:45
Group C:	"Being a Leader"	10:30
Group D:	"Church?"	10:30
Group E:	"Being a Leader"	11:15

11:45 Committe Meetings: Session #1 begins

Liturgy Committee
Entertainment Committee
Prayer Committee

12:30 Lunch (followed by outdoor recreation)

2:30 Workshops: Session #2 begins

Talk Schedule

Group A:	"Church?"	3:30
Group B:	"Being a Leader"	3:30
Group C:	'Church?"	2:30
Group D:	"Being a Leader"	2:30
Group E:	"Church?"	4:30

5:15 Committee Meetings: Session #2 Begins

6:00 Dinner

7:00 Workshops: Session #3 begins (this is wrap-up session to put on the finishing touches to your skit and your talk presentation)

8:00 Table Presentations: Entire group meets again to share the results of the day's work.

Conclusion

The teenagers who attended the Youth Parish Workshop were dedicated to the responsibilities and tasks they faced. During the weekend they produced a tentative plan for the establishment of a Youth Parish. They drew up a report describing their plans and the insights they had gained and presented it to the Pastors and the Religious Education Board of Flushing.

However, in the weeks that followed it became clear that a Youth Parish in Flushing would never be a reality. When presented with the actual plans, many of the pastors expressed grave doubts about the canonical legitimacy for instituting such a parish.

The teenagers were disappointed by this decision, but the lessons they had learned during the weekend and through meetings in the weeks following the workshop were invaluable. They had come to understand that the Church was not merely a structure or a bureaucratic organization. Instead, they seemed to view the Church as a community of people who believe in Jesus Christ and who come together to support one another, to reach out to those in need, to pray together, and to celebrate their relationship with the Lord.

Almost all of the young people who attended the Youth Parish Workshop went on to become the backbone of a youth program in Flushing that grew and eventually included over 150 other teens.

In a very real sense, through their hard work and willingness to minister to others, a Youth Parish had in fact been created in Flushing.

Needs Assessment and Program Development

Philip Ross Beaudoin

Philip Beaudoin's report on his work of setting up a youth program in a midwestern parish is presented here as a good example of how one person and the program he led grew as he directed more and more attention to the mentality and needs of the young people he hoped to serve. He reports coming to a "new view" of the young people, a view communicated by the young themselves. Out of that renewed understanding came a renewed and obviously much richer and varied program for teens.

Another valuable aspect of Beaudoin's report is the way he kept his data gathering, his research on young people, simple. He constructued a questionnaire not intended to be the last word in scientific objectivity or sophistication. Yet the survey was useful for his own purposes. His survey is offered here in hopes that it will encourage others to do a similar work of careful listening to youth.

I wish to alert the reader to a final feature of Beaudoin's acticle—his use of language. He uses a religious education and schooling language to speak of a parish program that is more traditional than some of the other programs represented in this book. What I myself find interesting is how, no matter what the language or the program, when we listen to the needs of youth, so many of us come up with similar approaches of stressing the informal coming together of teens and adults, and the resulting ministry of friendship. Further, Beaudoin sees his work with youth as work-in-progress, not as the final word but as an ongoing experiment in ministry to youth. More than anything else, that mentality of continuous learning by doing seems to be what characterizes all the writers in this book.

My earliest experiences in high school religious education taught me that some sort of a written needs-assessment tool was a basic necessity for getting a viable program "off the ground." By trial and error I was time and again forced to conclude that my personal intuitive evaluation of "where my students were at" was terribly off target, and that I had to find some way of getting an accurate reading of the psychological, religious, moral, and educational needs of my students.

Finally, as a director of religious education at a large parish with a newly formed high school religious education program, I ran across a youth survey formulated by Father John E. Forliti for the Minnesota Catholic Conference. This survey seemed to be what I was looking for. However, it did not go into the personal life and feelings of the students as much as I felt we needed to.

About that same time, I found a questionnaire printed in *Psychology Today* magazine that dealt almost exclusively with personal life and feelings. In consultation with the other teachers in the program, I decided to combine parts of both sets of questions along with some of our own, to try to achieve some overall view of the youth we were dealing with.

The result of this effort is the survey included here. It is not perfect by any manner of thinking. There are changes I wanted to make, but because of my lack of knowledge of copyright laws I did not feel that I could tamper with the copyrighted portions (for which we have received permission to reprint). However, from our experience, I would suggest changes in the vocabulary used in the survey because it is beyond the comprehension of some of the students. Oral explanation at the time of conducting the survey can take care of some vocabulary difficulties. Also, I would change the second "category" of the series of questions numbered 38 to 68 from "Some" to "Not Very Much." The students themselves explained that the "Some" category was a "cop-out" choice, and use of a negative reading for this column would force responders to make a choice between category 2 and category 3.

This survey may not be suitable "as is" for every junior/senior high school situation, either. Some users may need to delete and/or add some questions that pertain to their own particular circumstances.

The benefit of this type of survey, it seems to me, is that its analysis gives the coordinator and teachers some broad insights into the needs and interests of their students and the personal stance their students now have on a variety of topics. This type of survey is most beneficial when planning a new or revising an existing high school program. It can also be used periodically at the beginning and/or end of a school year to survey changes within the students in an already functioning program.

In our own particular situation, we used the survey to help us revise a "pilot" junior/senior high school CCD program. In July 1975 I had come to St. Mark's Parish, Independence, Missouri, as director of religious education and high school coordinator. A high school program had been underway, with about thirty-five junior and senior high youths participating. Discussions with teachers, parishioners, and youths revealed that the text and other materials used needed to be changed.

With little time available before classes started, and very little youth contact established at that point, I went through a text-evaluation process with the teachers and a few interested parents. We decided on *Hi-Time* and *Accent on You* as suitable texts for the year. With a few old and some new teachers and some new texts, involvement in the program increased to about seventy youth (ninety-five registered and about seventy regularly attended).

As the fall months passed, it became clear that we needed to make still more changes to meet the needs of our youth. But we weren't sure what all those needs were, nor quite where some of our students "were at" in their personal lives. So it was at this point—around November—that I formulated the survey we now have.

We administered this survey on December 3, 1975, to fifty-one junior high and eighteen senior high youth. It took most students an hour or a little more to complete. I think that the fact that we did the survey at all said something to the students about our genuine interest in them—as they really are.

After the survey was completed, we analyzed the results by junior high, senior high, male, female, and total group. The raw scores were converted into percentages for each response. Because the questionnare dealt with some very personal topics, we told the students that we would keep the results in confidence.

The conclusions were not earth-shattering, but we certainly had a new view of the youths we were working with. Some of the things we learned through this survey really opened our eyes to who these young people were, what they were interested in, and what potential they had.

As a result, the teachers and I brainstormed some ideas for programming for the following fall. What we came up with was a series of elective teaching units, a "home base group" concept (see Appendix 1), and a special unit for concentration on social action projects.

Another result was that after consultation with students and an experimental class that tried the idea, we decided to mix grades, 7, 8, and 9 and also grades 10, 11, and 12 for weekly classes. That is, when the junior high youths make a choice of an elective, they join other junior high youths interested in the same topic, irrespective of grade. The same is true in the senior high. We have found no major problems with this setup, nor have the youths reacted adversely to it. Home Base Groups, however, are divided according to grade in order to foster greater communication and mutual support.

We also decided that, because of our experience with the youths and the responses to certain questions in the survey, it was advisable to have a sort of "catchall" unit of basic teachings at the beginning of the school year—at least this year. We realized that we obviously could not cover all of Christian Doctrine in three weeks, but we felt that we could open up some areas of searching for the students and also deal with a few specific topics that were obviously in need of treatment.

In addition to the unit teaching and home base organization, a number of other developments took place in our program the following year. Among these were the Day-Away Program, the Youth Choir, and the Summer of Service.

All facets of the renewed program were explained to the junior and senior high students before the end of classes in the spring and their input was incorporated into the planning.

In the fall, a parents' meeting was held before the beginning of classes to acquaint the parents with what we were going to be doing.

Enrollment in the fall of 1976 was 136 (98 junior high and 38 senior high) and average attendance about 95 (71 percent).

A look at the yearly schedule (Appendix 2) will give you an idea of how all the parts fit together. Appendix 1 explains each portion of our present program.

But our work is not finished yet. As I write this, we are planning a follow-up survey for this spring (16 months after the original one), and we are considering further alternatives for the existing program. We are thinking of and talking with the students about a student-and-teacher planned series of units for specially motivated senior high youths, a special "warm-up" unit or units for the seventh graders, and so on. Also being considered is a preparation time and a service for a "personal recommitment" for ninth graders already confirmed. These items are just part of the process so well known to most of us: needs assessment, program development, program evaluation, needs reassessment, and so on. . . .

I have found that religious education is a never-ending dynamic process. No program can remain unchanged for long: individuals grow (students *and* teachers); communities grow; times change. The Spirit is always at work among us. Such things as this survey can help us keep in touch with these movements of the Spirit.

APPENDIX 1
ST. MARK'S RELIGIOUS EDUCATION PROGRAM
Independence, Missouri 64055
1976-1977

Our overall JUNIOR AND SENIOR HIGH SCHOOL program consists of the following parts.

1. *WEEKDAY PROGRAM*. This is the "regular" weekly religious education program. These classes meet Monday and Tuesday afternoons (Junior High) and Wednesday evening (Junior and Senior High). There are three portions to this program. (See Appendix 2.)

a. *Home Base Groups.* These are small groups of seven youths and one adult. These groups meet once a month at the regular class time. The group stays together throughout the entire year. The purpose of these groups is to establish a community among the youths and the adult, and to provide regular contact and communication between the youths and the adult leader. (Due to an elective program in the classes, *regular contact* with one adult is not always possible because of the various choices of topics and teachers.) It is in these groups that goal-setting, evaluation of results of classes, choices of electives, etc., are accomplished. These groups are truly the Home Base for the youths.

b. *Class Units.* Topics are taught in units of three or four weeks each. Except for the first unit, the youths have a choice of one of three electives each unit. The first unit is a "basic teachings update"—or an opportunity for the youths to reexamine some basics of their Catholic faith and to formulate some questions suited to their age and maturity. The topics of all of the units are taught on both the junior and senior high levels. (Class size is around 15 students.)

c. *Special Projects.* During Advent the youths have an opportunity to be more active in expressing their faith-life—through creative projects. Such things as media, liturgy, drama, service, crafts, and so forth have a part in these project times.

2. *DAY-AWAY PROGRAM.* On the five days during the school year when there is no school due to teacher institutes, etc., we have a Day Away. Sometimes this will be held at a seminary not far away. The day is constructed around a theme (Respect for Life was October's Day Away), and is divided into input, discussion, and fun activities. Youth are involved in the planning and execution of these days.

3a. *YOUTH CHOIR.* The junior and senior high youth have their own choir and music group (guitars, trumpet, and flutes). This choir practices late Wednesday afternoon and members may choose to bring a sack lunch and eat together afterwards (with choir director and high school religious education coordinator, too). Those who attend the Wednesday evening classes just stay over for the classes. The youth choir provides music regularly for one of the Parish weekend Masses as well as for special CCD Masses, etc.

3b. *YOUTH MASS.* On certain occasions (about every six weeks or two months), the youths plan and completely carry out a parish Sunday liturgy. The youths accomplish (under adult supervision) everything from

making banners, providing music, writing various prayers, etc., to usher-
ing (including taking up the collection—girls and fellows). (This Youth
Mass is a regular parish liturgy, separate from the Masses that are a part of
the religious education program.)

4. *VACATION BIBLE SCHOOL.* Our senior high youth (in pairs) teach
the two-week Vacation Bible School to primary-age children each June.
The junior high youth are classroom helpers and help in the office, etc.

5. *SUMMER OF SERVICE.* During the summer, our youth serve in
various ways outside of our local (somewhat affluent) community. They
tutor the young in programs in the inner city, visit inner-city nursing
homes, and provide other services to those less advantaged than they are.

6. *YOUTH RETREATS.* Really a weak link—but being picked up somewhat through our Day-Away program. We provided one weekend retreat
for senior high youth last year. The diocese also sponsors SEARCH
weekends for 11th and 12th grade students. It is MOST DIFFICULT to
find a priest for retreat weekends as well as somewhat difficult to find the
facilities, get together a team, etc. . . . Yet, I feel that these experiences
are valuable.

7. *YOUTH GROUPS.* Both junior and senior high youth have their own
social groups which meet on alternate Sunday evenings. This part of the
program provides peer-group fun and social activities . . . jointly planned
and carried out by the youth and adult leaders.

APPENDIX 2
1976-77
CLASS SCHEDULE

Week of—

Sept. 20 Home Base

Sept. 27 Unit 1 ⎫
           ⎪ BASIC
Oct. 6   Unit 1 ⎬ TEACHINGS
           ⎪ update
Oct. 11   Unit 1 ⎭

Oct. 18   Home Base + Comm. Pen.

Electives:

Oct. 25   Unit 2 ⎫ GOD

Nov. 1   Unit 2 ⎬ JESUS CHRIST

Nov. 8   Unit 2 ⎭ WORSHIP &
                    LITURGY

Nov. 15   Home Base +
          VOCATIONS
          TALKS

          THANKSGIVING WEEK
          NATIONAL BIBLE WEEK

Nov. 29   A   P ⎫
         D   r ⎪
Dec. 6   V   o ⎪ social action
         E   j ⎬ media
         N   e ⎪ liturgy prep.
Dec. 13   T   c ⎪ drama
            t ⎭ study groups
            s

         CHRISTMAS VACATION

Jan. 3   Home Base
             Electives:

Jan. 11   Unit 3 ⎫

Jan. 24   Unit 3 ⎬ SCRIPTURE, O.T.

                 CHURCH HISTORY

Jan. 31   Unit 3 ⎬

                 ECUMENISM

Feb. 7   Unit 3 ⎭

Week of—
Feb. 14   Home Base + Mass with Parents

ASH WEDNESDAY

                        Electives:

Feb. 28   Unit 4 ⎫
             SCRIPTURE, N.T.
Mar. 7   Unit 4 ⎬

            DEATH, JUDGEMENT,
            HEAVEN & HELL
Mar. 14   Unit 4 ⎬

            MARY & THE SAINTS
Mar. 21   Unit 4 ⎭

Mar. 28   Home Base

HOLY WEEK AND EASTER
                        Electives:

            Jr. Hi: SOC. &
            PERSONAL
Apr. 11   Unit 5 ⎫ RELATIONSHIPS/DATING

            Sr. Hi: DATING & PREP
            FOR MARRIAGE
Apr. 18   Unit 5 ⎬

            CHRISTIANS IN
Apr. 25   Unit 5 ⎬ ACTION

            VALUES
May 2   Unit 5 ⎭ CLARIFICATION &
            CONSCIENCE
            FORMATION

May 9   Home Base + Celebration

Note: The *topics* are given here, some *sample titles* are:
"What's One About Three, or Who's Who in the Trinity"; "What's Right in a Rite or Let's Live the Liturgy"; "From Peter to Paul (The Sixth, that is)"; "Our Past is Present—Understanding the Old Testament."

APPENDIX 3
A SURVEY OF
ATTITUDES, VALUES AND NEEDS OF
HIGH SCHOOL AGE YOUTH

Compiled by
Philip Ross Beaudoin
Director of Religious Education
St. Mark the Evangelist Catholic Church
3736 Lee's Summit Road
Independence, MO 64055

The men and women who teach our religious education classes and work with our youth want to do a better job than they are presently doing. A helpful start is for them to know what you really think. This survey has been designed to help you express your feelings and opinions honestly. Would you please take a few minutes now to respond to this survey? Please respond to each item, following the instructions given. Be as accurate as possible, but do not delay on any single item. You may write in additional comments if you wish, but do not sign your name. All replies will be collected and tallied together to preserve your anonymity.

Instruction: Circle the number (only one) which best reflects your feelings or opinion for each item.

1. In general, how happy or unhappy have you been over the last six months?

   1 Very happy   5 Slightly unhappy
   2 Moderately happy   6 Moderately unhappy
   3 Slightly happy   7 Very unhappy
   4 Neither happy nor unhappy

2. Does your level of happiness change often or remain fairly constant?

   1 It changes very often   3 It rarely changes
   2 It changes often   4 It remains quite stable

3. How often do you think about how good or how bad your life is?

   1 Every day   3 Monthly
   2 Weekly   4 Almost never

4. Compared to you, how happy are most of your acquaintances?

   1 Much happier than I   4 Somewhat less happy than I
   2 Somewhat happier than I   5 Much less happy than I
   3 About as happy as I

5. In Aesop's fable "The Ant and the Grasshopper," the ant spent his time working and planning for the future, while the grasshopper lived for the moment and enjoyed himself. Which are you *more like?*

   1 The ant   2 The grasshopper

6. How confident are you that your guiding values are right for you and will last?

   1 Very confident   4 Not at all confident
   2 Considerably confident   5 I'm not questioning my values
   3 Somewhat confident   constantly
       6 I don't really have any constant
         guiding principles

7. How optimistic or pessimistic about your life would you say you are?

   1 Very optimistic   4 Slightly pessimistic
   2 Moderately optimistic   5 Moderately pessimistic
   3 Slightly optimistic   6 Very pessimistic

8. How optimistic or pessimistic are you about the future of the country?

   1 Very optimistic   4 Slightly pessimistic
   2 Moderately optimistic   5 Moderately pessimistic
   3 Slightly optimistic   6 Very pessimistic

9. How optimistic or pessimistic are you about the future of the Catholic Church?

   1 Very optimistic   4 Slightly pessimistic
   2 Moderately optimistic   5 Moderately pessimistic
   3 Slightly optimistic   6 Very pessimistic

10. During most of your childhood, with whom have you lived?

    1 Both natural parents   5 Adoptive parents
    2 One natural parent and   6 Foster parents
      one step-parent   7 Other relatives
    3 One natural parent   8 In an institution
    4 Step-parents

11. How would you describe your parents' relationship (while they were together if they are now separated or divorced)?

    1 Very loving and stable
    2 Generally warm and stable
    3 Stable but emotionally cold
    4 Generally cold and conflicted
    5 I don't know, or I grew up with one parent only

12. How would you describe your current relationship with your parents?

    1 Warm and stable, with few conflicts
    2 Cool and stable, with few conflicts
    3 Emotional ups and downs; periods of closeness alternate with fights
    4 I'm close to one parent, not the other
    5 Moderately conflicted, we fight a lot
    6 We had a big fight and currently aren't speaking
    7 Don't live with either parent

13. In general, how would you rate your physical health over the last year?

    1 Excellent
    2 Good
    3 Fair
    4 Poor
    5 Very poor

14. Which of the following have been true of you in the past year? (*Check all that apply.*)

    1 Frequent headaches
    2 Insomnia
    3 Nightmares
    4 Constant worry and anxiety
    5 Tiring easily
    6 Trouble concentrating
    7 Often feeling guilty
    8 Sometimes feeling that you can't go on
    9 Irrational fears
    10 Often feeling lonely
    11 Feelings of worthlessness

15. Which of the following drugs do you take fairly often? (*Check all that apply.*)

    1 Tranquilizers
    2 Sleeping pills
    3 Pep pills, dexedrine, amphetamine ("uppers")
    4 Morphine or demerol
    5 Codeine
    6 Cocaine
    7 Heroin or methadone
    8 Marijuana
    9 Psychedelics (LSD, Mescaline)
    10 Vitamins
    11 Beer or wine
    12 Hard liquor
    13 Caffein drinks—coffee, tea, cola

16. Which of the following have you experienced? *(Check all that apply.)*

    1 Sniffing (Glue, gas, etc.)
    2 Snuffing (aerosols)

17. Which of the following drugs have you ever taken without a prescription? *(Check all that apply.)*

    1 Tranquilizers
    2 Sleeping pills
    3 Pep pills, dexedrine, amphetamine ("uppers")
    4 Morphine or demerol
    5 Codeine

    6 Cocaine
    7 Heroin or methadone
    8 Marijuana
    9 Psychedelics (LSD, Mescaline)
    10 Vitamins

18. How many cigarettes do you smoke per typical day?

    1 None
    2 A few
    3 About half a pack
    4 A pack

    5 Pack and a half
    6 Two packs or more

    Specify brand _____

19. How many sexual involvements do you think most people of your age have had?

    1 None
    2 One

    3 Two or more

20. How many children are there in your family?

    1 One, I am an only child
    2 Two
    3 Three or four

    4 Five or six
    5 Seven or more

21. If you were starting your own family, how many children would you have?

    1 None
    2 One
    3 Two

    4 Three or four
    5 Five or more
    6 I'm undecided at present

22. What is your sex?

    1 Male

    2 Female

23. What is your age?

   1 Under 13
   2 13 or 14
   3 15 or 16

   4 17 or 18
   5 19 and above

24. What is your grade in school?

   1 Junior High

   2 Senior High

25. Where do you stand politically on most issues?

   1 Radical left
   2 Very liberal
   3 Somewhat liberal
   4 Moderate

   5 Somewhat conservative
   6 Very conservative
   7 Radical right
   8 I don't have a stand right now

26. Have you ever had any of the following experiences? *(Check all that apply.)*

   1 Mental telepathy
   2 Precognition (awareness of future events)
   3 Mystical or super-natural experiences

   4 "Peak" experiences—or special experiences in prayer
   5 Feelings of harmony with the universe

27. How important is religion in your home?

   1 Very important
   2 Moderately important

   3 Slightly important
   4 Not at all important

28. to 35.: How many hours each weekday, on the average, do you spend in the following activities? (Circle the appropriate number of hours for each activity.)

28. School and activities related to school.

   0   1   2   3   4   5   6   7   8   9   10   11   12

29. Time with your parents.

   0   1   2   3   4   5   6   7   8   9   10   11   12

30. Time with your brother(s) or sister(s).

0   1   2   3   4   5   6   7   8   9   10   11   12

31. Time doing leisure activities, sports, and hobbies.

0   1   2   3   4   5   6   7   8   9   10   11   12

32. Sleeping.

0   1   2   3   4   5   6   7   8   9   10   11   12

33. Time with friends.

0   1   2   3   4   5   6   7   8   9   10   11   12

34. Working for pay.

0   1   2   3   4   5   6   7   8   9   10   11   12

35. Watching television.

0   1   2   3   4   5   6   7   8   9   10   11   12

36. How satisfied are you with this allotment of your time?

1 Very satisfied   3 Somewhat dissatisfied
2 Somewhat satisfied   4 Very dissatisfied

37. If you could change lives with another person, would you do it?

1 Yes   2 No

If you said Yes, who would it be, and why?

Instructions: Circle the number on the left (only one) which best reflects your feelings for each item.

		VERY		
NONE	SOME	MUCH	MUCH	
38. 1	2	3	4	I would like more opportunities to participate in social activities (dances, parties, etc.).
39. 1	2	3	4	I would like more guidance in reaching decisions about vocation, career, and college plans.
40. 1	2	3	4	I would like a better understanding of my feelings, moods, and desires.

		VERY			
	NONE	SOME	MUCH	MUCH	

41.   1   2   3   4   I would like a better understanding of my parents, teachers, and other adults.

42.   1   2   3   4   I would like more help in understanding other people my age.

43.   1   2   3   4   I would like more opportunities to meet with friends just to be together.

44.   1   2   3   4   I would like a better understanding of my own sexuality (what it means to be a man or a woman).

45.   1   2   3   4   I would like more opportunities to plan and participate in "youth liturgies."

46.   1   2   3   4   I would like more opportunities to be of service to other people in my neighborhood or community.

47.   1   2   3   4   I would like more help in developing responsible values and attitudes toward sex in interpersonal relationships.

48.   1   2   3   4   I would like more reinforcement of my own self-worth and value.

49.   1   2   3   4   I would like more opportunities to plan and participate (lector, song leader, usher, etc.) in "regular" parish liturgies.

50.   1   2   3   4   I would like more opportunities to develop personal relationships with adults beyond my family.

51.   1   2   3   4   I would like more help in improving communications with my parents.

52.   1   2   3   4   I would like more help in developing friendships in which I can be myself and be accepted.

	NONE	SOME	VERY MUCH	MUCH	
53.	1	2	3	4	I would like to study modern moral problems such as abortion, mercy killing, and man's responsibility to respect life, from a Christian perspective.
54.	1	2	3	4	I want to know more about the Bible and what it should mean to us today.
55.	1	2	3	4	I would like to gain a better understanding about how the Sacrament of Penance (Confession) relates to my life.
56.	1	2	3	4	A topic of real interest to me is marriage and family life.
57.	1	2	3	4	I want a deeper appreciation of the meaning of Jesus.
58.	1	2	3	4	A study of death and dying interests me.
59.	1	2	3	4	I would like to learn how to pray to God in a more personal way.
60.	1	2	3	4	I think I should know more about the ecumenical movement with Protestant churches.
61.	1	2	3	4	I would like to explore more deeply the question of freedom and authority.
62.	1	2	3	4	Faith and what it means to believe as a Christian have interest for me.
63.	1	2	3	4	I would like to study more about the history of religion.
64.	1	2	3	4	I would like a thorough background on the Church's teaching about race, poverty, hunger, and other social problems.

	VERY			
	NONE	SOME	MUCH	MUCH

65. 1   2   3   4   I would like to explore in more depth the Christian's responsibility in the face of war and human conflict.

66. 1   2   3   4   I could use help in knowing what to do about chemical addiction (drugs and alcohol).

67. 1   2   3   4   As a Catholic I need to now more about the Church and what it is trying to do.

68. 1   2   3   4   I could use guidance on the moral implications of stealing, lying, and cheating.

Instructions: Circle the number of the item which best reflects your feeling or opinion (circle one).

69. How often do you participate in youth programs (CCD, discussion groups, social activities, Youth Group, etc.) sponsored by your parish?

| 1 Never | 3 Half of the time |
| 2 Sometimes | 4 Most of the time |

70. How do you estimate your involvement in school activities (other than studies)?

| 1 Almost nothing | 3 Average involvement |
| 2 Some involvement | 4 Very great involvement |

71. How often have you been involved in community programs (politics, social service, etc.)?

| 1 Never | 3 Quite often |
| 2 Occasionally | 4 Almost continuously |

72. Do you feel you are part of your local parish?

| 1 Not at all | 3 Quite a bit |
| 2 To some extent | 4 In almost every way possible |

73. What term would you use to describe yourself as a member of the Church?

    1 "Catholic"
    2 "Christian"
    3 Other _____
    WHY? (if you want—on other side)

74. In the past six months how often have you gone to church?

    1 Rarely or not at all
    2 About once a month
    3 About twice a month
    4 Once a week or more

75. Have you ever participated in a retreat or similar experience?

    1 Never
    2 Once
    3 Two or more times

76. Are the Sunday Mass liturgies in our parish meaningful to you?

    1 Very seldom or never
    2 Occasionally
    3 Frequently
    4 Almost always

77. Do you feel that the use of guitar instead of organ helps you in your participation at Mass?

    1 Definitely
    2 To some extent
    3 Not very much

78. The last time you received the Sacrament of Penance (Confession) was:

    1 Within the last 3 months
    2 Three months to a year ago
    3 One to three years ago
    4 Over three years ago
    5 I have not yet gone to Confession

79. In the past six months how often have you prayed or talked with God?

    1 Not really at all
    2 Once in a while
    3 Frequently
    4 Every day

80. To what extent do you feel your religious values or convictions influence the way you act?

    1 I don't have any
    2 Hardly ever
    3 Sometimes
    4 Quite often

81. If you were to observe someone taking a watch from a store without paying for it, what would be your reaction?

    1 That is a wrong action
    2 That is wrong if you get caught

    3 It's not wrong to rip off a watch like that

82. If you saw someone break into a home and you did not report the incident or say anything to anyone about it,

    1 You would be guilty of wrong—by omission
    2 You would be smart by keeping your nose out of it

    3 You wouldn't be either right or wrong by keeping quiet

83. Which of the following statements do you consider to be true?

    1 A morally wrong act and "sin" are the same thing

    2 A morally wrong act and "sin" are two entirely different things

84. "Doing your own thing"—

    1 is generally the best way to operate
    2 is seldom the best way to operate

    3 must be balanced against objective right and wrong and the benefit or harm to others

85. How would you describe your relationship to Jesus Christ?

    1 Personal or close
    2 Remote

    3 Somewhere in between personal and remote
    4 Practically nonexistent

86. How do you think of Jesus Christ?

    1 As God—though looking like man
    2 As man—though chosen by God for special purposes

    3 As both fully God and fully man

87. To what extent do you think you would be able to explain your religious beliefs to someone else?

1 Not at all
2 In some things

3 In many things
4 In almost everything

88. Do you consider that Mary is . . .

1 No more or no less important than any other Christian
2 The center of many pious devotions—especially for the elderly and certain groups

3 The Mother of the Church and the exemplary Christian

89. Which statement best characterizes your belief in God or a Supreme Being?

1 I don't believe in God
2 I believe in an impersonal supreme being or spiritual force that does not direct individual lives

3 I believe in a personal God who has little or no direct involvement with individual lives
4 I believe in a personal God who directs and controls my life
5 Not sure

90. Do you believe in life after death?

1 No, I don't believe in any kind of life after this one
2 I am unsure

3 Yes, I believe that there must be something beyond death
4 Yes, I have definite beliefs about the afterlife

91. Do you see the saints as . . .

1 Heroes and models for your life (who lived much like you)
2 Monks or other pious people who lived lives very different from your own

3 I don't really know

4 Other: _____

92. How would you describe your relationship (faith, worship, involvement) with the Church (parish, religious education program, etc.) and its meaning for your life?

1 Irrelevant (lacking meaning)
2 Somewhat meaningful

3 Quite meaningful
4 No opinion

93. Assuming you were not a "born" Catholic, what religion would you choose for yourself? _____
    Why?

94. What are your present feelings toward the way of life of priests, brothers, and sisters?

    1 Very favorable   3 Mostly unfavorable
    2 A mixture of favorable and   4 I haven't given it much thought
      unfavorable

95. Do you feel you have a purpose and direction for your life?

    1 Not sure   3 To some extent
    2 No, not at all   4 Yes, to a rather high degree

96. Are you happy with your present life as a student?

    1 Seldom   3 Often
    2 Sometimes   4 Almost all the time

97. How would you describe your feelings about completing this survey?

    1 Positive, glad I got a   3 No feeling one way or the other
      chance to share some of   4 Negative because: _____
      myself
    2 Somewhat positive   _____
    _____   _____
    _____   _____

Take a minute to look over your responses. THANK YOU for your cooperation and help.
Do you have any additonal comments or observations?

Adult Training Program for Youth Ministry

Richard Costello

Possibly this report on training adults to work with teens could be placed in a later section of this book, that dealing with developing leadership. It is placed here, however, since it represents an attempt to lead adults in local parishes to learn the skills of listening and responding to teens in a creative, flexible way. Readers interested in helping adults respond more fully to teens will enjoy Costello's approach.

Costello started with adults who were more comfortable working with teens in highly structured situations, such as classrooms. He wanted to help them become comfortable with teens in other more flexible situations. He saw as the chief task of adults working with teens not one of first teaching them something, but of first focusing on them and of listening to them. He wanted his adults to reverence teens at the same time they were becoming better at relating informally with them. His efforts may have been successful simply because he himself reverenced the adults he worked with and went with them step by step, always giving them an opportunity to voice their fears and hesitations.

Does this sound familiar? "Interested adults *desperately* needed to help with the high school program. Please contact the rectory or the religious education office for details."

The odds are pretty good that if you walked into any parish, U.S.A., in September, you would find this announcement or something similar in the bulletin. Even if a parish is fortunate enough to

38

get adult volunteers for its high school program this way, too often these same adults quit in frustration halfway through the year. A typical parish repeats the bulletin petitions in January.

It's true that we might produce something edible by reaching into the refrigerator, randomly pulling out five or six items, and throwing them into a covered dish in a 350° oven for 45 minutes, but our chances are remote at best. Yet we apply the same haphazard recipe in recruiting adults for work in youth ministry. A general appeal for help in the parish bulletin *may* interest adults who have sensitivity and a facility for dealing with youth, but the odds for this are no better than the possibility that we will get a gourmet dish from our refrigerator casserole.

I think we need to take a new look at our recruitment and training of adults for youth ministry.

My experience in youth work has convinced me that the most beneficial way of recruiting adults is by personal invitation. But identifying those adults within the parish community who obviously have the ability to minister to youth is a first necessary step. There are a number of different ways to locate these adults and I will list here some that I have found effective:

1. Survey the teens in your parish about the quality of their relationship with their parents. If teenagers indicate to me that they have excellent rapport with their own parents I immediately consider these adults as good possibilities for youth ministry. It isn't always true, but usually if parents can relate well with their own teenagers they will do the same with others.

2. Ask the teens in your parish if they know any adults, possibly teachers or bosses, whom they like and feel would be good at working with youth in the parish.

3. Offer an adult education program in the parish on topics such as "Understanding the Adolescent" or "The Faith Development of the Adolescent." Often adults with ability to work well with youth can be identified at such meetings and discussions.

4. Contact volunteer agencies in your area to find out if there are adults successfully working in volunteer programs with young people. Many of these same adults may be parishioners, and they may be exactly the kind of adults you are looking for.

There are many other possible ways of identifying potential

youth ministers for your program. It would be unfortunate if these adults are "out there" in our parishes but have never become involved because no one ever challenged them to use their gift of ministering to teens. The key, therefore, is personal contact and personal invitation.

As necessary as it is to identify the right adults for youth ministry, it is even more important to provide them with the proper training. Often the adults who volunteer in September and quit in January do so because they aren't growing themselves. Hence they feel inadequate to the task. Working with youth becomes a difficult experience for which they have not been prepared.

Because I believe that little or no preparation is the primary reason many well-intentioned adults cease working with young people, I would like to propose some guidelines for developing a realistic training program. There are three basic guidelines that I have found helpful in training and in working with adult volunteers.

1. Adults who wish to work with youth must be willing to try to articulate their own faith experiences. They need not be theologians, but they should be adult Christians who are struggling to understand the presence of the Lord in their own lives, and who are willing to talk about their struggle. A training program should show them what it means to share their faith and how it can be done.

2. Adults who work with youth must attempt to find in one another's company a sense of Christian fellowship and support in their ministry. Without mutual support, prayer, and a sense of community, ministry will always become a discouraging task. Training programs must help build this sense of community interdependence.

3. Adults who wish to help youth grow in an understanding of their faith must be willing to continue the same quest in their own lives.

These simple guidelines were my blueprint for designing the following training program.

The Program

The Youth Worker Training Program ran for twelve weeks. It was divided into three four-week sequences.

Sequence One   Personal Growth of the Youth Minister

Sequence Two Theological Input
Sequence Three Practicum in Program Planning

Sequence One–Personal Growth of the Youth Minister

Sequence One was based on the belief that youth ministers cannot successfully help others to grow unless they themselves are involved in a growing process. Effective youth ministers are actively involved in growing and are prepared to take the next step in their own spiritual journey, unsettling though it may be.

Most of Sequence One consisted of assignments that the participants were asked to complete between the 2½-hour meetings. The majority of the meeting time was spent in sharing "homework" results and exploring together the implications. The assignments to be done in preparation for each of the four-week sessions were as follows:

WEEK I—Assume that you are put in a classroom with an assortment of twenty teenagers and must remain there for twenty-four hours. Assume further that you have no books, no weapons, no pencils, paper, blackboard or other equipment. Assume further that you are asked to communicate the message of Jesus in this situation.

What would you do? How would you begin?

How would you see yourself in that situation? (E.g., as one who should control the situation to prevent damage.) What would your initial feelings be and why? What message would you be trying to make the teenagers aware of? Specifically what would you be trying to tell them? How could you judge whether or not that message was successfully communicated?

Now set up a time chart and try to sketch out hour by hour how you would spend this time.

NOTE: If you have envisioned yourself as a "teacher" in this situation, do it again and envision yourself as an "adult participant" with no investment in the property and no direct commission to be in that classroom.

WEEK II—What do you think Jesus would want to say to a typical teenager today? (If you cannot imagine this, think of a teenager who lives on your block—whom you know at least by first name—and imagine what Jesus would want to say to him/her.) Specifically—write it down—describe his actions, his words, his mannerisms, the tone of his voice, where the dialogue would occur.

NOTE: If you find this hard to do, open your New Testament and read what Jesus said to Zacchaeus, the rich young man, and the woman taken in adultery.

Next, write down what *you* would like to say to that same teenager. Be specific.

What is the difference between your message and that of Jesus?

Is it possible to communicate the message of Jesus if you are not committed to trying to first live the message yourself?

WEEK III—Map out a schedule of activities that you can engage in to make contact with teenagers and get to feel at home with them (at least two per week, each contact a minimum of one-half hour).

Write out what you can do to begin making this kind of contact. Think of your opportunities (lunch hour, social involvements, etc.); think of yourself, what you could honestly do and what would come off as "phony."

After each actual contact, take time out to write a paragraph on how you felt in making the contact and why. Then write a paragraph on what you learned during the contact.

WEEK IV—Administer the following questionnaire, over a cassette tape recorder, to ten teenagers of various descriptions over the next week. Tell them you are taking a course on adolescents of today and want to get their opinions on a few things.

1 Do you feel that school is a good preparation for life?

2 What's the basic problem with parents today?

3 What's the most important thing in your life right now?

4 What does being a Christian mean for you?

5 If you were a teacher what would you try to do for your students?

6 What do you think about this interview?

7 What questions, if any, would you like to ask me right now?

8 Would you like to learn more about Christianity?

NOTE: Before you begin this project, try to guess what the teenagers would say by doing the test yourself as though you were a teenager.

After engaging in these experiments, what can you say about:

—The needs of today's teenagers.

—The questions of today's teenagers.

—The attractive points of today's teenagers.

—The negative points of today's teenagers.

—What I would like to do for today's teenagers.

—What, honestly, I feel I am capable of doing.

The exercises in Sequence One were designed to help the adults discern the validity of their call to youth ministry.

Through the various exercises, especially as they were analyzed, discussed and prayed over at the 2½-hour weekly meetings, the adults were able to clarify the objectives of youth ministry and begin to develop a working methodology for their future ministry.

Sequence Two–Theological Input

Sequence Two was designed to offer theological input to the adults.

The topics and content for these sessions grew out of the questions and misconceptions that surfaced as a result of Sequence One. As a leader of the training program I had to listen carefully to the adults to discern in what areas of theology they needed the most clarification. The four-week program in Sequence Two dealt with topics such as: Scripture, Christology, Revelation, Grace and Sin, Development of Conscience, Ecclesiology, etc. In some cases this four-week session was expanded when we felt that more input was needed. Along with the content of each session, the adults were supplied with resource readings that formed the basis of their preparation for each session.

Sequence Three–Practicum in Program Planning

The last four-week segment of the training program was a Practicum in Program Planning. In this sequence the adults were asked to design a one-hour program for a group of twenty teenagers. The group leader provided the adults with resource material and suggested to them a topic or theme for the program. The adults were organized into teams, at least two adults to each team. The group leader then contacted a group of twenty teenagers who were already involved in a youth program. He explained to them that we were conducting a training program for adults interested in working with youth and that we needed their help. The youth became the pilot group that the adults worked with to test their program design.

Once the adults had run their program with the teens each week, the entire group of teens and adults held a debriefing session. The youth were asked to critique the program and offer their suggestions on what they liked, what they didn't like, and what recommendations they could make for improving the design or the manner of presenting the material.

The practicum provided the adults with an opportunity to test their program design in a realistic situation while at the same time it gave them valuable input as to how they came across. It also allowed the teenagers an opportunity to minister to adults. Perhaps the most significant result of the practicum was that it allowed all participants to see clearly that they are in ministry together.

Conclusion

The three elements of the training program were designed to help adults to discern the validity of their call to ministry, to provide them with some theological updating, and to offer them a practical opportunity to plan programs.

As I indicated at the outset, however, unless the adults themselves are growing spiritually in their ministry, they will become frustrated and quit. It seemed to me to be important, therefore, to build into each of the sessions an opportunity for spiritual growth through prayer. As the participants continued in the training program, they developed a sense of trust in one another, a trust that eventually enabled them to share their prayer with one another. The participants saw these prayer sessions not as a flourish or "add on" to the program, but rather as an integral part of it. They understood that their own willingness to pray with one another and with the young people was a necessary prerequisite for growing in faith.

As the leader of the training program, I felt that it was also important to allow participants time for gathering socially. Between the first and second sequences I structured breaks that provided opportunities to simply enjoy one another's company. These social opportunities went a long way toward helping the adults develop a genuine concern and friendship for one another.

Through personal contact in our recruitment and a well organized training program we were able to diminish the necessity for our SOS bulletin announcements. We had discovered a core of adults who were not only willing but also able to lead youth toward fuller involvement in a community of faith.

Young Life Ministry:
Room for Catholic Youth Ministers

Jeffrey Johnson

It was in 1969 that I first heard of Young Life. While supervising a CCD program in a parish near Washington, D.C., I listened to the bitter complaints of two fifteen-year-old girls. Why did they *have to* attend CCD when they already attended Young Life, which was so much better? The following evening I went with them to a Young Life session. Since then I have not ceased to be impressed with the method of this ministry.

Young Life claims to serve all Christian denominations, but in my own mind I had always inserted the word "Protestant" between "Christian" and "denomination." Jeff Johnson has shown me the place for active Catholic support of this interdenominational ministry. Writing as a Catholic professional in youth ministry, Johnson shows us, especially through his own personal story, an inside look at the origins, philosophy, and methods of Young Life. Rooting themselves in what they call "relational ministry" and the ministry of friendship with teens, Young Life ministers are traveling the route that must be followed by any successful ministry to youth. If Catholic parishes followed this single foundational aspect of Young Life ministry, they would be well on their way toward fostering a renewed ministry to young people.

Even though Young Life ministers work on an area basis, as Johnson makes clear, I have put his article in this section on parish because the Young Life aim is to direct young people back to their own local churches. In addition, this article raises the serious possibility of several parishes' hiring a youth minister to work with the young people of an area. Since the primary affiliation of youth is not likely to be with a parish, but rather within a somewhat complex network of relationships involving school, sports, peer friendships, jobs, and even possibly parish, an area-wide ministry to youth seems sensible. Many Catholic dioceses have been experimenting with area-wide youth ministry for several years now. A good example is the youth ministry teams developed for the northern counties of the Santa Rosa, California, diocese by Father Don Kimball.

Finally, all of us concerned about ministry to youth must take seriously, appreciate, and learn from any helpful initiatives on behalf of youth, no matter from what source.

During the past six years a group of Catholic youth ministers have been using the methods of an evangelical organization called Young Life to reach young people in St. Cloud, Minnesota. The story of our area was a familiar one—high school CCD classes that no longer attracted students, failure of a release-time program, frustrated parents, pastors, and parishes. In this context, two of us began a Young Life club in St. Cloud and soon I realized that the strengths of Young Life's ministry matched the needs of the Catholic Church in our area. The purpose of this article is to explain Young Life's style of youth ministry and how we have incorporated this into our local and diocesan approach to youth catechesis.

The strength of Young Life centers around the ability to evangelize, disciple, and call into ministry the high school kids who are totally uninvolved with a local church. I am convinced that this outreach and relational style of ministry can complement any program of youth catechesis, whether in a parish or a school setting. My belief comes from the fact that my first faith experiences, leadership training, and invitation into ministry came through Young Life.

Young Life began in Dallas, Texas, with the work of a young seminarian named Jim Rayburn. Jim was a deeply committed Christian who loved kids and could effectively communicate his concern for them. The time was 1940 and Jim was working with a Bible-oriented Christian group called the Miracle Book Club. He had an effective ministry going with this group, but found that he naturally gravitated toward kids outside the Church. Jim began hanging around the high school in an effort to make friends with those untouched by church programs. These kids soon responded to his easy-going manner and were attracted by his acceptance of and concern for them.

As Jim attempted to love them unconditionally, he won their respect and friendship. It was easy for Jim to gather these kids together for an evening of fun and music and finish with a short talk on the Christian faith. The response was tremendous. Kids heard the story of God's personal concern for them made credible by Jim's individual concern for them. Those early years were filled with summer camping trips, tent meetings, and school assemblies, but mostly hours of hanging out with kids.

Jim soon realized the sound scriptural approach of his ministry, for just as God came into our world as a human person in order to communicate His love, Jim was entering the high school world in the understandable form of an adult friend. As Jim saw it, he was "winning the right to be heard." The key to his success was friendship, genuine caring for young people that communicated God's concern for their individual lives.

As his ministry grew, Jim recruited fellow seminarians and other adults to help him establish the "Young Life Campaign." Young Life's style of reaching out to kids with the Christian message was radical for its time and place. Within the neutral setting of the high school world, Young Life was especially successful with kids who were uninvolved in their local churches.

In a few short years Jim's vision spread beyond Texas as Young Life grew in numbers of clubs, staff men and women, and support from interdenominational groups of adults. Today Young Life operates in about 125 communities in the United States and in 13 foreign countries. There are about 400 full-time staff and 5,800 volunteer leaders working in 1,120 Young Life clubs. Young Life also owns properties that will serve 16,000 kids in the summer.

THE 5 C's IN OPERATING A YOUNG LIFE AREA: CLUB, CAMP, CAMPAIGNERS, CONTACT, COMMITTEE

CLUB—A typical Young Life club looks much the same as Jim's original one. The group gathers in one of the kids' homes for an hour on a school night. The atmosphere is informal, beginning with lively, sing-along music meant to release energy and begin to focus the group's attention. Next comes a skit of some sort, involving the kids and/or leaders. The leader may get three of the biggest guys in the club up front, dress them in bibs and baby hats, and have them drink cokes from baby bottles. The skit gets the group to laugh at itself and is usually followed by some announcements about a weekend camp or special event. After some quieter, more thoughtful music comes a short personal talk about Christ and the Christian message.

The club is a vehicle for meeting new kids and strengthening existing relationships and proclaiming the Gospel in an informal setting. The dynamics of the meeting—the music, the humor, and the informality—are all geared toward creating an atmosphere to present the story of Christ in an attractive and digestible form. Young Life staff describe their meetings as designed for non-Christians, i.e., ones who have not heard or accepted the Gospel. The club is meant as an outreach tool, not as a complete catechetical program, in the belief that a relationship with Christ is the necessary basis for all doctrines and values.

The uniqueness of the Young Life Club lies in the leader's ability to present the story of Christ in a personal and understandable form. The basics of the Christian faith are covered in a year's messages in such a way that kids feel free to come and go with no pressure to accept anything. This style of presenting the faith is coupled with the belief that the Word proclaimed does convict the hearts through the work of the Holy Spirit. Ever since Jim Rayburn's humorous yet powerful messages moved those Dallas kids, Young Life has given special attention to presenting Jesus in an attractive and identifiable way. When effective proclamation is coupled with an attractive model of the Christian life-style, the impact of the Christian message is significant.

CAMP—As other youth organizations have found, retreats are the richest context in which kids can experience the Christian message. Young Life also uses weekend retreats and week-long camps to build new relationships with kids. The program provides quality time for friendships to develop by having other staff people run the clubs, skits, recreation, meals, etc., freeing the local Young Life leaders to experience everything with their groups.

CAMPAIGNERS—The follow-up group to both club and camp is called Campaigners, small Christian growth groups that focus on Bible study, discussion, and prayer. Kids deepen relationships as they learn to apply the Scriptures to their own lives and pray conversationally. The group's effectiveness is dependent upon the leader's ability to model a credible Christian life-style.

CONTACT—From the leader's perspective, the core of his ministry is "contact work," the unstructured time spent in building relationships with kids. Contact work is creative loafing in the adolescent world, hanging out at the focal points in a community that attract kids—primarily the high school or extensions of the high school subculture. It means hours spent at the school, going to games, practices, concerts, shopping centers, fast food restaurants, all for the purpose of meeting and talking with kids on their turf.

COMMITTEE—From the Church and greater community's standpoint, the most important element is the core of committed adults who form the Young Life Committee. These men and women are local community people who are responsible for the financial, spiritual, and moral support of total Young Life ministry in a community. They provide the budget of an area, staff salaries, camp expenses, leadership training, etc.—all from donations solicited from the community. In this way, Young Life can exist in an area only as an expression of community concern for young people.

Because Young Life is not the total Church, it cannot provide a total ministry for youth. Acknowledged weaknesses include follow-up after high school, the sacramental dimension, and involvement of Young Life kids in the needs of their communities. Within the Church's total ministry to youth, Young Life sees itself as an extended arm of the local Body of Christ, offering God's love in a unique outreach of friendship.

My own involvement with Young Life began when I was a sophomore in high school and my group of friends started going to our school's club. At Young Life I heard the story of Jesus in my own language and saw this message lived out in Jack and Andy, our two club leaders. Through club, winter camp, and Campaigners, I learned that faith was not merely attending Mass, receiving the sacraments, and being a good person, but involved a personal relationship with Christ.

During my junior year my mother was concerned that I receive some Catholic doctrine and so I reluctantly attended my parish's CCD program. My last CCD class had been in sixth grade in preparation for Confirmation, and I found the high school classes even more boring. The difference was that now I had a personal faith and found weekly quizzes too detached from everyday life to help me grow in my faith. I am certain that I learned some facts from those classes, but they would have been meaningless without my faith experience through Young Life. It was in the boredom of those CCD classes that I first asked the question "Why can't the Catholic Church do something like Young Life?"

This question was to stay with me. After graduation, I attended the University of Notre Dame and there met a man named Chuck Lehman who was doing groundwork for Young Life in South Bend. During my sophomore year he invited me to visit a meeting and soon after asked me to join him in leading the club. For the next three years I led music and learned from a leadership perspective the essentials of club and Campaigners while building relationships with high school kids.

During my senior year I learned about "Youth Leadership, Minnesota," a training program created by Young Life staff members concerned about preparing qualified leadership for the future. Youth Leadership places men and women in churches or youth agencies for field experience while they pursue graduate studies, usually in theology. The thrust of the training is relational in style and is supervised by an experienced youth minister in the trainee's community. Through the guiding friendship of Dave Phillips, Youth Leadership's director at the time, I received additional training while in the M.A. theology program at St. John's University, near St. Cloud.

During those two years another Youth Leadership student and I began Young Life in St. Cloud, first by introducing ourselves to the school administration and churches in the area. We met a few kids through Young Life contacts, invited them to a club meeting, and began building relationships from there. After four kids attended a Young Life camp that summer, we began a Young Life club in the fall while considering how to expand our ministry.

The question I had asked in high school CCD class was to be answered in the ministry being developed in the St. Cloud area. The following spring we gathered the pastors of the local churches together to further explain Young Life and ask them to support the ministry in St. Cloud. Four parishes supported me for the next two years to do the work of a Young Life staff person, and since then I have focused my work in one church while joining the Catholic diocesan staff in youth ministry.

During the last six years, we have developed our leadership team from the community and colleges in the area and from that group has come four of the eight youth ministers in our area. All of us are using the Young Life style of ministry to some degree—club, Campaigners, weekends, team leadership—as well as doctrinal classes, liturgies, social and recreational activities. Our greatest weakness is the lack of adult leadership from our own parishes, for the majority of our forty leaders come from the colleges in our area. We are pleased that five of our present leaders have come through our Young Life clubs, but we recognize the need to sink deeper roots into the adult community of our parishes.

Our individual programs differ, but we all agree on the primary importance of contact work. We have been blessed with sympathetic school administrators who allow us to circulate freely in the high schools that we serve, only one of which is Catholic. We are further blessed with generous pastors and parishes that are freeing our time to work relationally with young people. Our experience in this predominantly Catholic area confirms what Jim Rayburn found forty years ago, namely that life changes come from "one life touching another."

PRINCIPLES OF YOUNG LIFE'S MINISTRY

Friendship has been the most essential element in Young Life's style of ministry—the belief that a personal friendship is the best vehicle to share faith with a young person. Adolescence is a time of transition from childhood to adulthood, a time of profound physical, emotional, and spiritual changes, a time of identity formation. Unfortunately, this is the time when an adolescent is moving away from familiar institutions—the family, church, or neighborhood, the traditional sources for adult friends. Young people today see most adults in authority roles such as teachers, bosses, priests, policemen, and consequently are left to their own peer relationships for guidance and friendship.

Young Life attempts to work with the sociology of the adolescent world by discovering the key focal points for kids in a community and being there. To expect kids to come to a church program can at times go against the flow of their lives; rather we must take the initiative and bring our concern where they can hear it. Beginning with Jim Rayburn's concern for the outsiders, this outreach orientation has tuned leaders into the needs to which they must address the Christian message.

One Young Life staff man named Don Johnson uses the following drawing to explain his approach to outreach.

Christian Ministry to Those "Without"
(Colossians 4:5)

The Uninvolved and Unconcerned

The Involved but Unconcerned

The Concerned but Uncommitted

The New Disciple

Company of the Committed

There are varying levels of relatedness to Christ and His Church, from the uninvolved and unconcerned to the "Company of the Committed," Elton Trueblood's term for the Church. Believers seek to reach out to all segments of the world in hopes of inviting them into the fullness of life in Christ. Applied to youth ministry, the varying levels of involvement might look like this:

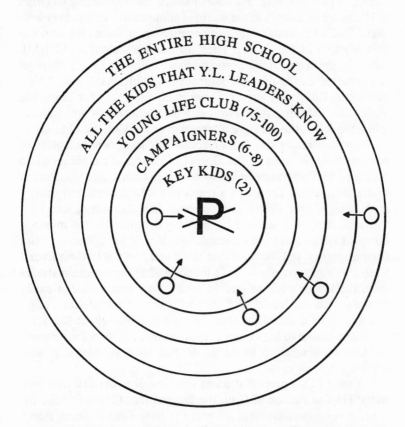

Our ministry would then be seen as an effort to invite the young people we encounter one step closer into the Christian life. When each person of a leadership team has his own set of relationships established in different parts of the high school world, the impact on a school can be significant.

Theologically, this ministry through friendships could be called "Incarnational Evangelism," literally bringing the good news in flesh. God's most complete revelation of Himself came in the person of Jesus so that His message of love could be understood by mankind. Likewise, the Church's concern for young people must find its expression in adults committed to sharing their faith in a personal way. As Jesus pitched his tent among us (John 1:14), so we must walk in the world of adolescents, to discover with them God's understanding and acceptance of them. We can see this lifestyle in Paul's first letter to the Thessalonians (2:1-13), where he describes how he brought those believers to faith through his personal caring and uncompromising faith. As Young Life's president, Bill Starr, says, "There is no substitute for living life with kids," sharing their hurts and joys, successes and failures while modeling the creative alternative of the Christian life-style.

Another major strength of Young Life has been the ability to present the essentials of the Gospel in clear and simple terms to young people who have failed to hear it in their churches. Part of that effectiveness comes as a result of contact work, but mostly from being simple, direct, and personal. In a club setting kids hear the basic story of Jesus told by one truly commited to the message he speaks. Jim Rayburn's formula was simple yet effective: "Get their attention, tell them a Bible story and apply it to their lives." Club messages usually include humor and always contain stories from the leader's life related in such a way that kids can easily identify with the leader and then with the scriptural story (e.g., Zacchaeus as a social outcast, up a tree). Throughout the year, messages also give kids practical application of Gospel values and definite challenges to being or deepen their relationship with Christ.

Young Life's presentation of the Gospel is divided into four parts: (1) The Person of God, the incarnation; (2) man's need for God, a relational concept of sin; (3) how Christ meets man's needs—the words and work of Christ; and (4) Christian commitment and life-style. Club leaders vary their use of this message scheme, covering the sequence in a month, semester, or a year's time. The impact of the club messages is that the young person can hear the Good News as a unified story.

Lastly, the key to any successful youth ministry is the adult leadership. Young Life has always put its best resources into training and creative development of new forms of ministry. The quality of ministry in a Young Life club or any youth ministry is directly related to the quality of the relationships and faith-life of the adult leadership. Fellowship brings forth ministry. When Christians gather to share their lives and faith and pray together, ministry emerges as a natural expression of that fellowship. Ministry without fellowship is merely "youth work." When fellowship truly happens, young people can see a leadership team as a community of believers giving witness to Christ, a visible model of the Church in their midst.

PRACTICAL APPLICATION

1. *Outreach: A Ministry of Friendships*

If we believe that faith is best communicated through friendships, how does our ministry reflect that belief? Ministry to the total young person requires that we know the high school world, its atmosphere, its pressures, the heroes, the outcasts, its rhythm of life, and its needs in order to speak God's Word within this world. This direct contact outside a "religious setting" is essential to a ministry that seeks to truly serve young people. I know that the quality of my ministry is directly affected by the number of hours that I am able to spend with kids outside of meetings; there is no substitute for contact work.

Do you know the adolescent subculture in your area? If not, take some time for some informal sociological research: Where are the kids? What are their hangouts? Who are their favorite teachers? Talk to school administrators, favorite teachers, parents, fast-food restaurant managers, policemen, Protestant youth ministers—anyone who is knowledgeable about the high school scene, and become an expert on your area. Then ask the question: "Where can I spend time to build relationships with young people?

This outreach mentality moves us from being concerned only about the ones who come to our program to offering ourselves in friendship to those outside the influence of the Church. We do not have to look far in the New Testament to see the concern of Jesus and the early Church for outsiders.

2. *Proclaiming the Good News*

When do most young people (or any people) tune out of a sermon? Usually when the talk ceases to be personal and is simply moralizing. Young people are most interested in other people's lives, what makes adults tick, and how they make their decisions. In preaching or speaking to young people we must begin with their interests—human lives—and more importantly with our own lives and faith. Adolescents need to see transparent adult examples of faith who are willing to share their personal stories of faith and are able to express the story of God's love for them. The Scriptures are revelant to the adolescent's world, but we must do the translating not only with a new paraphrased version, but with our lives.

The question for us, then, is "Have our young people truly heard the Good News of God's love for them—personally?" If not, perhaps we need a new setting within which to present the message. A new combination of music, humor, and informality might open some ears to God's acceptance and love.

3. *The Call into Ministry*

The greatest source of leaders for Young Life is from within its own ranks, i.e., the kids themselves. It is not unusual for a Young Life staff person to tell of his initial involvement with Young Life through first meeting a leader at school, being invited to a club, then perhaps to a weekend or week-long camp. The next step might be a work-crew assignment, a month of volunteer work at one of the Young Life properties, then perhaps training as a leader during college. Finally, after graduate training, that person may be invited to join the full-time staff. Many others serve as volunteer leaders and committee people or use their experience within their local churches.

I believe that this is a modern model of the early Christian style of deepening involvement in the Church; namely, evangelization, discipleship, and the call into ministry. Through an outreach style of evangelization, Christian growth groups, and gradual leadership training, a totally uninvolved young person can be invited into the fullness of the Church's life. The challenge facing us is to create ways of gradually inviting young people into the ministry and leadership of the future Church.

4. *Fellowship* → *Ministry*

If true ministry is indeed based on Christian fellowship, what does that mean for our group of leaders or teachers? It means that young people will go no further or deeper than their leaders go. If leaders are not praying together it will be hard to ask the group to pray; if you cannot speak personally about your faith, it will be difficult to get the kids to express their own faith. Many Young Life leaders spend as much or more time with other leaders as with their kids to insure a spiritual depth that focuses the leadership group on God's love. This is also the best way to reproduce one's own ministry, to give away what one knows about youth ministry for the benefit of more young people. The questions for us all are, "How much quality time do we spend with our leaders? What would happen if we were more involved with their lives?" Perhaps we need to rewrite a few job descriptions around the needs of the relationships involved in Christian ministry. Notice how relational and spiritual the "job descriptions" were among the Apostles in the early Church.

5. *Schools and Religious Education Programs*

The challenge to any structured program is to include relationship-building activities within the existing curriculum, both for teachers and capable volunteers. We are emerging from a time when we taught faith intellectually by utilizing only educational vehicles to pass on the faith. If we believe that the student-teacher relationship is of prime importance in learning faith, how does that appear in our lesson plan? We know how authority can stifle relationships with young people, but do we offer some nonauthoritarian settings for our teachers?

I know of a Catholic Young Life leader teaching junior high CCD in a parish who insists on staying with the same group of kids for three years. One of his relational tools is a "secret notebook," a journal that kids write in at the end of class and pass on to Gene. During the week he replies to their questions or comments and returns them at the beginning of the next class, and Gene assures me that they are filled with some deep thoughts and feelings. This style of education tells kids that their teacher is more concerned about his relationship with them than with mastering a certain grade-level text. It tells them that they are important, a message our young people deeply need to hear.

CONCLUSION

Young Life's philosophy of ministry to the unchurched of the adolescent world speaks prophetically to our Church's efforts in youth catechesis. The Church needs to develop the tools of outreach ministry through incarnational evangelism, solid Christian growth groups that teach and disciple believers and graduated levels of leadership involvement that call young people into ministry. In shaping our youth ministry around friendships, we can invite young people into the greatest friendship available—a living relationship with Christ.

Young Life Focus: Friendship

William S. Starr

This statement on the ministry of friendship so central to Young Life is offered here as background to Jeffrey Johnson's preceding overview. The kind of friendship that William Starr describes here is also called "fellowship" in other contexts. The New Testament Letters and other early Christian writings are themselves eloquent testimonies of the kind of friendship the Gospel summons us to and that also summons us to the Gospel.

When a man is asked to resign from the presidency of a company he has served for eighteen years, what happens to him? When a woman is transplanted to Kansas and all the people she knows are back in Washington, D.C., how does she cope? When we measure life by how much we produce, by tasks performed, by Management by Objective, where is the place for being a friend? When it takes so much effort to be a success, how much is left over to *be?*

In our society I see little room for people to have as their objective the simple pleasure of being with a person in order to be a Friend. I have come to a sharp realization that Friendship is not essential to the accomplishment of the goals in most people's lives. Thus, Friendship is a very rare kind of love; it is not coaxed, paid off, shoved, dragged, enticed in a hundred ways, to do the work at hand. We can camouflage the unpleasant tasks, make the humdrum sound exciting; but the objective of management is primarily to get on with the show.

Even in marriage Friendship can be skipped—it is not an essential in our day. The Eros kind of love is certainly present; and the concept of commitment can be fully regarded in a marriage where there is no true Friendship. In the lives of most people Friendship comes way down the line. To take the time to build a Friendship for the sake of sharing deeply is indeed rare; and the Friendship level of love is a very deep level.

C. S. Lewis has written so eloquently in *The Four Loves* about Friendship: " . . . the least *natural* of loves; the least instinctive, organic, biological, gregarious and necessary. It has least commerce with our nerves; there is nothing throaty about it; nothing that quickens the pulse or turns you red and pale. It is essentially between individuals; the moment two men are friends they have in some degree drawn apart together from the herd. Without Eros none of us would have been begotten and without Affection none of us would have been reared, but we can live and breed without Friendship. The species, biologically considered, has no need of it."

To me, Friendship is the most costly love, because it is all expenditure. There is no return to be expected. If there is a return, that is a bonus. Friendship asks and expects no payment. It doesn't fit into the categories that we understand, such as doing something out of obedience. A child obeying his parents may be acting out of love, but the obedience is probably to please the parents, to get along in the family, to make things run relatively smoothly. Seldom does a child think of being a friend to her mother or father. The act of obeying is trying to accomplish some end. It's when we're not trying to get anything done, that it is a Friendship kind of love.

Between the rearing of our first children, and the rearing of our last one, I see such a difference. Ruth and I are old enough to be Richie's grandparents, and it gives us such a different feeling. I feel I can be his friend without manipulating him to my goals. I was not able to do that with the first children because I was trying too hard to be a good father. I'm not trying to be a good father, per se, to Richie; I am offering the littly guy *myself*. It's a beautifully relaxed thing. I'm not looking for any return; but I'm getting an overwhelming response!

The other evening I was deeply moved, and the tears were

rolling quietly down my cheeks. Richie, noticing, climbed up in my lap and said, "I hardly ever get to see you cry, Dad." Together we talked about the meaning of tears and we shared the goodness of being able to feel deeply.

Through the centuries Friendship has been revered as the most "spiritual" of Love's expressions. Homer, as far back as 850 B.C. set down his obervation that two friends were as "two bodies with one soul inspired." Diogenes in 200 A.D. expressed the same thought, "A friend is one soul abiding in two bodies."

Friendship is strangely separate from the material affairs of life. We will go out to dinner with companions or acquaintances, and have a great time; but meeting the everyday needs of life is basically an interruption, a distraction of the always-too-short time which friends have together. "Let him be to me a spirit," Emerson says in his essay on Friendship. "A message, a thought, a sincerity, a glance from him I want, but not news, nor pottage."

Because we are all mutually tied to a loving Father, I think God wants us to love each other in a deep respectful way. We all have one Ancestor, and He is our Creator. All created things are tied together because we are tied to Him. I can see how right the Environmentalists are—the animal lovers, all those people who care about the endangered species. Because we have a common Father, we are all inter-related in a sense. We exist together because of a common tie outside of ourselves, beyond ourselves. That makes Friendship, with a person or with an animal, the most logical expression of love imaginable, because we are, in fact, related to each other.

Companionship is the first step. This is the matrix out of which Friendship is born. This goes on in mess halls, locker-rooms, pubs, country clubs, boats, parks, kitchens, backyards. Activities such as hunting, fishing, sewing, shopping, lunching, playing cards are often referred to in terms of Friendship, but these "friends" are more often "companions." This is not to disparage companions; rather, it is to distinguish between them.

Lewis explains: "Friendship arises out of mere Companionship when two or more companions discover that they have in common some insight or interest or even taste which the others do not share and which, till that moment, each believed to be his own unique treasure (or burden) . . . It is when two such persons discover one another, when . . . with immense difficulties or amazing speed, they share their vision, it is then that Friendship is born. And instantly they stand together in an immense solitude . . . The very condition of having Friends is that we should want something else besides Friends. Where the truthful answer to the question, 'Do you see the same truth?' would be, 'I see nothing and I don't care about the Truth; I only want a Friend,' no Friendship can arise—though Affection of course may. There would be nothing for the Friendship to be about; and Friendship must be about something, even if it were only an enthusiasm for dominoes or white mice. Those who have nothing can share nothing; those who are going nowhere can have no fellow travelers."

It strikes me how infinitely more we have to be about than dominoes! It's a little different to me than God *commanding* us to love each other. That is the *agape* kind of love where no mutual interests draw people together; that is an act of obedience to please the Father. You cannot *command* somebody to be a friend. Emerson says that "we talk of choosing our friends, but friends are self-elected. Reverence is a great part of it." Friendship comes as the result of seeing that the essence of life is in giving when there is no end to be accomplished—when you have no right to any claim on anything other than that you both happen to belong to God.

The truth stands out to me as I read the letter Paul wrote to the Christians in Thessalonica. He says, "You know what manner of men we were among you *for your sake*." And I see Paul being a friend. If a person is going to live out this example as Paul did, (I Thes. 1:5) he quite forgets the end result in the intensity of primary living. Paul's purpose was not to get people to *do* anything; he was a man with a rare truth who lived with them *for their sake*. Then if the Holy Spirit opened the hearts of his friends to hear the words that were appropriate to the truth of the Gospel, then those words would take place. In Paul's case they did; but that was not why Paul became a Friend to the Thessalonians. Because he was gripped by the truth and tenderness of Jesus Christ, his life was destined to be spent in intense pursuit of all that life was meant to be. A life that spilled over in enthusiasm ("Do you see the same truth?" or "Do you care about the same truth?") would have had great appeal to the truth-seekers in Paul's day. Being joint seekers of the same truth, the same beauty, the same God, offers a blazing and compelling attraction whenever we are willing to live among people *for their sake*.

This kind of love that is neither pushing nor grasping is unbelievable in our world. It is a love of mutuality, of equality, where you are neither masculine or feminine. It goes beyond sexuality, beyond nationality, beyond role or profession. It is being God's human creation, willing to risk being human. Unembarrassed by material advantage, or prestige, two human beings come together in a simple common search, on a common journey.

It looks to me as though God meant for love to be lived out on a unique basis of equality; He made man in His own image. Then when He walked in the cool of the Garden of Eden He looked for His friends, and found them hiding from Him. His play for equality was short-lived; and from Genesis 3 to Acts 2 this quality is missing in the Biblical record. What God intended in creation was to be revealed in the new humanity. What happened on the day of Pentecost brought the disciples into a celebrative, joyous relationship that broke language barriers, and introduced a communion of love, such as human beings never had known.

Being a friend is what we're about in Young Life. I'd like to suggest that while we see the birth of Jesus Christ ranking at the top of all human history, we do not want to limit ourselves to *talking* about the theology of incarnation—except as it forms a model for us. Rather, we consider it as methodology. The deeper we go into our own hearts, the more likely we are to get a vital response back from others. The response is overwhelmingly good when they can read vibrations that say, "Here is somebody who isn't after a thing. He doesn't want me to do anything, to give up anything. He is just offering himself unconditionally."

Like Martin Luther, I feel that as the Friendship ripens, there will be a natural sharing in words of our very best understanding of the Gospel. It is an integral part of Friendship to share the deepest of all personal things. Once you have reached this level with someone, you want them to understand certain things you would not care at all to share with others. The Gospel to me is not something you throw around, or exhibit in an impersonal fashion on a billboard. It's like when God told Moses, "You're on holy ground. Get your shoes off." That's the way I feel about the Gospel. When you get down to that level of sharing with a person, it is holy ground.

It is audacious for us to think that any human experience by itself is sufficient to convey the immense good news of the Gospel. We have to put words to it eventually, even though in doing so we stumble. The Holy Spirit of God graciously takes that truth and uses everything He has going for Him; so the Truth we speak is perhaps better understood if we have made even the earliest steps of friendship. While sharing a discovery can add new dimensions to the Friendship, it can also drive a wedge between two people. Expressing innermost thoughts is always a risk. Friendship may be jeopardized; but you don't throw out the friend because something happens that you can't understand. You work it out on the basis that there is some reason for this disturbance.

This, to me, is why Friendship is a vital aspect of propagation of the Gospel. If, indeed, something does alienate or separate or hurt, Friendship is the force that makes two individuals willing to go back and pick up the hurt and look at it together. What did happen? What are we finding out? On the other hand, without Friendship, if offense takes place, who cares? Who will bother to want to repair the damage?

The Gospel I understand is given life in the Incarnation. If we think we can dispense with this, giving certain words to a total stranger, then it seems to me we have not grasped the Gospel at all. It seems to me that the Gospel is embedded in the Incarnation. In the human involvement we begin to call forth a new being.

Ugo Betti, in his play "The Burnt Flower Bed," expresses this truth: "Nothing else matters half so much. To reassure one another. To answer each other. Perhaps only you can listen to me and not laugh. Everyone has inside himself—what shall I call it?—a piece of good news. Everyone is a very great, very important character. Every man must be persuaded, even if he is in rags, that he is immensely, immensely important . . . Don't stand on top of him. Don't stand in his light . . . Give him great, great hopes. He needs them, especially if he is young."

If we put evangelism in the same category as other tasks, we become task-oriented. Then I fear we've missed the whole point. God could have spread the word about His love by dropping leaflets on the world, but He didn't. He took the time and trouble to take human form and come to us personally. He spent a period of years in an attempt to express to His friends what was in His heart.

Because we too are tied to space-time concepts, I believe God expects us also to exercise this non-essential kind of love in getting His job done in our society today. This one vehicle, humanly speaking, that gives us some chance of success is Friendship. Understood correctly, relational evangelism is based on a deep level of Friendship. Floodgates that are normally closed just naturally swing open to reveal an inner truth, an inner tenderness and beauty. This Friendship is a goal toward which we work. I long to see this happen with all our leaders—this highest kind of human experience.

Purposes of Young Life

Young Life Board Statement

In some ways this third piece in our "Young Life Trilogy" is the most valuable, since it is the statement of purpose of the Young Life organization. As such, it lays out for Catholics a full statement of what Young Life is trying to accomplish for young people. In addition, it offers a good view of some of the procedures of Young Life, thus complementing the previous two articles by Johnson and Starr.

I myself am impressed at how well thought-out the Young Life ministry is. Young Life does not try to do everything for young people. It tries to do a few things well while using other community agencies for services outside its own competency.

My hope in presenting this statement of purpose is that it may provide a sort of paradigm against which parishes, areas, or dioceses can develop their own statements of purpose in dealing with youth. I have found too few Catholic parishes and dioceses that have worked out a coherent approach to youth ministry. As in other areas of life, our unconscious and unexamined presuppositions can sometimes be actually dangerous or at least counterproductive.

THE CONSTITUTION OF THE YOUNG LIFE CAMPAIGN

ARTICLE I   The name of the corporation is "THE YOUNG LIFE CAMPAIGN."

ARTICLE II   The purpose shall be to proclaim in deed and word the Person and work of Jesus Christ to the world adolescent community (with emphasis upon the North American young person) by any and every means as God directs.

A. To introduce the Gospel of the Lord Jesus Christ to young people who are not personally committed to Him.

B. To establish personal, unconditional friendships with young people as essential in the proclamation of the Gospel.

C. To encourage, among young people who are personally committed to Christ, the development of a Christ-centered life which shall manifest itself in an active concern for the spiritual and physical needs of mankind.

D. To encourage committed Christian young people to an active participation in the church.

Under the direction of the Board of Directors and the Staff, these general aims shall be implemented by such activities as neighborhood meetings in different communities, by camping programs, by evangelistic meetings, and by printed publications.

YOUNG LIFE IN THE BROAD PERSPECTIVE OF GOD'S WORK

Young Life in the Church

Historically we have viewed Young Life as part of the Church . . . in mission to the world. This fact has been stated in many ways, but may be confusing to some staff and friends.

When Young Life goes into any area, we realize that the movement of God is already taking place there among His people, and we are joining in and enhancing that movement. God doesn't arrive when we arrive—He's been there!

With this in mind, we cannot ignore other believers, Christian organizations and ministers in the area. Every effort must be made to establish accountable relationships between our staff and those leaders who share our overall objectives. Though progress may be slow and discouraging, we must not let down in our attempts to harness our contribution with others in the community of believers. Practically speaking, we would hope every Area Director would seek a regular, working, praying, accountable relationship with a group of other Christian leaders and ministers.

Out of this relationship may come grand new opportunities for outreach in the community. Worship congregations have resources which when combined with ours may serve to expand God's purposes in remarkable ways. Their most obvious resources are *volunteer leadership potential, Christian nurture opportunities,* and *finances.* Our resources? . . . *What we have learned about relating personally to kids, the approach to proclamation of the Gospel and Presentation of the winsome Saviour, the camping ministry,* and *concepts of leadership.*

The Lord is laying upon us the conviction that we cannot reach kids everywhere without a broader view of how we may work with and influence local congregations. Young Life can be a model in the community—a resource for motivation, training and encouragement—that ends up with a lot of young people reached with an incarnational approach through leaders who may call it by a different name but who are committed to those things we have learned and shared.

In summary, we affirm that:

1. All Young Life staff should be responsible, involved members in a local church congregation. (This does not mean we must teach or give heavy time involvement, but rather to worship and serve as the Lord enables.)

2. Area Directors should seek accountable relationships with Christian leadership in the community.

3. We are to pray and work toward mutual involvement and sharing of experiences and resources with the local worship congregations.

4. Those kids we influence for personal commitment to Christ are to be encouraged toward local worship congregations for nurture and service.

5. We recognize the existence of other Christian organizations that may even at times appear competitive for Christian support. We should take the initiative in our approach to these people in hopes for honest dialogue and creative fellowship and service.

Young Life and Community Agencies

As in the case of church relatedness, we see the necessity for leaders to become familiar with other helping and reconciling agencies at work in the community, and to cooperate with and learn from these agencies. This is not for "public relations" reasons, but rather what we believe about the quality of our outreach, our limitations, and the great help these agencies can be to our ministry.

For example, too few of us understand the complexity of the problem of alcoholism—what happens to the family of the alcoholic—the unbelievable effect upon the growing youngster in the home. There are people who have given their adult lives to dealing with this immense social problem of our day. One out of six kids we work with comes from a home affected by alcoholism. We have little choice as responsible, incarnational leaders. We should learn from these special agencies and establish working relationships with them.

Do we know what local resources are available to us in the fields of mental health, law enforcement, health care, drug rehabilitation, remedial and special education? It is true, the Young Life leader has a specific calling in the relational proclamation of the Gospel—all the more reason to work with the resource agencies which can help the people we are dealing with.

In summary, we affirm that:

1. We as staff and leaders in a community will take the initiative to study agencies, and be in contact with them for resources beyond our own as we deal with young people. Where we find qualified agencies we will utilize their services in order that we might maintain our focus upon our primary task.

2. We have never considered ourselves experts in every personal and social problem, but we want to be good students, always learning and equipping ourselves for a "whole person" ministry to kids, for we know that man's more obvious needs (physical, etc.) are related to the ultimate need of his relationship with God in

Christ. Whenever possible, we want to minister to these obvious needs, too.

OUR MINISTRY

Contact/Club

We have not outgrown the basic principle of establishing unconditional relationships with kids who need Christ—and the proclamation of the Gospel in a club-type setting. Even though there will be situations where the traditional club ministry may not work best, we affirm the contact/club approach as a valid Young Life strategy and calling for our day.

Young Life in any area must have trained leaders majoring in the difficult and sometimes discouraging work of direct relationship-building with non-Christian young people, wherever they are. In most cases this will lead to an opportunity to share Christ in a club meeting of some kind—a meeting designed for the non-Christian.

In summary, we affirm that:

1. All Young Life outreach is to be characterized by grass-roots contact by leaders with uncommitted young people, recognizing that many who claim church membership actually do not attend or are anti-church in attitude. We are determined to reach out to these young people wherever they are, building unconditional friendships.

2. Proclamation of the Gospel, by deed and word, be it in the small or large meeting, or individually, is to be a learning situation for non-Christians. These may follow different programmatic and cultural forms, but the test is: What are the kids learning about our Saviour, and what does it mean to be committed to Him through redemptive faith?

3. Young Life leadership aspires to be in the front ranks of outreach strategy—seeking new approaches, innovation—trying by every means possible for a cutting-edge ministry with hard-to-reach kids.

City Ministries

The Lord has blessed Young Life with remarkable results in our approach to suburban-oriented young people. This work must continue and expand. The future is bright for reaching more of these kids who will take community leadership roles in years to come.

When we speak of a commitment to the city and to minorities, we do not mean a shift of emphasis from our suburban ministry to something else more important. Some have read it this way—that Young Life is not excited and challenged anymore by its opportunities in suburbia. On the contrary, we seek by every means possible to reach typical high school kids.

What we are saying is that we believe God is calling us to look at our communities in their entirety. We know the incarnational principles of outreach will be effective wherever applied, whether in the cities or suburbs. Like our Lord Jesus Christ, we, too, are called to go into all the world around us. It is our mission to help raise up more Christian leaders for our work among minority groups in the city.

Our track record has not always been too encouraging. Sometimes we have hurt for leadership and funding in our urban ministries. Failures have taught us lessons, and successes have encouraged us. We are not giving up. We must find ways to reach all sorts of kids in all kinds of living situations and cultures.

In summary, we affirm that:

1. The commitment made years ago to city kids is very much with us today, and we will pursue every means possible for leadership and funding.

2. In areas which include suburban people, city and minorities, the strategy for expansion is to show commitment to all of them.

3. Since suburbia holds so much of the power and financial resource in a community, we cannot allow our friends there to go unchallenged by the needs of the city.

Young Life leadership is aware that these goals will not be reached automatically just because we state them. We hope that help is on the way. It may come in new forms of organization, or through our Urban Vice President and his colleagues, or fresh new approaches for funding. We all have been frustrated, wondering how to "grab the handles." May God help us in our struggle together!

Whenever opportunity and personal calling enable efforts in *rural* situations, we welcome and encourage them. We feel a weight of obligation, however, for a mission-wide move toward unlocking the urban possibilities at this time.

Camping

It is expected that any Young Life area will be involved in year-round camping ministries. We are convinced of the effectiveness of being with kids for an extended period of time in a new and different environment. Our incarnational approach thrives in these situations.

In recent years we have seen innovations to meet many objectives—stress camping, bike trips, Campaigners camps, urban plunges. This trend should be encouraged. Some of our most creative effort will continue in these directions.

However, the one-week camp at a major Young Life property is still for the purpose of *outreach* to kids who need Christ, or for those who are so new in their understanding of the faith that they need to hear the Gospel carefully reviewed.

In summary, we affirm that:

1. The camping experience for urban and suburban young people is a valid and effective means for ministry—outreach and nurture.

2. Some of the camping effort is for the purpose of Christian nurture, but the Young Life emphasis in its major properties will be outreach to kids who need Christ.

3. Each Young Life staff person normally will be expected to participate by bringing kids to camp from his area and having a camp staff assignment during each summer.

4. Every area will take advantage of what we have learned about camping with young people and utilize this in a camping program with adults, the purpose being not only to expose them to what it is we do with young people but also to have the privilege of exposing them to the attractiveness of our Saviour.

Junior High

Recent developmental trends among young people have caused us to lower our Young Life age to the junior high level. We find that these kids are quite capable of understanding and appropriating the life-changing concepts of the Gospel. Due to contemporary social pressures, some young people by the time they are in high school have already tasted enough of life to appear harder to reach, and in some cases to become embittered or apathetic.

In the highly mobile urban scene, there is even more of an urgency to reach the younger kids before some of them are forced into destructive patterns associated with high density populations and limited opportunities.

We have discovered that one very effective means for outreach to the junior high is through our high school and college-age Christians. Effective clubs have been run by these young people under staff guidance, with positive things happening in the lives of the young leaders themselves.

In summary, we affirm that:

1. The strategy for future expansion in Young Life areas will include junior high-age outreach.

2. In most cases the junior high program will be enhanced by short-term involvement of high school or college age Christians, trained and carefully supervised in leadership responsibilities.

International

The dynamics of relational outreach to young people seem to be common to all cultures . . . people respond to unconditional friendships and genuine love, national boundaries notwithstanding.

We have made a commitment to reaching all kids everywhere. This will not require us to tool up for the task of doing it all ourselves with a traditional Young Life U.S.-style operation. Rather, we will respond to those Christian people in the world who want to establish Young Life-type concepts in their own cultures, with their own national leadership, financial autonomy and responsibility, and with their own God-given strategies for reaching young people in their land.

In summary, we affirm that:

1. We are to have a global concern for young people who have yet to hear the claims of Jesus Christ.

2. Our strategy will be either to send advisors to foreign lands for a few years helping indigenous leaders adapt our principles into their culture, or to make available our U.S. training resources to any qualified leaders from other countries.

3. We have no desire to build a world-wide Young Life organization, but rather to see young people in the world exposed to the beauty and truth of Christ because of His life-changing capacity contained in His redemptive act upon the cross in whatever cultural and organization setting God would provide.

Christian Nurture

Though the primary thrust of the Mission is outreach to those who are not committed to Christ, we are to take very seriously our role in helping new Christians to a basic understanding of personal growth and responsibility in the world. This will mean emphasis upon study of Scripture, disciplines of prayer and worship, responsibility to the Church, Christian fellowship, active concern for the spiritual and physical needs of mankind, and living in obedience as disciples of Christ.

Our task is not to indefinitely follow up Young Life kids, with the assumption that if we don't nobody will. The Holy Spirit will be at work in these lives to take them into fresh, new dimensions of Christian experience. We fail any young person if we do not expose **him to** the magnificent scope of the Church around the world, and **his** responsibilities and opportunities therein.

In summary, we affirm that:

1. Young Life leaders are responsible to help committed young people understand the basic ingredients of Christian growth and responsibility, and to establish teaching situations where they may receive this instruction and encouragement.

2. Our goal is to lead these to a full appreciation of the Church of Jesus Christ, the resources therein, the breadth of involvement by people in the world, and its task in sharing the Good News in word and deed.

3. We do have a responsibility to stay in touch as best we can

with former club kids—helping them into growth situations and encouraging them in their walk with Christ. Many times this follow-up activity can best be handled by a volunteer leader on the local team.

4. We recognize that the growth and development of a believer in Jesus Christ is to take place over a whole lifetime, and that Young Life has but a very short time to contribute to the total process of one's growth and development. For the most part, we will simply have the privilege of getting them started in the new adventure of living their life for our Redeemer.

OUR LEADERSHIP

Personal Welfare of Staff

Where do we get our encouragement and refreshment? What do we do with our own personal problems and needs? Is Young Life supposed to meet our total emotional, psychological, spiritual needs? (Some have tried to go this route and have been hurt.)

Young Life is an avenue of expression of the call of God upon a person's life for mission. Warm and significant relationships are often created among staff colleagues. This is only natural when people go through heavy and joyous times together in an incarnational ministry. Other staff are often the people closest to us in heart and spirit when difficult personal needs arise.

We must recognize the danger of casting too much of ourselves upon Young Life, or considering it to be our only family. This can be devastating and a great hindrance to growth. The family of Christ extends so much further. We must take advantage of those relationships beyond our Mission.

In summary, we affirm that:

1. Young Life is a fellowship of staff who have special needs that can often best be met by the ministry of another staff person. We should be sensitive and available to our colleagues for this personal ministry. We also recognize that there will be many other Christians outside of Young Life making a very valuable contribution to the needs of our staff.

2. All staff should seek involvement in a small commitment

group broader than the confines of Young Life where sharing and growth can be enhanced.

Staff Training

Training must continue to be a major emphasis of our Mission. The Lilly grant has made us aware of the effectiveness of certain programmatic approaches to training. So much of the quality of our ministry will depend upon this focus.

In summary, we affirm that:

1. Each staff member is to have an assigned supervisor of his training (Regional Director for most staff) who has responsibility and authority to pursue to completion a basic curriculum of staff training. Their basic curriculum is to include all of the following:

a. Basic Academic Curriculum—O.T., N.T., Bible Survey, Theology, Church History, Ethics and Philosophy of Religions. (These are the core courses of the Institute and M.A. programs.)

b. Psychological Training.

c. Practical Field Work Training—kids, community and committee relations, leadership, office, fund raising.

d. Supervision under a trained Area Director during training period.

e. Urban Sensitivity.

f. Evaluation—of trainee, trainer, program, Area Director.

g. International Philosophy of Young Life.

h. Troubled Kids Training.

i. Personal Spiritual Growth and Nurture.

2. The assigned supervisor is also responsible for encouraging and monitoring continued learning efforts, structured and/or personal initiative learning, for as long as the person is on staff.

3. There will also be a special training program devised for every volunteer in the work, with each of these volunteers being held accountable to an Area Director, and where an Area Director is not present to the Regional Director.

Team Concept in the Area

Our unique, specialized ministry to the adolescent opens doors to all levels of ministry with adults. Time factors make it impossible for area staff to follow and develop each of these opportunities. A group of committed people can do it together, however.

Leadership teams are forming, sometimes around one high school, where people can use their God-given gifts. A high level of commitment to one another and to the Lord is characteristic of these teams. No longer is there a "lone-ranger" feel to the area, where one person carries the total weight of the ministry on his shoulders.

In summary, we affirm that:

1. Club situations are best handled by a group of leaders. There may be a diversity of age and personality—so much the better in order to reach the sociological groupings of the local adolescent scene. The senior leader in this situation is responsible to see that gifts are being utilized and team members communicated with and encouraged.

2. We are to involve people at all levels of the area ministry, giving them a chance to utilize gifts and to feel an integral part of the Young Life team.

3. The local committee is an integral part of any Young Life area team. This group of men and women is to be involved in prayer support, financial support, community information and promotion of Young Life, planning and evaluating (with staff) the area ministry, and in spiritual partnership with area staff.

4. Opportunities for ministry with adults will arise—beautiful ones. Members of the team can take advantage of these. Responsible staff are to remember that these opportunities have come because of our clear focus upon kids who need Christ, not primarily upon adults. Without the ministry to kids, there most likely will be no sustained effectiveness with adults.

5. The opportunity for working with adults is not simply a secondary privilege arising out of our ministry with young people, but has also become a definite responsibility of ours. Young Life must share what we have learned with the Body of Christ at every opportunity. Working with the adult provides us the vehicle for sharing not only the beauty of the Gospel but all that God is teaching us about communicating this message to the kids. This becomes one of the finest methods available for the giving of ourselves away.

EPILOGUE

We realize that this is not a complete statement of all the things Young Life believes. We have considered the more mission-oriented tasks before us. Matters of personal habits and disciplines are largely left unsaid. However, we respect the relational nature of our ministry that demands our lives be a demonstration of the Christ we represent.

Part II

Developing Diocesan Programs

Reflections on Spirituality and Ministry

Timothy D. Fallon

Some readers are certain to wonder why Timothy Fallon's reflections on the relationship between spirituality and ministry find their way into this section dealing with the diocesan task in youth ministry. The reason is that Fallon's paper itself represents an effort to help those working with youth in a diocese to achieve a unified vision of themselves as followers of Jesus serving youth. As Director of Youth Ministry for the Diocese of Kalamazoo, Fallon developed his statement over a period of months in consultation with many persons in different ministries in that diocese.

Fallon believes the foundation for any effective ministry is one's relationship with the Father who has sent the Spirit of Jesus into our lives. Cut off from that foundation, ministry devolves into a mere running of programs and keeping of schedules. On the other hand, ministry enriches the quality of one's spirit-life. Because he is attending to fundamental matters, Fallon sees also the relationship of youth ministry to the wider community. One can see the trajectory of this sort of thinking: it leads to collaboration among the various ministries and eventually one unified ministry of the Church.

▲

REFLECTIONS ON SPIRITUALITY AND MINISTRY

Next time you get together with a group of youth ministers, try this. When asked how you've been, say: "Well, I'm not as busy as I used to be, but I feel better about my ministry." I'll give you odds that the first response is either silence or laughter. I'm amazed at how youth ministers tend to assume busyness and even overwork are part of our calling. I have only recently become aware that when someone asks me how my day was, I am apt to say: "I was swamped!" or "Things weren't too busy." Without even being aware of it, I often describe the quality of my day in terms of my activity level.

It is important to reflect critically on why we tend to be so busy, whether we need to be, if such busyness is an effective way to meet others' needs, whether it is a subconscious response to our own need to be needed, and what effects such an approach to ministry has on our spirituality. In these pages I invite you to reflect with me on this last point—the relationship between our spirituality and our ministry. I will focus these reflections on my own ministry, which is a pastoral youth ministry at the diocesan level. However, from my discussions with other people in other ministries, I get the impression that these insights apply in some degree to all ministry.

I
SPIRITUALITY AND MINISTRY ARE INTEGRAL

To me, spirituality is faith expressed in life-style. This means that my interior life is enfleshed in all I am and do. The lived-response to God's presence in Christ in my life permeates and shapes my entire life. Certainly this means that spirituality has to do with the type of prayer life I have, the quality of my participation at liturgy, and how I minister to others. However, it also has to do with my response to the hitchhiker I see on the way to an appointment, how I relate to the secretaries in the office where I work, and whether I take the time to relax when I need to. The quality of my spirituality—how my faith is expressed in my life-style—is the central focus of my life as a Christian. All other concerns flow from how in touch I am with God's presence in Christ and how well I am able to reflect that presence in my life.

Ministry, it seems to me, is responding in faith to the needs of others. Thus, ministry is that dimension of my spirituality—one essential aspect of it—that deals with my being for others. My ministry expresses my faith and must be shaped by it. Thus questions about the nature of my ministry—whether I am invitational or manipulative in my approach to people, whether paperwork or persons are a priority of my ministry, whether busyness or presence characterizes my life—are also questions about the nature of my spirituality.

Spirituality and ministry are integrally related. Both are based in faith, and are concerned with my response to God's presence in Christ. Spirituality is the totality of that response in all dimensions of life—"in thought, word, and deed," as we used to say. Ministry is that particular dimension of my faith response—that dimension of my spirituality—that has to do with how I give my life for and to others. Thus ministry is an integral aspect of spirituality—the two cannot be separated.

Having said that spirituality and ministry are integrally related, I must also say that it does not seem to me that this integrity has been consciously operative in the life of the Church as I know it. Because we have neglected this integrity, especially in shaping most existing ministries in the Church, we have tended to emphasize "doing" rather than "being" in both spirituality and ministry. Thus busyness and fatigue rather than spiritual vitality haunt many youth ministers. We need to focus on the integral relationship between spirituality and ministry, call it to center stage, and critique present structure and practice in light of it. First let me share a biblical reflection on this relationship.

Near the end of John's Gospel (21:15-19), we find Peter and several of the other disciples on the beach finishing the breakfast Jesus had prepared for them. Peter has experienced the bitter agony of betraying Jesus. Now, in his enthusiasm to be his friend, the repentant disciple has come to Jesus by swimming to shore from the boat. Three times Jesus confronts Peter with a probing question: "Do you love me?" Peter, becoming more upset but also more determined with each response, three times declares his love. Each time Peter declares his love, Jesus calls him to minister to his flock. Peter's ministry is rooted in this intimate moment of reconciliation and love.

We, too, receive our call to minister in the intimacy of our relationship with the risen Lord. Because we respond faithfully to the Lord, we are his ministers. We must, then, consciously keep in mind that it is our relationship with the Lord that makes our response—our ministry—imperative. The uniqueness of our faith relationship has a fundamental influence on the shape of our ministry. Unless our ministry is rooted in and integrally related with our spirituality, it makes no sense.

This integral relationship between spirituality and ministry is reflected both in the individual Christian person and in the Christian community as a whole. It is true for me, and it is true for all of us together. My interior life is reflected in my life-style. When I haven't reflected or taken time to be quiet, I find myself distracted and disinterested in conversation, wanting to get about my busyness, leaving the person I am with in the room but away from in my heart. So, too, the shape of the community's faith life is enfleshed in our communal life. If we haven't shared our faith with one another, but have only carried out the parish business (balancing budgets, hiring teachers, having festivals), we can't still our hearts to hear God's word or celebrate his presence in Eucharist in a meaningful way.

The relationship between spirituality and ministry is reciprocal. Not only does the shape of my spirituality influence the shape of my ministry, but the shape of my ministry influences the shape of my spirituality. For example, my sensitivity to Christ's presence in others might lead me to minister through a visit to a care facility for the profoundly retarded. However, it might also happen that being with a family at the time of a death would lead me to more fully experience the meaning of Christ's death-resurrection in my own life. Thus, ministry both shapes and is shaped by spirituality. Because spirituality and ministry are integral, each influences the other. However, even in this mutual relationship, spirituality remains primary and is the central focus.

II
THE FUNCTIONAL APPROACH CONTRASTED WITH THE PERSONAL APPROACH

Because the integration of spirituality and ministry has not often been conscious, youth ministry and other ministries have often developed on a functional model based on "doing." A diocese wants to do something with young people and so an Office of Youth Ministry or Office of Youth Activities is created. (These two terms—Ministry and Activities—should reflect very different realities.) The functional approach leads to creating *offices,* and diocesan staff persons immediately feel pressured to *do* something that shows *results:* teach classes, give workshops, begin programs, and on and on. (The analogy for the parish seems obvious.) Much of this tendency toward producing results, toward accomplishing the task, is undoubtedly related to an American pragmatic business model that thrives on *functional* goals. Thus, Church ministry becomes unintentionally shaped by a product-oriented mentality of getting the job done. Unfortunately, the result is that in many cases effective administration becomes a higher priority than does the value of personal presence and the need to grow in faith through our relationships in community. When someone drops by to see me, I am so caught up in the papers on my desk that the person is a distraction rather than an opportunity to encounter another.

In this functional view, spirituality—far from being at the heart of the Church's ministry—tends to be one more thing to get done, one more activity on the treadmill of life that must be accomplished before I can get on with other things. It is often like my grace before meals—something to perform before the real activity begins. Rather than spirituality's being a liberating force in my life, it is one more oppressive activity. Rather than spirituality's being a central focus for my ministry, it moves off into a corner for rainy Saturdays with nothing to do or for that occasional retreat experience, which may be an "R & R" in disguise.

On the other hand, when I begin to view consciously my approach to ministry in terms of my spirituality, the nature of faith becomes the norm for developing the shape of my ministry. Thus "doing" becomes less central; the functional takes on its proper perspective. My being in relationship with the risen Lord is the critical focus of my life, hence of my ministry. Who I am is viewed as more important than what I do. Doing is still important as an extension and expression of myself, but my personhood is central.

As persons, we must express ourselves. The artist must paint, the dancer must dance, the poet must write. Yet we are loved and called to God not because of our own achievemer⸱ ᵇut because of his enduring love. Thus the biblical view consistently takes being in relationship to God as the central focus of life. Our words and actions are important to the extent that they express this relationship, but the relationship is of prime importance. This priority of person over function and of being over doing must be normative for shaping our ministry because the Gospel is normative.

III
IMPLICATIONS FOR YOUTH MINISTRY

Critically reflecting on youth ministry with a consciousness that spirituality and ministry are integral could surface any number of pertinent points. Here I have chosen to elaborate three that have far-reaching implications in my own ministry. These are: that reflection on spirituality should be a primary pastoral concern of the American Church, that community is at the heart of ministry, and that spirituality could provide a context and direction for dialogue on how youth ministry relates to other ministries of the Church. I have expanded each of these in what follows. However, the most important point I'd like to make is that what is at stake here is not several items for implementation, but rather a consciousness—that man is whole, that faith is as big as life, that spirituality and ministry are integral. This consciousness must pervade our lives and ministries. These "for instances" are spelled out in order to illumine this consciousness in my own ministry. In reflecting with me, I invite you to explore the implications for your own life.

A. *Reflection on Spirituality*
A critical priority of the American Church should be that of enabling people to reflect on their own spirituality, on how their faith is expressed in their life-style. Youth ministry is significant, it seems to me, because it reveals this priority, and it is and will be a vital ministry within the Church to the extent that it can help us address this priority.

First, let us look at how youth ministry *reveals* people's need to be able to reflect on their own spirituality. Youth ministry becomes a priority when the Church is losing its ability to help youth grow up in faith. By its very nature, it indicates a problem in passing on the faith. Parents are concerned with a "crisis of faith" in their children and they insist that the Church address this problem. Educators see that youth don't know their faith and become concerned to teach it. Pastors see youth disregard the Church as an influential force in their life and want to take steps to remedy this. However, these phenomena reveal as much about the quality of faith of the adult community as they do about the so-called problems of youth. Youth do not grow up in isolation, and for the most part they reflect—although often with more intensity—the struggles of the entire Christian community. Youth are not alone in their faith questions and searching—we all experience them.

One of the major reasons why the adult community is having problems passing its faith on to youth is because we are not in touch with our own spirituality. Parents, unable to speak of the value of worship for themselves, wonder why their kids question going to church on Sunday. Adults, unable to speak in personal terms about the meaning of faith in their lives, wonder why youth don't seem interested in religion. We need to foster the ability to reflect on spirituality—in ourselves and with each other. Too often our faith is off in the corner, tacked on at the end, and peripheral to critical issues of our life. As a result, when youth come to scrutinize it for their own lives, they find it excess baggage in a transient world where it's important to travel light.

It seems to me that youth ministry can held us *address* this priority of reflecting on spirituality in several ways. First of all, we can address it by helping youth become more aware of their own spirituality and by helping them develop the ability to articulate their faith. This skill of reflecting on the everyday is an absolute essential for a vital, growing faith. In *Motivating Adults for Religious Education,* Kevin Coughlin writes of this need within the adult community. Likewise, it seems to me that the ability to reflect on experience is probably the most important skill that we can offer to youth today. Secondly, by using youth ministry as a "teachable moment," we can minister to the adult community—and particularly to significant adults working with youth—by helping them develop the ability to share their faith with young people. Thirdly, we can minister to the whole Church by providing a context—that is, an environment—where dialogue on spirituality takes place between youth and adults. Such dialogue should be based on the idea that each group has something to give and something to gain from the interaction. It is from this type of dialogue that mutual growth in faith can begin to happen, and youth will come to be viewed as an integral part of the community of faith.

B. *Ministry in Community*

When the integral relationship between spirituality and ministry is conscious in shaping our ministry, community is seen to be an essential element of that ministry. We are, as Church, a community gathered in response to God's presence in Christ in word and sacrament. Community is not a "side-effect" of or an addendum to our spirituality—it is at the heart of our response to God as Father and Jesus Christ as our brother. This understanding of God gives us a new understanding of ourselves as sisters and brothers, and of all humankind as a family. When we are called to God in Christ, we are called to each other.

There are two aspects of this communal nature of ministry that I would like to explore here. Ministry is *person-centered,* and it is *relational.* These two are intertwined, and much has been written on each. The recent USCC publication *A Vision of Youth Ministry* would be an example of this writing, as would Michael Warren's *A Future of Youth Catechesis.* Both *Five Cries of Youth* and *Bridging the Gap* by Merton P. Strommen emphasize these points, even if in different words. Here the point I would like to make is that these ministry-dynamics flow directly from the nature of our faith. Also, it seems to me that, in spite of all that is known of person-centered and relational ministry, they have yet to pervade youth ministry as we know it.

Sometimes when you ask a person how things are going, the response is "Well, I'm here." When you stop to think of it, though, one of the most important things we ever have going for us is our personal presence. "I'm here" is perhaps the most significant statement we can make. Ministry is a way of being with and for others so that we are "at their service"—responding to their needs and concerns. When we consciously shape our ministry on our spirituality, *person* emerges as central while function and programing take a secondary role. My person as a minister meeting the person of the other is crucial. Thus the needs and concerns of the total person are an important basis for shaping our ministry. Programing is not an end in itself; rather, personal growth is the goal. Luke's account of Jesus' meeting Zacchaeus (Luke 19:1-10) exemplifies this. Jesus is not so concerned with the sins of Zacchaeus—what he has done—as he is with Zacchaeus as a man. Jesus becomes present to Zacchaeus. This affirmation of him as a person calls him to repentance. (Here much of what Henri Nouwen has written on hospitality in *The Wounded Healer, Reaching Out,* and elsewhere comes to mind.)

Persons are essentially related, and so person-centered ministry is also relational ministry. These are two sides of the same coin more than they are separate principles. Both are expressions of the communal nature of ministry. To say ministry is relational means that it consists of whole-person interaction. Again, the story of Zacchaeus is exemplary. Jesus is not concerned with Zacchaeus as a tax collector (and hence, a sinner), although it is this role that alienates him from his fellow countrymen. Rather, he relates to him as a man, as a whole person.

Roles have a way of expressing power or authority—as that of a parent over a child or a teacher over a student. When we relate in terms of roles, we relate unequally. The focus is on how we are different—in what area you are an expert and I am not, and so on. On the other hand, when we relate personally—that is, in whole-person interaction—we focus on our sameness. We accept each other as we are. In whole-person interaction, we are equal and I am as open to grow from my encounter with you as you are to grow from your encounter with me. We relate in a mutual give-and-take in which each of us has something to give and something to receive.

It is not new to say that ministry consists of relationships between whole persons more basically than programs. Strommen, for example, in both *Five Cries of Youth* and *Bridging the Gap,* stresses mutuality as one of two key dimensions in the faith community's outreach to youth. What I think is important to say, however, is that the *reason* for our stressing this priority of relationships is the nature of our faith. Faith is relational (communal) and thus so is ministry.

In applying the communal focus of ministry to youth ministry, many reflections might be made. Here, I would elaborate only four.

1. *Modeling:* Youth ministers at all levels should model an approach to ministry that has a communal focus. Thus both we as diocesan-level ministers and our ministry should provide a living "for instance" for parishes. This type of modeling is not a static concept that implies an ideal after which all others should strive nor is it a perfection. We should never imply that we "have arrived." Rather, we should model our *very struggling* to be communal, person-centered, relational. Thus, for example, our meetings should not be administrative and functional only, but should incorporate this as one small aspect of a faith-filled convening (i.e., a coming together) in which people grow together, rather than commiserate shared exhaustion.

In modeling, the professional youth minister should be a catalyst and stimulus for the efforts of the community, not a remedy for their inadequacy. The minister should model for the community the type of presence with youth that is possible. He is an extension of their responsibility, not a substitute for it. The parish cannot hire someone to pass on their faith for them—they must learn to do it for themselves. They can hire a professional to help them, and recognize that some among them have more natural gifts than others with youth. However, it is their own responsibility. Thus every minister should draw others together into a seminal community in order to develop a shared vision of how it is possible for youth and adults to grow together in faith. Together, they can make a shared commitment to make that vision a reality.

2. *Priority on Person-Resources:* Our time and energy as ministers must always be spent on persons. In my diocese this means clarifying that the purpose of the diocesan presence in youth ministry is to form key youth and adults as ministers. Such formation means calling people together at the parish level, at the regional level, and at the diocesan level to develop a shared vision of what youth ministry is and can be. To me this means realizing that

managerial skills that show people how to organize might be important but will never be enough by themselves. Rather, the key is in persons with a healing and enabling presence. Such a presence can be refined through interpersonal skills to enable people who are growing to call others to do the same.

3. *Listening Presence:* Ministry with a communal focus, which is a ministry of presence, is in my experience most effective when it begins as a listening presence. For me, this does not imply that it is passive or "mind-less" in its listening. Rather, it means that we take youth seriously, and relate to them with sensitivity and understanding. This means that we don't presume to know their needs, but let them tell us about their lives. Then, as their experience and needs unfold, it means we need to be able to respond from our own experience. A listening presence means laying aside our hidden agendas, not trying to trick them into wanting what we would like them to, reverencing their uniqueness as individuals, and trusting them to shape their own lives. It means being able to lay aside our institutional presuppositions that ask youth to relate to us on our own terms.

Think of how many of our programs ask youth to come to our buildings and fit into preset patterns of interaction we have designed. We are comfortable with what we have planned. But are they? Yet, if we have a person-centered ministry, we should be concerned with their comfort more than our own. We as ministers should be willing to lay down our comfort to be at their service.

4. *Valuing the Process:* I often have adults call me to say "Why don't you get a group of youth to . . ." These people mean well and often have good ideas. However, I have found that a good idea by the *wrong person* is not a good idea. We need to develop youth ministry in such a way that it calls forth from within rather than imposing from without. To me this means that the process of ministry is critical. Only when people are able to be involved directly in shaping their own approach will they really be able to "own" it. For this reason, I do not see how programs can be packaged from one situation and implemented "as is" in a variety of other situations. What we as ministers need to be able to do is to be with people as they struggle. This doesn't mean we need to have an answer or be the expert so much as it means we must be a

partner on the quest. Our gift and our skill need to be the ability to call forth in others the creativity to shape their own faith—a faith as big as life, a faith able to continue to grow and re-form.

C. *Relationship of Youth Ministry to Other Ministries*

There is much talk these days about the relationship between various people who work with youth—catechists, youth ministers, retreat leaders, school personnel, and so on. The underlying theme of collaboration—as expressed, for example, in the recent USCC publication *A Vision of Youth Ministry*—seems clearer in theory than in practice. Even though these discussions are important, they are only one dimension. As important as it is to integrate all the various ministries to youth, it is equally important to integrate youth ministry with other ministries in the Church. This latter dialogue should also surface, and undoubtedly is beginning to. I would not want to try to predetermine its direction, much less its result. Still, it does seem to me that a consciousness of the integrity of spirituality and ministry would allow for spirituality to be the context of such discussions and suggest a possible direction.

In my own dioceses, there are slight beginnings of such a dialogue on the relationship between youth ministry and the other ministries of the Church. There are several reasons why we are able to enter into such a dialogue that might not be possible elsewhere—we are a small diocese with little history, all ministries in the diocese are in emerging stages, and youth ministry is clearly viewed as a pastoral ministry. Because youth ministry is seen as a pastoral ministry, the needs of youth are seen in context of the total life of the Christian community. Integrating youth as a vital part of the community and enabling them to accept as fully as possible the responsibility of participation in the community are important goals of ministry. Thus as a minister I approach youth uniquely, but gradually this approach to youth touches all aspects of the community: shared responsibility (should youth be on the parish council is only the most superficial level of this), Christian service (how can youth be helped to minister to others?), Christian worship (how can the faith of youth be celebrated in the ritual prayer of the community?), and so on. Thus, youth ministry needs to be integrated into the life of the whole Christian community. The youth minister is not detached from the community working with one interest group, but his ministry goes to the core of community life and touches all aspects of the community's concern.

It can be seen, then, that while various ministries begin from a unique perspective, as the implications of each ministry are explored and extended the ministry will gradually be found to be in some relationship with other ministries. This has profound implications for reshaping those ministries, and for allowing structures to emerge that both reflect and allow various ministries to be integrated with each other. It is not possible to predetermine what these relationships are, or what implications they will have. The point is, however, that the central focus of spirituality could provide a starting point and context for such dialogue.

Conclusion

One morning while I was working on these reflections, I was so preoccupied by them that I went through the entire Liturgy of the Word without ever being aware of the readings. I laughed afterwards when I thought how much that proved my point—but how far I still have to go to live all that I know. What is important for me to realize in this, however, is how much I need the support of others to form and re-form my life and my ministry to consciously reflect the centrality of being and personhood. The point of writing down these reflections is not to have a definitive statement that indicates the struggle is over and the victory won. My purpose is to surface a dialogue that must begin within each of us and among all of us if we are going to continue to shape our lives according to the Gospel and call others to do the same. No one of us can do it alone. Together, I have much reason to be hopeful.

RESOURCE READINGS

Kevin Coughlin, *Motivating Adults for Religious Education,* 1976 NCDD Research Paper. The extensive footnotes in this work are very helpful in suggesting additional reading.

Henri J.M. Nouwen, *Out of Solitude: Three Meditations on the Christian Life* (Notre Dame, Ind.: Ave Maria Press, 1974).

Henri J.M. Nouwen, *Reaching Out: The Three Movements of the Spiritual Life* (Garden City, N.Y.: Doubleday and Company, Inc., 1975).

Henri J.M. Nouwen, *The Wounded Healer: Ministry in Contemporary Society* (Garden City, N.Y.: Doubleday and Company, Inc., 1972).

Merton P. Strommen, *Bridging the Gap: Youth and Adults in the Church* (Minneapolis, Minn.: Augsburg, 1973).

Merton P. Strommen, *Five Cries of Youth* (New York: Harper and Row, Publishers, 1974).

Understanding the Diocesan-Level Task

John Roberto

John Roberto's description of the diocesan-level task complements Timothy Fallon's reflections in the previous article. Currently Director of Youth Ministry for the Diocese of Richmond, Roberto began paying close attention to the interface between management theory and youth ministry in his earlier work directing youth ministries in the Diocese of Bridgeport, Connecticut. Here he summarizes his experience and learning on this topic in a closely reasoned article that will bear careful scrutiny and rereading by those responsible for organizing youth ministry at the diocesan level.

Roberto's approach is clearly one of encouraging each diocese to find the organizational model best suited to its own local needs. Again, as parish youth ministers must attune themselves to the needs of the specific young people in a local area, so those directing diocesan efforts must, according to Roberto, do the same thing at a different level. Another valuable aspect of Roberto's focus in his stress on planning for the future, a matter for special attention in youth ministry.

▲

There is much confusion, discussion, and even controversy these days about the diocesan responsibility in youth ministry. Questions abound: "Who is responsible for youth ministry?" "What do we mean by the concept 'youth ministry'?" "Why have a diocesan approach to youth ministry?" Questions such as these, as well as the confusion throughout the country, make the diocesan task more difficult and most important. One important fact that must not be overlooked is the serious difficulty the Church has had over the past decade ministering to young people. Recent research has documented the fact that almost 65 percent of all young people (high school age) are not receiving any formal religious education.[1] The report infers, at least, that this figure probably represents the total percentage of young people not being reached by the Church with any form of youth ministry. This one statistic alone should stop us cold in our tracks and lead us to ask some fundamental questions about the Church's ministry with youth. The diocesan-level task is crucial and is a serious one. This article outlines a basic process any diocese can use to develop a holistic ministry with youth. No matter how unique a diocese may be, there are fundamental principles and planning steps that constitute the diocesan-level task.

A. *Theory and Principles*

   In the midst of the confusion surrounding the Church's ministry with youth, *A Vision of Youth Ministry* has been developed to shed some much-needed light and direction on the purposes and scope of youth ministry. The product of over fifteen months work, three separate stages of writing, and consultation with youth ministry people across the country, and published by the United States Catholic Conference's (USCC) Department of Education, this document goes a long way toward unifying the Church's ministry with youth. It describes youth ministry as "the response of the Christian community to the needs of young people, and the sharing of the unique gifts of youth with the larger community."[2] This description of youth ministry has four constitutive elements:

   Youth ministry is *TO* youth when the Christian community exercises its pastoral role in meeting young people's needs.

   Youth ministry is *WITH* youth because young people share with adults a common responsibility to carry out the Church's mission.

   Youth ministry is *BY* youth when young people exercise their own ministry to others, particularly to their peers.

   Youth ministry is *FOR* youth in that adult youth ministers

attempt to interpret the needs of youth and act as advocates in articulating youth's legitimate concerns to the wider community.[3]

In this view, youth ministry is a multidimensional reality, it is a multi-ministry. The components of youth ministry, as outlined in *A Vision of Youth Ministry,* are *Word* (encompassing Evangelization and Catechesis), *Worship, Creating Community, Guidance and Healing, Justice and Service, Enablement* (of Youth and Adults), and *Advocacy.* These components define the scope of youth ministry; they "are brought into focus by a common dedication to the following goals:

Youth ministry works to foster the total personal and spiritual growth of each young person.

Youth ministry seeks to draw young people to responsible participation in the life, mission and work of the faith community.[4]

This document provides the foundation upon which a youth ministry is to be built. For our purposes it provides us with the basis, goals, components, and scope of a diocesan youth ministry. All diocesan youth ministry efforts in the coming years will be judged on their ability to actualize this vision.

A Vision of Youth Ministry offers many points for further elaboration. One of these is the very nature of youth ministry. I would like to offer a description of youth ministry that I believe has great import for understanding the diocesan-level task.

Youth ministry is a generational ministry of the Church that seeks to personalize the ministries of the Church *to, with, by* and *for* youth. This ministry is a convergent and confluent ministry, bringing together the many ministries of the total Church in response to young people. Youth ministry is a collaborative ministry, unifying and integrating past efforts into a holistic approach. By understanding youth ministry as the convergence and confluence of the Church's ministries, we gain an important insight—youth ministry makes no sense outside of an understanding of the Church's ministry. By viewing youth ministry as a convergence and confluence, we affirm the fact that the entire Church is responsible for ministry to youth. For a diocese this means that every diocesan ministry, not only its "youth ministry," has a responsibility to young people. I believe this insight has a great practical importance for the diocesan-level task.

If we truly realize that youth ministry represents a convergence and confluence of the Church ministries in response to young people, it is apparent that one office or department can never fully grapple with the breadth of youth ministry. Youth ministry is the task of the whole Church—every diocesan ministry has a responsibility to youth.

The preceding description of youth ministry surfaces several key principles that should guide the diocesan-level task.

1. *Youth ministry is a convergent, confluent ministry.* Youth ministry integrates the ministries of the Church in direct response to the needs (psychological, social, spiritual) of young people. It is a generational ministry; it is not in and of itself a unique, differentiated ministry. Rather, it is unique in the sense that it brings together the ministries of the Church in response to youth.

2. *The Church's ministry has a dual focus.* Ministry is *within* the church (internal) in that the gifts of faith are exercised within the Church; worship, building the Christian community, proclaiming the Word, caring for the needy, are but a few of the ministries within the Church. Ministry is also *of* the Church (external); i.e., it serves humankind by exercising its call to mission: bringing the Good News of Jesus to all peoples; offering itself, the Christian community, as a sign of a people transformed by the Spirit; and serving the many needs of all peoples through justice, advocacy, and service. For youth ministry, this dual focus must be present in our work. Youth ministry in its seven components seeks to address this dual focus—ministry *within* and *of* the Church.

3. *Christian ministry is ONE ministry.* The Church's ministry is a common enterprise where all Christians continue the work of Christ. Each Christian is blessed with different gifts to exercise, each has his/her own calling, charism, and competence. It is within the richness of a variety of gifts that the Christian community works to fulfill the mission and ministry of Jesus. This understanding for youth ministry signals an end to a fragmented, competitive

use of God's gifts, and calls all who minister to youth to exercise their gifts in *unity* for the good of all. A healthy understanding of ministry sees the integration and working together of the many gifts of the Christian community. This insight needs to be applied to our work in diocesan offices (as well as in parishes and schools) if youth ministry is to become a reality. It is a difficult task, but to understand the nature of ministry, and especially youth ministry, means that we need to develop wholesome relationships with and respect for each other in our ministry to youth. We need to work *together* in the one ministry of Jesus Christ.

4. *Christian ministry is shared.* Shared ministry, for our purposes, means that the broad scope of youth ministry demands a collaborative model with each person contributing his/her gifts, each sharing in the work of youth ministry. Ministry, and the work of youth ministry, belongs to no one person or office. Shared ministry means taking collegiality seriously, and recognizing that diocesan ministries work together with local efforts in a common ministry. Shared ministry means that every person, office, department, etc. takes seriously both his/her responsibility to youth and the responsibility to work together—each in his/her own way, according to personal gifts, talents, and abilities. Without a lived experience of shared ministry, of cooperation among diocesan ministries, of mutual support, youth ministry cannot be truly operative on a diocesan level.

5. *The diocesan-level effort in youth ministry is characterized by the principle of subsidiarity.* Essentially, subsidiarity means that the diocesan-level ministry does not organize programs and services which the local level can and should be doing for itself. Subsidiarity demands that a diocesan youth ministry act as catalyst, as enabler—serving parishes and schools so that the local level may establish ongoing, comprehensive youth ministries. This means that diocesan-level personnel and offices must evaluate their efforts so that what they provide will serve as an enabler, as a catalyst to assist the local level. The diocesan-level cannot "do for" parishes or schools what they should be doing for themselves. Oftentimes, the multiplicity of diocesan programs serves only to allow the local level to remain dependent. The hallmark of an effective diocesan youth ministry effort is its ability to enable local

leaders to develop their own youth ministries. The quality of a diocesan-level youth ministry effort can be measured by the quality of parish and school youth ministries. This is a demanding standard.

B. *Planning a Diocesan Youth Ministry*

Before describing the task of planning, it would be well worth analyzing the various models of diocesan youth ministry efforts. The past few years have seen a multiplication of diocesan youth ministry offices, often without any rhyme or reason. These offices often develop out of panacea planning: A diocese realizes that there is no youth office and creates one, or it becomes aware that other dioceses have youth ministry offices and therefore determines that it needs one too. Oftentimes this office is created and filled by a director working alone with no formal connections to other diocesan ministries. Since the office is often forced to carry the full load of the youth ministry effort, such an organization is unfair to the director as well as being unfair to the parishes or schools served.

Other dioceses organize their youth ministry effort out of an existing office (e.g., CYO Office or Religious Education Office). What these dioceses fail to recognize is the breadth and scope of youth ministry. It is a contradiction to have a Youth Ministry Coordinator (whose role should be to coordinate the diocesan youth ministry effort) operating out of one of these offices when youth ministry should encompass the total diocesan approach to young people, not simply one office's responsibilty. Somehow, we are "backing into the future" in our development of diocesan youth ministries. Our planning and development of diocesan youth ministry efforts must be in concert with the theory of youth ministry (especially as outlined in *A Vision of Youth Ministry*).

However, these situations do not characterize the total scene. There are excellent diocesan youth ministry efforts developing in many dioceses, respecting the theory and vision of youth ministry, and leading the way in the development of a comprehensive holistic ministry to, with, by, and for youth. I would like to explain these efforts by developing three models, which I believe have great promise. This is by no means the last word on diocesan models;

rather, new models are being developed each year. I have attempted to develop in broad strokes three basic models that respect the criteria I outlined in the first section of this article.

MODEL A   CONVERGENCE MODEL

The convergence model attempts to draw together diocesan ministries into a concerted, holistic ministry with youth. In this model, each diocesan ministry is expected to have a responsibility to youth. The structure of this model is to bring together all of the diocesan ministries in the form of a council, task force, or coordinating team. Each ministry is asked to send a representative to this council. This means the council will not only represent those agencies directly serving youth (like CYO or Religious Education), but also diocesan ministries such as social ministry, worship, family life, et al. The major purpose for such a group is to promote unity, collaboration, and integration of the diocesan youth ministry effort. Members of this group can establish goals and objectives for their work, act to integrate existing programs and services, and advocate new programs/services to existing offices or departments. This coordinating group is a step toward ending competition, poor communication, and overlapping efforts. The coordinating council serves an important function in the ongoing development of a total diocesan effort in youth ministry.

MODEL B   OFFICE MODEL

Many dioceses have established offices of youth ministry with varying responsibilities and staffing. The best of these office models bring together the various dimensions of youth ministry (often integrating CYO offices with high school religious education efforts) into the responsibility of one office and clearly define their relationship and interdependence with other diocesan ministries. Oftentimes (as I described before) an office assumes total responsibility for youth ministry without realizing that every other diocesan ministry is also responsible. By establishing clear and formal lines of interdependence with other diocesan ministries, the Office of Youth

Ministry can work with other diocesan ministries in establishing joint programs and services (e.g., working with the Worship Ministry on workshops for youth ministers, on liturgical planning for youth ministry, etc.). Such an office, organized in this manner, respects the broad scope of youth ministry and the principles of convergence, shared ministry, and the essential unity of Christian ministry.

MODEL C   DEPARTMENT MODEL

Some dioceses organize their youth ministry effort into a department within a broad office or ministry, e.g., the Department of Youth Ministry within the Office of Pastoral Ministry or the Ministry of Christian Formation. This model still respects the integrity of youth ministry if clear, formal lines of responsibility are defined. Frequently, departments of youth ministry are better integrated into other diocesan ministries because of the nature of the broader office. Often, joint planning is a mandate because the broader office operates as a whole. This framework allows youth ministry to plan with and interact with other ministries in a holistic approach. (For descriptions of actual diocesan models, cf. *Models of Diocesan Youth Ministry,* USCC, Department of Education, 1312 Mass. Ave. N.W., Washington, D.C. 20005.)

All three of these models represent systematic efforts to translate the theory of youth ministry into a diocesan approach. The programs and services they develop are unique to the needs and situation of each diocese. What concerns us in this article is their ability to reflect the broad scope of youth ministry. Despite my brief treatment of each model, they hopefully will provide a starting point for reflection for those dioceses beginning their transition to a youth ministry model.

Dioceses that are in the process of developing a holistic, integrated approach to youth ministry would do well to follow a few key steps. These steps have come out of my own experience in diocesan-level youth ministry. 1) *Analyze the Current Situation*—Who are the people and offices currently serving youth? What are their goals and objectives? What programs and services are being offered? Evaluate how well your constituency is being served and what are the needs of youth ministers and youth. 2) *Develop Healthy Relationships*—among the various diocesan offices serving youth. Offer opportunities for staff people to get together, to know each other, and explore what the talents, abilities, and gifts of each person are. 3) *Evaluation and Needs Assessment*—devise a format and technique to evaluate current efforts and gather information about current and future needs in youth ministry. 4) *Develop a Plan of Action*—from the evaluation and needs assessment, the committee (composed of representatives from the different offices and from the field) can set concrete goals and objectives, as well as an action plan for developing an integrated approach. A diocese can use one of the three models or develop its own model. After the general plan is developed appropriate authorities must be consulted, but the committee has done its job in drafting a plan. The above is but a bare outline of a process that may take years, but I hope it serves the purpose of helping dioceses begin the process. Once the transition has been completed, work can begin on the process planning phase.

Planning a diocesan youth ministry, like any organizational process, involves careful attention to the process by which goals, objectives, programs, and services are developed. There are numerous steps planners engage in throughout the planning process. Careful attention to the process of planning will help to insure successful operation of any organization; youth ministry planning helps insure that we develop programs and services that assist our constituency (parishes and schools, youth ministers and youth) in actualizing youth ministry in their local situations.

There are many fine resources at the disposal of diocesan planners. Below is a brief bibliography to assist the reader:

Arthur C. Beck, Jr. *Effective Decision Making for Parish Leaders*. Twenty-Third Publications, West Mystic, Conn., 1973.

John C. DeBoer, *Let's Plan—A Guide to the Planning Process for Voluntary Organizations*. United Church Press, Philadelphia, Pa. 19102, 1970.

John Forliti, *Program Planning for Youth Ministry*. St. Mary's College Press, Winona, Minn., 1975.

Norman Lambert, *Managing Church Groups*. Pflaum Publishing, Dayton, Ohio, 1975.

George L. Morrisey, *Management by Objectives and Results*. Addison Wesley Publishing Co., Reading, Mass., 1970.

"An Overview of the Steps in PROGRAM PLANNING." United Church of Christ, Council for Lay Life and Work (Order from: Central Distribution Service, P.O. Box 7286, St. Louis, Mo. 65177, Code # LW-0370-P2-8M-25ᵉ).

The planning process used in the summer workshop at St. John's University and contained in schema form in this article is from Norman Lambert's *Managing Church Groups*. This is probably the best written, most understandable, and most practical guide for church groups involved in developing goals and objectives, programs and services for their ministry. I am providing an overview of his planning process supplemented by other ideas I have developed over the past four years in diocesan-level youth ministry. No matter how unique one's diocese or which model one operates from, planning is an essential element in any ministry.

Before entering CMOR (Church Management by Objectives and Results), a preceding step I have found helpful for opening up the planning group to new possibilities for creating the future is called "futures planning." John Westerhoff has outlined this process in his article "The Visionary: Planning for the Future" in *A Colloquy on Christian Education* (Pilgrim Press, Philadelphia, Pa., 1972). Westerhoff describes four types of planning: annual planning, social-demand planning, panacea planning, and problem-centered or crisis planning. Each style suffers from being locked into the present. The creativity of the group is hampered, new ideas are never explored. Futures planning begins with the presupposition that the future will not be like today, but that the future will be different from the present. We create the future today by the decisions we make, often without any vision of what the future might be. Futures planning begins with a vision of the future and then looks back on today to see what has to happen in the interim so that the future vision may be realized. Westerhoff outlines the steps in futures planning. It is well worth the effort to adventure into the future; all kinds of new possibilities open up.

Once one has engaged in futures planning, one is ready for Lambert's CMOR (Church Management by Objectives and Results). This process "involves a clear and precise identification of what is to be achieved, the establishment of a realistic program for achieving it, and the use of concrete and measurable evidence to evaluate the success of the program."[5]

Lambert identifies four major areas of church management and fifteen steps within those areas. The following schema illustrates the total scope of diocesan (or parish) management. I have inserted extra ideas into his process and indicated the chapter of his book that details the individual step.

SCOPE OF DIOCESAN MANAGEMENT[6]

A. *Planning:* Determine what will take place.

1. *Writing a mission statement:* Determining the thrust and the limitations of our activities, i.e., programs and services (Chapter 4). "A clear mission statement will help an organization clarify its purpose, define the limits of its authority and responsibility, and discover areas where there is duplication of effort or where important responsibilities have not been assigned." (p. 28)

2. *Developing data for objectives* (Needs Assessment/Data Gathering): Determining the areas within which objectives will be written, surfacing needs, and evaluating them against Christian guidelines. (Chapter 5)

Lambert discusses in detail two methods for assessing needs:

A. *Forecasting*—using data from the past to predict the future.

B. *Problem-Solving*—focusing on perceived problems in the organization with the intent of reducing or eliminating them.

In addition there are two other methods I have used in assessing needs:

C. *Surveys, Interviews, Questionnaires*

In addition to gathering problems from one's constituency, one seeks out their needs or concerns in youth ministry. Surveys, interviews, or questionnaires to the constituency should uncover their real needs in their local situations, and secondly should determine how they see one in a diocesan position responding to their local situations. Inquires are directed to leadership people, adults working with youth, and/or youth themselves. The *Youth Research Survey* (developed by Merton Strommen, et al. at the Youth Research Center in Minneapolis, Minn.) is an excellent tool for just this purpose. The survey has wide usage throughout the country. The book *Five Cries of Youth* was developed out of Strommen's survey of 7,050 church youth. (For more information about the Youth Research Survey write: Youth Research Center, 122 West Franklin Ave., Minneapolis, Minn. 55404.)

Another variation worth exploring would be to have each parish or school evaluate your programs/services at the end of each year, and in doing so list their needs and concerns for the coming year and how they see you, at the diocesan level, responding. One way to implement this idea is to distribute an evaluation form in which one has listed all programs and services offered in the past year. Beneath each program or service, ask respondents to evaluate: 1 (Excellent), 2 (Good), 3 (Poor), 4 (Needs Improvement). Ask whether it is an essential service to be continued, or not essential at this time and better discontinued. Also ask for their comments and suggestions. Following this procedure for each program and service should uncover some very valuable information.

D. *Hearings and Sounding Sessions*

Another technique is to draw together a representative group of one's constituency to share their needs, concerns, and hopes for the coming year in youth ministry. The best way to get at needs and future programs/ services a constituency thinks should be offered is to set up a process in which the participants can share with one another in small groups (perhaps using a discussion sheet with key questions to answer) and then feed their input back to a leader. The diocesan staff's job is to listen to their input, not to critique it. Often the list will be long, unmanageable or beyond one's responsibility to meet, but the process is still important. One might end the meeting by proposing ideas developed for the coming year and asking for a critique.

A variation on this technique is to hold regional meetings across a diocese to call forth leadership people (youths and adults) to share their needs/concerns and their expectations of the diocesan office. These sounding sessions are very good at building grass-roots support for one's work. Devise a process for the day or evening, use small group discussions, give the participants a chance to share and give their input, and explain how the input is being used.

Whichever technique chosen or devised, needs-assessment tools are a way of building trust and mutuality among the people served. By sharing in the diocesan programming for the coming year, people have a sense of ownership, and feel that one has listened to them. These two ingredients are essential for successful diocesan youth ministry, for when programs and services are announced for the coming year, a constituency will feel a part of those programs/services and in turn participate and cooperate with those directing the diocesan-level program.

Summary of Planning Steps

1. *Gathering Data:* Some basic categories for gathering data about the people for whom one is planning are: expectations, attitudes, understandings, behavior, experience, concerns, responsibilities, pressures. (For more information, cf. "An Overview of the Steps in PROGRAM PLANNING.")

2. *Data Analysis:* There are four steps in analyzing data: collate the responses, analyze trends in the data, look for underlying factors in the trends, and narrow the data to the scope of the work. (For more information, cf. "An Overview of the Steps in PROGRAM PLANNING.")

3. *Writing Objectives:* Deciding the exact results to be achieved and writing them in understandable form. (Chapter 6) "Objectives are desired results that the organization wishes to attain during a specified period of time. These results should be 1—within the scope of the organization's mission statement, 2—based on real needs that can be documented and verified, and 3—Christian in nature." (p. 33) (Note: Many organizations first develop broader long-range goals for their work and then develop objectives within each of their goals. Often the goals are written for a 2 or 3 or 5-year time span, while objectives are written one year at a time.)

4. *Programming and Scheduling:* Establishing a plan of action and time requirements for achievement of an objective. (Chapter 7)

5. *Allocating Resources:* Determining and assigning the work hours, materials, and money required to reach an objective. (Chapter 8)

B. *Staffing:* Matching the human resources to the desired objective. (Chapter 9)

6. *Determining personnel needs.*

7. *Selecting and recruiting personnel.*

8. *Training and developing personnel.*

C. *Leading:* Bringing about the human activity required to accomplish an objective. (Chapter 10)

9. *Assigning:* Charging individuals with task responsibilities.

10. *Delegating:* Sharing a portion of one's authority with subordinates.

11. *Motivating:* Influencing subordinates to perform in the desired manner.

12. *Coordinating and communicating:* Achieving harmony of group effort and the proper flow of information and ideas.

D. *Controlling:* Exercising authority to assure accomplishment of objective. (Chapter 10)

13. *Establishing procedures and policies:* Setting consistent and systematic methods for handling repetitious tasks and making predetermined decisions whenever possible.

14. *Making Corrections:* Comparing actual performance with planned performance and bringing about any needed improvement.

15. *Evaluation:* Conducting a self-study of effectiveness in reaching objectives. Some techniques for evaluation include: questionnaires, rating scales, verbal evaluations, small group discussions, projective methods, checklists, interviews, observation, open evaluation meeting. (For more information, cf. "An Overview of the Steps in PROGRAM PLANNING.")

Each year this process is recycled. Preferably, one will have engaged in futures planning before CMOR, which will allow a look at how well one is approaching a vision of the future. At this point now one is ready to recycle the CMOR process, beginning with reevaluating a mission statement and gathering data through a needs assessment.

Lambert notes some preliminaries before engaging in the CMOR process that are worth repeating.

> CMOR is built around the concepts of participatory decision-making, ongoing evaluation, and the achievement of desired results. Before an organization implements CMOR, it should have specific results that it expects to accomplish by the CMOR process. An objective for implementing CMOR should be written, along with a program, schedule, and the allocation of resources. Such a procedure will aid in evaluating the effectiveness of CMOR, and also will be good practice in its application.[7]

This article outlines a basic planning process for a diocesan-level youth ministry, as well as establishes a foundation in theory and principles upon which to build. The future of youth ministry will be shaped by the decisions we make today, by the structures we create, by the theory upon which we build, by the ministry we create through diocesan programs and services. Diocesan-level youth ministry is a serious task because of the critical situation we find surrounding us. It is also a joyful task of continuing the ministry of Jesus Christ with young people.

NOTES

1. "Attendance at Catholic Formal Religious Education Programs By Children and Youth in 1974 and 1975." Msgr. Wilfrid Paradis and Dr. Andrew Thompson (USCC, Publications Office), 1976.

2. *A Vision of Youth Ministry*. USCC, Department of Education, 1976.

3. *Ibid*.

4. *Ibid*.

5. Lambert, Norman, Managing Church Groups (Dayton, Ohio: Pflaum Publishing, 1975). p. 5.

6. *Ibid*., p. 5-6 (The schema is taken from these two pages.)

7. *Ibid*., p. 26.

Youth Sharing Ministry: The Philadelphia Program

Marisa Guerin

In early 1976 I was asked by Father Frank Schmidt, director of Youth Activities for the Archdiocese of Philadelphia, to spend a day in Philadelphia examining the various aspects of the youth program there and giving some feedback on what I saw. At the time, I knew almost nothing about that archdiocese's youth work except its heavy investment in Catholic schools. What I saw there on my short visit I found very exciting. Over the years, a well-organized, richly varied ministry to youth had developed, partly through Frank Schmidt's organizational genius. The program included a leadership development effort for inner-city youth that made use of survival-type camping trips, a national venereal disease hotline, and many social-action projects.

What I found most significant, however, was the role given to young people in each of these programs. The day I visited, many teens were at the Youth Center busily going about their tasks. Every time I asked Father Schmidt a question about one or other aspect of his programs, he would call over a young person to explain his or her efforts. I could see that he had put much of the program right into their hands. Some of the teens were engaged at the time in organizing the youth of all the country's dioceses for a project related to the Bicentennial Eucharistic Congress. Using a WATS telephone line, each person seemed to have her/his own desk and file of information on the various dioceses being phoned.

Since that time, I have been searching for someone familiar with the Philadelphia program to write a report on how it works. Such a person is Marisa Guerin, the youngest staff person in the Department of Education at the U.S. Catholic Conference and one who participated in the Philadelphia program as a teen. Marisa's own work as a specialist in youth

110

activities at the Bishops' Conference reflects the Philadelphia approach of leading by putting responsibility into the capable hands of others. Her report shows us what can happen when the proper vision and proper planning are implemented at the diocesan level.

▲

"Kids have something to give, too . . . but we have to be invited to find our place. Around here, the people are friendly. The staff are involved with us. We grow together, as persons and as Christians."

In his comment, Juan Velez reflects the feelings of many of his peers about being a part of the teenage leadership of the Philadelphia Archdiocesan Department of Youth Activities (DYA). Though his words are simple and straightforward, the experience to which Juan refers is a signal achievement of the Philadelphia DYA, an authentic enablement of youth that has been the cornerstone of its success in ministry.

In the Archdiocese of Philadelphia, the DYA shares the responsibility for youth ministry with the offices of religious education, Catholic schools, and others. Although the rambling downtown offices of the DYA can give the appearance of youthful chaos, the observer soon notes that the activity conveys the spontaneity and energy with which the DYA's ministry is carried out by its young leaders.

Over the past ten years, the DYA has grown in scope and effectiveness, currently reaching thousands of young people with a broad-based program of community-service work, parish youth organizations, leadership development, spiritual growth programs, athletics, and cultural activities. This complex network is administered by the director of the DYA, Monsignor Francis X. Schmidt. Affectionately described by a friend and co-worker as someone who "can't think in less than four figures," Monsignor Schmidt is a dynamic person with a rare ability to turn visions into realities. Exemplifying the approach of his whole staff, Monsignor Schmidt brings humor, candor, and genuine friendship to the young people he meets, and in affirming them, invites them to "find their place" in service to others.

The adult staff at the DYA offices maintain a relatively low profile; their desks and activities do not dominate the office space. At times, it can be difficult to locate the adults amidst the numbers of young people conducting meetings, answering telephones, planning and organizing programs. The support and competency of the adult staff is critical to the success of the DYA, but it goes hand in hand with a commitment to sharing the ministry with youth. The confidence and ease of the youth leaders is genuine, because it is clear to them that they have their own, valued role in the ministry of the Church.

What is the key to the effective enablement of young people as sharers in ministry? If personal enablement for ministry is correctly seen as a guiding principle of ministry, this question is a very important one. An exploration of the approaches, traditions, successes, and failures of the Philadelphia DYA staff in this effort may prove helpful to a broader development of this aspect of youth ministry. However, a brief preliminary sketch of the work carried on under the auspices of the DYA is necessary in order to provide the proper context for the remarks that follow.

The largest single component of the DYA is the Catholic Youth Organization (CYO), a parish-based ministry to youth that in 1976 involved 13,000 teenagers in spiritual, cultural, service, social, and athletic activities. As in the majority of DYA programs, the primary thrust of CYO is a youth-to-youth ministry that enables young people to give and to grow. Organized on regional and diocesan levels, the CYO leadership structure is very open to young people, giving them responsibility for the development of their own programs, and providing them with weekend experiences, workshops, and other opportunities for growth in leadership. Although the adult advisors are essential to the success of CYO, the kind of adult needed for work with youth is a St. John the Baptist . . . one who is able to pave the way for growth of the young people, but willing to step aside when a young person is ready to take on a greater level of responsibility.

In every locale, the needs or particular circumstances of the community shape the most effective approaches to ministry. In Philadelphia, one such circumstance is the existence of an extensive Catholic school system that includes approximately 30 high schools. To provide the teenagers attending these schools with broader opportunities for self-discovery and service to others, the Community Service Corps (CSC) was established in 1966. Ten years later, based in 31 diocesan, private, and public high schools, the 6,000 teenage members of CSC volunteered their time in an impressive list of creative programs, some of which include: Operation Incentive, a city-wide tutorial program; Operation Santa Claus, a Christmas toy collection through which the teens distribute gifts to close to 1,000 needy families; and Operation Golden Touch, offering companionship and service to the elderly. CSC also sponsors the annual National Training Institute for Leadership and Service, a six-week summer program conducted by youth leaders for their peers.

Originally a CSC project, another important component of the DYA is Operation Venus, a nationwide toll-free hotline providing information and referral to teens on the subject of veneral diseases (Toll Free Number: 800/523-1885). Created in 1970 in response to the alarming incidence of VD among teenagers, Venus receives over 125 calls a day, all handled by trained high school volunteers. The staff of Operation Venus emphasizes the serious nature of the responsibilities carried by these teen volunteers, stressing the importance of capable and supportive adult staff in the area of training and administration.

The Shalom Program under the auspices of the DYA is a nationally recognized drug-abuse prevention program, operating on the principle that negative behavior such as drug or alcohol abuse is offset by personal development and growth in maturity so that young people become capable of informed, responsible choice. Shalom provides trained counselors to high schools where they conduct a broad-based program of prevention, early intervention, screening, and referral for drug-abuse problems, as well as group experiences in decision-making, communications, and self-awareness. Teens who demonstrate interest and ability are trained as peer leaders in these programs, and provide a valuable support function for the Shalom specialists.

Discovery Leadership Institute (DLI), administered by the DYA, is a long-term multifaceted program to develop leadership among inner-city poor male youth, especially from minority groups. The young men who participate in the DLI program are provided with workshops, classes, outdoor experiences, and community service jobs, as well as the opportunity to form harmonious community relationships with one another. The DLI staff expresses some of the positive outcomes of the program in terms of personal growth for the young men, the satisfying experience of a meaningful job, and the growth of concern for the affairs of the community. As in Operation Venus and other DYA programs, the young people who have come through DLI have exhibited a definite tendency to further their training and education in the direction of the helping professions, due in part to the variety of occupational models available for them to observe during their time in the programs.

The DYA sponsors a large number of Christian Experience programs such as the Search retreat model, most of them conducted at the Archdiocesan Camp Neuman Conference in Bucks County. These weekends or one-day programs are conducted by teenage team leaders or young adults, and provide youth with the chance to grow in relationship to God and to further their own self-discovery. An outgrowth of the Search program is a senior religion seminar held in Cardinal Dougherty Catholic High School on Monday nights for the duration of the school year. Using the young-adult team approach, service projects, and experiential learning coupled with input sessions, the seminar is an example of the extended use of the peer ministry approach in catechesis and service. There is a touch of irony in the fact that so many members of the seminar classes apply to become team members for the following year that some of them must be turned away. Apparently, the call to ministry extended to young people through their participation in these types of programs is in advance of structures and roles for youth to commit themselves to.

The formation of youth is also carried out by the DYA through a broad program of athletic activities, and through the benefits of participation in the Scouting and Agape Campfire organizations.

The kinds of ministry outlined in the above programs are not in themselves unique to the Philadelphia Archdiocese, or to Catholic ministry, for that matter. What is notable about the DYA is rather the significant leadership role exercised by the young people in these programs, and the high degree of ownership and commitment they feel. To the young leaders of DYA, the matter of youth involvement can be as simply expressed as basic common sense . . . how, they ask, can an effective program *for* youth be run unless it is developed and administered *with* youth? From a broader perspective, however, a variety of reasons and approaches underly the enablement effected by the DYA.

Physical Circumstances

The DYA operates from a strong central diocesan base. Because the Philadelphia Archdiocese is primarily urban and suburban and served by an excellent public transportation system, young people from almost every area of the Archdiocese are able to meet, work, and conduct programs at the central offices when necessary. Also, the highly visible human needs of an urban area area a constant reminder of the responsibility for Christian service and presence among the poor, homeless, and lonely. The large Catholic population and established Catholic structures that characterize Philadelphia can be an asset to youth ministry, since channels of contact and communication are well established. On the other hand, the traditional priorities and institutions tend to set limits on the forms of ministry that can be effectively carried out. And clearly, the availability of parish, high school, and camp facilities for youth is a plus for the work of the DYA. However, although many factors in the Philadelphia situation tend to optimize resources, the DYA staff members stress that large numbers of Catholic adults or youth are not the primary criteria for success. The actual youth leadership group that is the focus of personal and ministerial enablement in Philadelphia is relatively small, and the critical factors in their growth are relational rather than material.

Approaches to Enablement

At all times, the adult staff of the DYA seek to identify youth with leadership potential from among those participating in DYA programs. Many young people are unaware of their own abilities, and unlikely to come forward on their own. Likewise, some youth who are very willing to volunteer their time and effort are limited in their effectiveness by their own great needs. An ongoing practice of companionship with youth, accompanied by attentive observation and followed up with special invitations to responsibility, is the basis for adult enablement of youth.

The attitudes, values, and ego needs of adults who work with youth are an important determinant of their success in developing youth leaders. Monsignor Schmidt and other members of his staff believe that young people are good, that they have talents, insights, and gifts to share with others. To be able to act on this belief, a person who works with youth must be personally mature, secure in the knowledge of his or her own worth, and genuinely respectful of the person of the youth. A relationship of respect and trust entails a certain amount of risk, and this must be accepted as part of the entire process. No young person *or* adult is perfect, and all continue to grow and learn. There will most certainly be times when the outcomes are totally unexpected, when leaders disappoint, or when crises develop. The effective adult enabler must be ready and willing to support young people in their responsibilities, but should also refrain from stepping into a difficult or unexpected situation to "save" it for the youth. The DYA staff strive for flexibility in their dealings with youth and exercise careful judgment in the responsibilities they invite young people to take, but in the end their relationship to the young people is much the same as that of a good coach to good athletes—the coach can support, train, and encourage the players, but can't play the game for them.

In order to attract young people and to be able to offer them a ministry that meets broad needs, the DYA operation involves a balance of opportunities. Young people have a need for respect, for affirmation, for the knowledge that they are needed by others. The programs and service opportunities of DYA enable youth to contribute their best to others, and be treated as persons with something to give. The peer relationships work out important identity and intimacy issues. For this reason, there is a high degree of social interaction encouraged and facilitated in the context of the work of the DYA. The fact that boys and girls work together on most projects and activities is a definite plus for the many Catholic youth in Philadelphia who attend sex-segregated high schools. The context of service, spiritual growth, and personal affirmation contributes to a healthy and Christian influence on the friendships and romantic relationships these youth become involved in through their participation in youth ministry.

The DYA provides young people with a faith community that is especially receptive to their own questions, needs, and celebrations. Although the DYA meets these needs partially through liturgy, group prayer, scripture study, and retreat weekends, perhaps the most crucial gift is the personal relationship of the youth with believing adults. Monsignor Schmidt accurately notes that it is very important to "waste time" with the young people. The deepest questions and most complex understandings can be worked out openly between an adult and a young person only after enough time has been spent together cultivating the field of friendship.

When a young person accepts the invitation to responsible participation in the work of the DYA, he or she makes a decision that leads to an experiential learning process of great value. Building upon the formal education and personal formation effected by family and school, the concrete experience of responsibility creates a daily challenge to a teenager. The situational pressures of organizing a meeting, coordinating a project, facilitating group process, and relating to authorities are real-world experiences that test and shape the teenager's self-knowledge and confidence. Reflected on with adults from a Christian perspective, these experiences can provide important maturity to teens who would otherwise be catapulted into pressured situations during the college or young-adult years with less available support from the Christian community.

Concretely speaking, the approach of the DYA to the development of youth leaders is highly structured. An intricate bureaucracy provides young people with titles, roles, and office space related to their work. To those who have little patience with the details of bureaucratic management, it is important to realize that in some ways a carefully delineated structure is a support and defense for the youth. The role expectations are clear, and honest evaluation of their successes and failures is possible. The structures are not imposed on the youth, but created and managed on their own. In addition, the fact that duties and responsibilities are clearly identified enables teenagers with much potential to take on systematically broader responsibilities, leading in many cases to an adult commitment to ministry. Because so many young people in this various program, are responsible for a certain amount of their own financial support, particularly those from disadvantaged backgrounds the department is committed to the provision of "enabling funds" for the youth leaders. Enabling funds are apportioned based on weekly time sheets, at a minimum but adequate rate. Finally, Monsignor Schmidt and the other adult staff members attempt to offer all possible unique and valuable workshop or travel opportunities for the young people, sending them as delegates to regional or national meetings, funding their participation in high-level training workshops, and organizing recreational opportunities of a diverse nature.

Positive Outcomes

Perhaps the greatest advantage of the youth-enablement process that goes on through the DYA is the constant revitalization of youth ministry that continues to make the DYA effective in its own work, and that flows outward to enhance and strengthen the other ministries taken on by the youth who have moved past their high school years and into families, colleges, parish ministries, priestly and religious life.

There are, however, some specific results of the human development approach that can be seen in the lives of the young people who are or have been a part of the DYA. One such result is the development of personal identity, self-worth, and confidence associated with the testing of one's abilities in the context of an affirming community. In addition, new abilities are discovered, and the complementary talents of diverse people within a community can be appreciated. During the adolescent years, the clarification of personal values and behaviors is especially critical. By providing a wealth of experiences, adult role models, and active learning opportunities during this formative period, the programs of the DYA have a directional impact on the lives of youth that has real momentum and a foundation in reality. The lasting effects of involvement with DYA is attested to by adults and young people, particularly in the area of higher education and professional choices tending toward helping professions or more explicit ministry. Also the network of relationships established through DYA with persons of similar values and life-styles is an ongoing support for the young adults who complete their high school years with DYA.

Through their participative experience of the Church as an institution, young people who work with DYA seem to attain a greater understanding of and love for the Church. In a sense, the faith community they experience on retreats or with their co-workers gives them a glimpse of the vision of Church that all believers strive to fulfill. Without that experience of community and without an awareness that the Church is the pilgrim people of God, still becoming, young people may grow into maturity fully informed of the doctrines and practice of the Catholic Church, but disheartened, impatient, and thirsting for the personal and community religious experience that enlivens faith.

Some Problems

Despite the remarkable depth and extensiveness of the youth leadership development conducted through the Philadelphia programs, there are specific difficulties that are experienced in the DYA that may be common to those in other areas and therefore worthy of note.

The high level of activity and the multitude of programs run by the DYA on occasion lead to the situation in which large doses of interpersonal or societal experiences go unprocessed, thus greatly diminishing the learning value of the projects. Without sufficient reflection, service experiences, management problems, spiritual encounters, lose some of their potential for providing growth, and in some instances may hurt a young person unless an adult or peer is available to share the feelings of the youth.

Because of the well-developed and pervasive Catholic high school system that characterizes the Philadelphia Archdiocese, the DYA programs are sometimes overly modeled on the school situation. This has the practical effect of reaching the young people where they are, but it can also work against the growth of parish-based, intergenerational faith communities.

The enthusiasm and commitment of the leaders in youth ministry in Philadelphia is sometimes a source of family tensions. Careful attention to communication with parents and involvement of families in appropriate projects is an important area of development for DYA.

Although the youth ministry efforts of the DYA are large and influential for teenagers, there is irregular continuity with other ministries in the Church on the campuses, in parishes, etc. If youth are being enabled to take their place in the ministry of the Church, then there is a responsibility incumbent upon the whole Church to prepare and to support youth and young adults in avenues for others.

Conclusion

The personal enablement and leadership development of the DYA in Philadelphia is not the most visible aspect of its work. However, it is certainly the core of its ministry and the source of the creativity and energy that moves the more highly visible complex operations. And in the last analysis, there is no program, no model, no set of behaviors, that can guarantee success in this type of endeavor. The models and programs and rules can only facilitate and guide what is more fundamental—the personal dedication of the adult staff to their youthful co-workers, and an abiding respect and thanks for the gift of each young person who becomes a part of the DYA community. By effectively adding skills and structures to an attitude of personal Christian relationship, the DYA has continued the growth of their ministering community. The way is uncertain, and there will be times when financial and human resources seem impossibly low. But the work of all ministry is the work of Jesus Christ through his Holy Spirit; with him, the work of ministry to youth and with youth will grow.

Part III

Developing Leadership

Manalive:
A Program for Enabling

James Kolar

As far as I can determine, the Manalive Program of the Archdiocese of St. Paul-Minneapolis is the largest one in the country attempting in a systematic way to prepare young people for ministry. Readers can judge for themselves the sort of careful reflections behind the program from the following report by Jim Kolar, coordinator of Manalive. The following are some of my own reflections after reading this account of Manalive; they may be useful to the reader.

1. I am impressed with the intelligent care taken to supervise and understand the experience of these youth ministers. Involved here is not just an effort to get people into ministry, but also the hard work of staying with them and serving their needs at each step of the way.

2. We have here (and in the other reports on training for youth ministry) a possible model for all training in ministry of any sort. Here field work dominates; in seminaries, it takes a decided second or third place. Even recent documents on priestly training stress, and perhaps overstress, academic preparation, while they understress field work. The best of the new deaconate programs in the United States are more like Manalive than like the "hothouse" model of most seminaries. Unfortuantely some deacon training programs are still aping the worst features of seminary training.

3. It is certain that these field-developed and seminary-developed ministers will have to work together, and closely together, in the future. Unless they are able to do so well, we will eventually have seriously divergent, rather than seriously coordinated, ministries in the Church.

4. All the training programs described in this section stress spirituality in one way or another. This stress suggests much soundness in the present and much hope for the future.

5. Finally, this section of the book might profitably be studied by persons working with young adults in seminaries. Seminarians will have something to learn from these experiences of their sisters and brothers in ministry.

------------------------------------ ▲ ------------------------------------

In September 1973, a program of youth ministry entitled "Manalive" began in the Archdiocese of St. Paul-Minneapolis. It originated as a response to two sets of data that were gathered and pulled together from 1970 to 1973. One set of data had to do simply with the number of baptized Catholics in the archdiocese who were between the ages of 13 and 18. Out of 60,000 adolescents who were baptized Catholics, 10,000 attended one of the 17 archdiocesan high schools. Another 9,000 were involved in some type of parish-centered program—principally a program that was designed and structured to be educational. This meant that 41,000 youth were not involved in any formal program or process of religious education. As religious education was the predominant form of youth ministry, it seemed correct to assume that those 41,000 had little or no consistent or ongoing contact with the Church.

A further piece of statiscal data that emerged was that there were three priests who were engaged full time in youth ministry on a diocesan level, two at the Catholic Youth Centers and one at the Catholic Education Office. There were also 100 professional religious education coordinators in parishes on a part-time or full-time basis. The coordinators' primary responsibilities were twofold: the design of curriculum and the recruiting, training and supervision of volunteer adult teachers or moderators. The actual contact with youth was incidental. There were also other persons involved to one degree or another in some form of ministry to youth on a part-time basis—e.g., priests, lay volunteers. Normally these persons had little actual time to give to youth.

The second set of data surfaced from the results of an extensive survey that was given to over 4,000 Catholic adolescents from representative sample groups. (The Catholic youth surveyed represented urban, suburban and rural areas, and included youth from parochial and public schools.) The survey instrument itself was designed by the Youth Research Center under the direction of Dr. Merton Strommen. The instrument was constructed to bring out the religious attitudes, beliefs, values and practices of the youth it surveyed. It was designed around six major categories: family relationships, personal growth and peer group relationships, personal battles and moral issues, feeling for other people, institutional church and religious participation. I will not attempt to explore all the data and correlations that the survey revealed, but rather I will simply try to isolate some of the data that was particularly influential in the origin of Manalive.

As a person goes through the data, the single most recurring area of interest and need that is in evidence is perhaps best assumed under the word "relationships." From that perspective it is possible to sift through that data in a relatively rapid manner. For example, 60 percent expressed a concern about their relationship with themselves in terms of a negative self-attitude; 64 percent expressed a desire for more self-respect; 38 percent were bothered quite often by a fear of personal failure; 25 percent were overly conscious of personal faults and guilt; 34 percent expressed that at one time or another they had considered suicide. Slightly under 50 percent were bothered by a lack of positive relationships with their families—especially regarding unity, closeness and love; 25 percent were disturbed by the strained and argumentative relations their parents had; 25 percent complained that their parents had little interest in them; one out of three felt that their parents didn't understand them, were too strict, didn't trust them, or didn't like some of their friends. Forty percent stated that there were not enough social activities in the home.

In relationships with their peers, 40 percent expressed distress over cliques that closed off relationships; almost one-half were bothered by the unfriendliness and lack of care of their peers. Three out of four felt that there was an unhealthy amount of peer pressure to follow the crowd.

Regarding their relationships with God, 61 percent were troubled a lot because they didn't have a deep faith in God; 58 percent were troubled because they didn't have a close relationship with Christ; 37 percent were troubled because God doesn't seem to hear them when they pray.

From a different perspective, yet one that dovetails into the previous data, 9 out of 10 said they were looking for a place where "they can experience acceptance in a group of people who really care about each other." The same percentage said they wanted "to develop greater ability to show a loving concern for others." Ninety percent wanted help in "learning to be more of the real me when I am with other people," "understanding myself and my problems," "in discussing my doubts and conflicts openly." Eighty percent wanted the "friendship and encouragement of adults I can count on." Nine out of 10 surveyed said they wanted help "in experiencing a closer relationship with God." Eighty percent expressed a desire "to attend meetings where I can experience the presence of God" and "to learn to speak naturally and intelligently about my faith."

As these two sets of data—the statistical information and the results of the survey instrument—were analyzed, the picture of youth and ministry to them came into much sharper focus. Over two thirds of the Catholic adolescents were not involved in any form of Catholic education, and as education in a formal sense was the predominant thrust in ministry to youth, it appeared that 60 percent had no consistent contact with the Church. From the youth research survey instrument it became quite clear that the vast majority of youth had felt needs concerning their relation with themselves, their families, their peers and God. Furthermore, they expressed a strong desire that the Church help them experience, explore and understand how these different relationships could be deepened and strengthened. It was apparent that a ministry to youth that was designed on an educational paradigm was not going to meet these needs. What was needed was a model or paradigm that would be structured on the basis of those dynamics that are operative in the field of human relationships.

After studied consideration, it was decided that a form of youth ministry that was going to reflect this data should be structured according to four basic lines. First, it should be relational form of youth ministry. The youth worker would not be a religious educator or a teacher in the formal sense. Rather, he goes out to seek out youth in those places where they normally associate, and once there he is to initiate and cultivate personal relationships with the youth through his interest, care and availability. Second, it should be parish based. The worker would be a member of a parish staff and would gain the strength, support and vision that the staff would provide. Also, as part of a parish staff, the worker would have identity as a "Catholic youth minister" from a particular area church. Third, it should be centrally administered. The recruitment of workers and parishes, the initial and ongoing training, the supervision and evaluation, and the administrative functions would be carried out by the personnel hired by the primary governing body—the Board of Directors. Also, the central administration would provide the community base for the workers themselves in terms of their own care and support. Fourth, it would be based on a young adult who would have the desire and ability to work full time in this form of ministry for a two-year period. It was envisioned that this ministry would be an opportunity for young adults who had the potential to enter into this experience of challenge and growth for themselves. The name for the program was to be "Manalive" after the quotation from St. Ireneus that "the glory of God is man fully alive." In September 1973, the first training program took place and Manalive was underway.

Since the doors of the St. Paul Catholic Youth Center opened at the end of that first three-week training and orientation program in September of 1973, we have passed through a rather large expanse of relatively uncharted territory in the field of Catholic youth ministry. When we began we had a fairly clear picture of the landscape we would be covering. The needs of youth, their desire to enter into the world of their primary relationships—with self, family, peers, world and God—and to recognize or establish significant landmarks in that world had been identified. Yet as the first workers actually began to make their way through this landscape, it became painfully clear how little was actually known about the territory they had entered. As the exploration continued, landmarks emerged and trails were established. Normally, these landmarks and trails emerged in the context of trying to work through difficulties that cropped up as their ministries developed. What I propose to do is to lead you along the paths that have emerged and

to point out some of the major landmarks that have been discovered.

Saving the Saved Syndrome

One of the first major difficulties encountered was a fairly
simple one—to whom is the ministry of Manalive directed? Ini-
tially the program had arisen in the context of a discussion that
focused on the 66 percent of Catholic youth that were not involved
in Catholic schools or parish-based religious education programs.
This 66 percent was called the "unchurched," the "unattached," or
the "disaffiliated" and "unsaved." It was assumed that the other 33
percent was churched, attached, affiliated and saved, and that
Manalive should not spend any time with youth in that category.
As one pastor put it, those youth are not "fair game" for a Manalive
worker. Rather the worker should deal exclusively with the lost 66
percent. With experience, some of it painful, it became evident
that these so-called "churched" or "saved" youth had as many, if
not more, needs as the "unsaved" did. And that these so-called
"good" kids, even though they didn't have serious trouble with the
law, or the school, or their families, did have quite definite needs
that were not being met at the Catholic high school or in CCD class,
needs that could be met through a positive relationship with a
Manalive worker. Further, we discovered that youth themselves
did not establish their peer group relationships along the distinctions delineated by ecclesiastical statisticians. Consequently the
workers found that their ministry was not focused so much on a
particular group, but on a particular way of relating and ministering
to youth. When this was clarified we were much more comfortable
and prepared to more accurately form the expectations of pastors,
parish staff and parishioners and workers.

Finding Some Legs to Stand On

Written into the heart of the program was the concept of
ongoing meetings with all the workers. It was recognized that this
would be a way not only to provide continuing education, but also
to provide for the supportive and caring relationships among the
workers themselves. But we soon found a further benefit for these
gatherings. The first workers were in a definite sense scouts or

explorers. They would go out with a sense and direction for what they were to do. They would come back sharing what worked and what didn't, their positive and their frustrating experiences. They would trace out the contours of the ministries they were developing. After nine months a pattern seemed to be developing. This pattern was fashioned into what became fondly referred to as the "Manalive Platform." The platform became an instrument to sharpen and firm up the basic perimeters of the program. It became something the workers could stand on, and as such, it was a support for their ministry. The platform itself is held up by four basic legs. The first leg arose as we realized how difficult it was for the worker to enter into the complexities of a particular parish staff and parish situation. Most workers were a bit naive about how a parish operates and they needed preparation to enter as comfortably and efficiently as possible into parish life. Also they needed to learn how to become visible in the parish and the area as a Manalive youth worker. Lastly they had to know how they could familiarize themselves as quickly as possible with the agencies, schools, "hangouts" in the area. The pre-contact leg of the platform was designed to meet these needs. The second leg of the platform arose as we began to deal with all the concrete factors involved in reaching out to and relating to youth. These factors are suggested in the following questions: How do I receive the okay to go into public school? How can I learn about the composition of the school? How can I initiate conversation with youth? What should I talk about? The contact leg of the platform was designed to meet these needs. The third leg came about quite naturally as workers had to develop ways to bring the individuals reached through contact into some type or form of group experiences. What kind of group experiences work, how to organize them, how often, with whom, where? All these questions led to the development of this third leg of the platform. It is simply called the post-contact or grouping stage. This is a most flexible stage composed primarily of those group activities that work, and how to make them work. The fourth leg developed as the workers began to have youth come to them who had been involved in stages two and three and who now were at a place in their own growth where they wanted to learn more specifically about how God works in their lives and how they can grow more intensely and more rapidly in their own personal and spiritual lives. Also a high percentage of these youth had leadership potential and the workers needed ways to develop this. So the discipleship leg of the platform was developed. This platform has been the backbone of Manalive for the last two years. We have evaluated it with the workers each year and they have found it to be accurate. Each year during a total program review with the workers, the platform is modified and updated.

Supervise or Improvise

During the first year there was no full-time administrative person in Manalive. Consequently the contact with the workers on a regular basis was limited to the initial and continuing training days. As time went on their need for more support and regular contact with a central administrative person became more and more evident. By the beginning of the second year a full-time associate director was named. In order to obtain more concrete information from the workers about their day-to-day activities, the associate director had them keep daily time sheets that provided a concrete picture of how their days were spent, as well as providing a standard against which they could compare their yearly job descriptions. This system provided an opportunity for the associate director and each worker to get together regularly to go over the time sheets and job descriptions, and to evaluate how time was being spent, what things were working, what wasn't working so well, and so to provide a kind of in-the-field supervision.

The workers were also assigned into geographical teams of two or three. These teams then, under the guidance of the associate director, drew up a contract between themselves as to how they could support one another, and how they could concretely aid each other in their particular ministries. Ideally, these persons in a team could provide a proximate source of support and feedback for one another. In most situations, however, these teams did not function for any amount of time. The workers over a period of time, as they more and more developed their own styles of ministry, found less of a need to maintain this team structure. Also for their own support they tended toward those workers whom they felt closer to personally, not geographically. Within the last year we have utilized one of the parish staff as a contact person for the worker. This person becomes involved before and during the initial training program and agrees to assume the day-to-day supervision of the worker. The associate director, contact person and worker then get together at periodic intervals to assess the progress of the program in their parish. Quite naturally, the ongoing training days still provide a good opportunity for a type of supervision.

I would like to mention one particular experience that was common to all the workers during their first year—learning how to deal with their expectations. It was characteristic of them to be high achievers, as was amply indicated in their personal and academic backgrounds. They were motivated by high ideals. With this blend of ingredients their approach to their ministry was one in which they expected a high degree of success in a relatively short period of time. Although a substantial portion of the initial training was designed to surface their expectations and to temper them with a more realistic picture of their work, they nevertheless had a hidden-agenda set of expectations. As they began their ministry, they had a real vision of what they expected to happen, of youth responding to them and to their faith, of working in harmony with a parish staff that had established common directions and goals, and of being joined to the other workers in a bond of unity and single vision. As time passed, the vision became clouded with frustrations, disappointments and difficulties. Part of this was due to their inability to meet their self-imposed standards and timetables. Part was due, also, to the discovery that the parish staff in most cases did not have their goals worked out, and that the other workers were not all that "common" in their vision. During the sessions with the associate director and other workers it was possible to work through these expectations. As that was done, there was normally a pronounced relief on the part of the workers and they were able to be not only more realistic but more effective in their relationships with youth, parish staff and other workers. And, perhaps as important, there emerged a deeper sense of the original vision, a vision tempered—not extinguished—by experience.

Ministering to the Ministers

As Manalive was in its planning stages, we felt the real need to incorporate into the program some way of maximizing the positive relationships among the workers themselves. We felt this was important for a number of reasons. It was clear that the heart of Christian life was the fellowship that exists among believers themselves and that this fellowship was characterized by relationships that were centered in the Lord and expressed in ways that were congruent and consistent with that center. As a person prepared for a Christian ministry it seemed only logical that he should do so in the context of a community that was striving to center itself in just such a way. This perspective for a training program would offer to the worker candidate the opportunity to experience, reflect on, and evaluate the environmental dynamics and their effects that are operative in a community that has originated and is structured in this way. We hoped that there would develop among the workers themselves a sense of what community is and how it functions. More particularly, we knew that the workers would need one another. There is, at times, in ministry a feeling of personal inadequacy, isolation, disappointment; and it is a great support to have developed positive ongoing relationships with persons in the same ministry and living the same life-styles. They would, then, be able to share in and reflect on the commonality of the experiences they were going through. As time went on and workers developed in their own styles of ministry, some rather pronounced trends began to emerge. It became clear that there were some rather varying expectations on the part of workers apropos of their relationships with one another. Some workers settled into a "lone ranger" style and were quickly absorbed into their respective parishes. It is true that all of the workers fell into a kind of jealousy about their particular parishes and how they spent their time. Because of their desire to get established and due to the great needs each saw in his area, they went through a period in which they were reluctant to give time or effort to anything or anybody apart from their parish. Most worked through this syndrome. Yet one of the enduring sources of conflict was that when one worker needed another—for a joint activity or just to talk—there was none available. They were all too busy. A few workers even established the policy that they were so busy and indispensable they couldn't take a day or a week off, even for themselves.

As these problems surfaced, we began to devote some time to try to clarify what workers actually expected from one another and what they could realistically expect. We decided that workers should expect the following things from one another:

— a basic Christian attitude in terms of their relations—openness, honesty, correct ways to handle conflicts, etc.;
— an active presence in the continuing training sessions;
— morale support—availability and open ear from one worker to another when it's needed;
— a common front because they are all in the same work;
— an active care and interest in the lives of each other;
— help in planning and staffing joint ventures—summer camps, retreats, bike trips.

Although these points and many more were agreed on, the range of the discussion was significant. The spectrum ran from those who had a "lone ranger" attitude—all they wanted or expected was help in staffing activities and to receive new insights and information that would be specifically helpful to their own work—to those who looked at relationships with other workers as a kind of repair shop where they could get the dents and bumps from their ministries taken care of, to those who had a desire to get into the lives of the other workers and actively to support and care for them. We discovered that if a person had developed a "lone ranger" or "repair shop" attitude, whether by design or default, it was a difficult thing to work through.

I must point out, however, that as we discussed these ways of operating, we offered to each worker the choice of what type of relationship he would like to have with other workers. They all chose the active caring style. Some recognized that the way they acted and related was not in that style at all, but they wanted to work toward that. Before leaving the workers I would like to share some further information and reflections. They deal with the growth of the workers themselves.

There is no question that the workers are a unique and talented group of people. They come form a highly diversified set of backgrounds. Some come from college or graduate schools, others from

professions or trades. Some had a great deal of experience in youth
work, others had little. They were all at different places in their
own spiritual and personal journeys. Yet all possessed the common
desire to share their lives and their faith. Furthermore, they had
the maturity and personal abilities and skills needed to be effective
in this form of ministry. It should be noted that although these
requirements may appear to be quite simple, only one out of five
people who apply is accepted into the program.

As the workers reflect on their ministry, a consensus emerges
that this form of ministry provides them with real channels of
growth in their own lives. In private discussion, continuing training
days, through questionnaires and taped interviews, a mountain of
data about the ways in which they have grown has been gathered. I
would like to share some of these areas.

Concerning Their Own Personal Lives and Life Direction

"Changes you from the inside out; cleans out our lives so they
might be more in accord with God's design";

"A time of testing, growth, change—finding out what it means
to live a Christian life";

"Allows a person to 1) discover their gifts, 2) learn how to use
them in a Christ-centered life of service. This is brought about by 1)
the community of workers, 2) the demands of the ministry itself";

"Developed the capacity to be sensitive to people on all
levels—physical, emotional, psychological, intellectual, spiritual";

"Taught me to live looser, freer and cheaper than I thought I
ever could";

"To enjoy a simpler life-style—a style that is more concerned
about God's things."

Concerning Christian Life and the Church

"How contrasted the world's values are with Christian
values";

"How Christian life is totally inclusive—every area of our
lives is involved";

"More accepting of the humanity of the Church and the people
in it—more accepting of people's weaknesses";

"Growing dependence on God's presence in my life";

"The need for Christian community where I can know and be known";

"Through ministry the Lord has been freer to work swiftly and thoroughly in many areas of my life, to bring about more consistency in what I believe and the way I live my life."

Concerning Their Ministry

"To be a minister is to be a hand of Jesus—a hand that heals, accepts, forgives, soothes—anything I say or do gains its credibility from that";

"Ministry—service to others when I feel like it or not";

"To be a missionary to young people—having your interest invite them into God's presence";

"To help the youth see the reality and presence of Jesus in their lives";

"To provide channels of growth to young people so that they have a valid and realistic opportunity to decide whether or not to follow the Lord";

"To be a consistent, true witness of Christ, to develop personal relationships with them, to meet their needs, to represent them to the pastor and parish";

"To offer to youth alternatives to the world's ways";

"I definitely want to stay in ministry—but I'm willing to submit my resignation to the 'lone ranger' club."

Perhaps one term more than any other describes how they understand their ministry and their growth in it. Manalive, for them, is a program of how to be a midwife, for it provides the opportunity to help bring to birth in themselves and others the uniqueness and giftedness that God has blessed each person with in a loving and caring way. The frustration and difficulties only serve to highlight the joy and beauty of the birth that is taking place.

How Do You Evaluate Relational Ministry?

The need for a process of evaluation was one that arose very early in the program's growth. In a real sense, it was necessary to discover what the effects of Manalive were, and to see if those effects were ones that met the needs the program was designed to accomplish. A kind of on-going evaluation was structured into the program itself. This was done by means of the job descriptions drawn up by each worker that detailed their objectives, goals and performance standards. As these performance standards were explicit, concrete and time-bound statements of how the worker would attain each goal that he had established, it was possible to discover whether or not the standards had been met. That in turn provided the basis for an evaluation or review. The daily time sheets also provided a way to evaluate how each worker actually spent his time in comparison with the stated goals and performance standards. if there arose a substantial discrepancy between the time sheets and job description, it was quite readily detectable and again provided a basis for an evaluative review. A further dimension to the ongoing evaluative process is the continuing training sessions. As part of that the workers and administration spend three full days a year doing a total program evaluation. The results of all this has been to reinforce the primary goals of Manalive and to reinforce the style and viability of the ministry that is emerging through these efforts.

From a more formal perspective an evaluation instrument was drawn up by which the whole program could be assessed in terms of its strengths and weaknesses. The single instrument was designed to be primarily a self-evaluative tool that could be utilized by the major components of the program, namely, the board of directors, the administration, the workers and the parish staff. It was composed of a series of criteria or goal statements that delineated the principal responsibilities of each component element. These criteria statements, as such, listed ingredients that are essential to Manalive and consequently provide a framework within which it is possible to assess Manalive's status and to make recommendations to strengthen it.

As one reads through the instrument it becomes readily apparent that only one section could be called self-evaluative—in that it deals with criteria that defined one particular person's primary area of responsibility. It was felt, however, that the perception of other persons outside one's own area, but who were involved in some capacity, could be invaluable sources of information. The data gathered was then shared at the appropriate levels in a constructive and growth-oriented way.

Concretely, the process we went through consisted of three stages. First, each person completed the evaluation form by assessing how well the goal statement had been accomplished according to a scale of one to four. Secondly, each component of Manalive then met to share and discuss their assessments with one another in an ordered sequence. Thirdly, the subcommittee on evaluation from the board of directors then collated the data in the form of an overall program evaluation and submitted it to each of the parties involved. It was extremely positive and manifested the effectiveness of the program as a whole. The primary weaknesses were in the areas of an adequate funding base, communication levels between the various components and certain aspects of field supervision and recruitment.

As the reader will have noticed, in our attempts to evaluate we did not include what might be considered the most vital component of the program—the youth themselves. After considerable discussion it was felt that it would be extremely difficult to use this instrument, or to design an effective instrument that could be used to gauge the impact that workers had on youth. For example, how could you isolate certain of the changes that youth experienced in their lives as being due principally to their relationship with a Manalive worker? It seemed that it would be quite impossible to qualitatively judge the impact of workers on youth. It was felt, in addition, that to give any formal instrument to most youth might insinuate a kind of manipulative atmosphere in the relation between those youth and their worker.

From a quantitative or statistical perspective, we know that a worker in a two-year period meets and knows by name 300 youth, and that he has developed an ongoing stable relationship with 100 of those youth. What this stable ongoing relationship means varies according to the youth involved. The impact the worker has on troubled youth, i.e., those from broken or bad homes, or those with drug problems, or those who are classified or classifiable as juvenile offenders, is fairly visible. There are many incidents of how these youth have experienced dramatic turnarounds in their lives, of how they deepened their own sense of self-worth, of how

they were enabled to relate to others in more positive and supportive ways and of how their awareness of God's presence and order
in their lives has been deepened. With other youth, those who do
not have such serious problems, at least from a societal or legal
service point of view, it is usually more difficult to note the changes
that have occurred in them. Sometimes the changes are noticeable
in their increasing ability to find worth in themselves; at other
times changes can be seen in their being able to talk with their
parents or families more openly and honestly. Some teens become
more involved with parish life and activities; others are able to
understand a bit more clearly how God wants to be present in and
works in their lives; still others became enabled to deal in more
positive ways with the conflicts and problems they encounter from
time to time in their lives. There are, of course, those who do not
appear to have been affected in any noticeable way. It is significant
that at an archdiocesan youth gathering in April 1975, when the
young people were asked what the single most important thing
their parish could do for them was, they said: Have our parish get a
Manalive worker.

The Needs of Youth as Experienced by Workers

During the course of our ongoing training sessions, the workers have shared what they have experienced and perceived the
needs of youth to be. I consider these perceptions important for
two reasons. One is that these workers spend the major part of
their days (and nights) for two years with youth from differing
backgrounds and in a variety of settings: one-to-one, small groups,
in unorganized and organized settings, in schools, shopping centers, homes, camps, churches, on the street, etc. Because of this
experience, their observations are most important. Secondly, the
perceptions of workers have naturally arisen within the context of
their relational experiences; that is, their perceptions have arisen,
been filtered through their own levels of awareness and understanding. Hence these perceptions reveal in a significant way a
great deal about the workers themselves. I have not attempted to
categorize their observations, nor will I comment on them. I will let
them speak for themselves. Youth have a need:

—to express themselves to God but don't know how;

—to belong to a group where they can experience Christian fellowship;

—to be accepting and accepted for who they are;

—to express themselves;

—to accept responsibility for who they are and for their actions;

—to help others out—to be of service to others;

—for somebody to identify with—a model they trust and respect;

—for discipline—internal and external—in a consistent way, especially within the context of being cared for as a person;

—for proper affirmation;

—to experience and to understand their faith concretely;

—someone to have fun with;

—a place to be and a place to belong;

—outlet for physical and emotional energy;

—peer group understanding;

—family understanding;

—to understand sexuality and dating;

—to find the importance of their individual selves;

—forgiveness—how to handle guilt in a constructive way;

—how to deal with feelings;

—experience of genuine Christian Community;

—still point in a turning world—need someone who can be restful, solid and stable influence;

—with all their dependence or external stimuli, need opportunity to develop inwardness and creativity;

—to test, experiment, question, explore;

—to know what it means to be mature and adult;

—to have a good time in a Christian setting;

—to experience and know that Christ is real;

Rearranging the Landscape: Toward a Holistic Ministry to Youth

As we reflect on the history of Manalive and the developments and growth that characterize that history, there is a dynamic that emerges that has some significance for the form that youth ministry should adopt as it moves toward the future. I would like to share in brief fashion some of the elements that should be included in that form.

It seems quite clear that the Church in this country, following the lead of our society as a whole, tends to look on education in a formal sense as the primary agent of socialization and as the best way of handling needs as they arise. For example, in secular society, when the number of traffic fatalities involving adolescents went up, a course in driver's education became part of the normal high school curriculum. In recent years, too, to handle the problems of unwed mothers and venereal disease, courses in sex education were introduced; when drug use increased, they added courses in drug addiction. The Church, in responding to the needs of adolescents, designed courses in religious education to meet those needs. Whether that education took place in Catholic high schools or parishes, the emphasis was still the same. In effect, education is seen as the primary agency in the Christianization process. Perhaps at a time when the broader society around the Church reflected values and beliefs that were rooted in Christian tradition and when the society as a whole understood and interpreted its experiences by those beliefs and values, it was possible to leave the primary responsibility for socialization of a Christian to the other agencies in our society, e.g., family, school, peer group, media.

In such a context, the Church was left to focus on the services of sacramentalizing and educating people in doctrine and tradition. Now, when society is on longer homogeneous but highly pluralistic, it seems that the Church must assume much more of the responsibility for the socialization and Christianization of her people. The Church then must adopt a strategy that affects the whole personal growth of the individual. It would seem that, rather than looking upon the Church as a dispenser of grace through Sacraments and through right doctrine that supports part of an individual's need so that she can somehow muddle through the morass of pluralism, the Church should work toward establishing an environment that would allow grace the space to move and grow. The Church should consider adopting a strategy that creates an environment composed of those dynamics that lead to an integrated and holistic Christian life. At the heart of such an environment would be a network of personal relationships that arise from a common ground or experience, develop in a context that is expressive and supportive of that common ground, and move toward the orchestrated, multi-leveled fullness that God intends His Body to be. This then could form the basis for the creation of a viable alternate society in which a person's life could be Christianized in a total holistic fashion.

More particularly in youth ministry this would require that the youth minister have relational, catechetical and organizational skills and that his ministry be orchestrated around those skills. Manalive workers have discovered that when they have developed trusting, open relationships with youth, that creates a kind of mutual or open space that is shared between the youth and the worker. This mutual space is composed of the relating and sharing of experiences, which in turn allows the worker to enter into the lives of the youth and to help them interpret from within what it is that they are actually going through. As the worker is able to concretize the meaning of Christian life through this mutual or open space, youth more and more need the support of other elements in their environment to integrate and deepen their growth in Christian life. They need to be part of an environment that is being shaped or contoured by the ways of thinking, acting, relating, that are expressive of Christian life. If this environment is not present, then youth are left with an inconsistent or truncated Christianity. What the Manalive workers are faced with is the need to discover or to create such an environment. They know that the success and effectiveness of their ministry, and their own lives, depend on it.

Leading Youth to Ministry:
The Orlando Experience

Edward McCarthy

For some years now, the Diocese of Orlando, Florida, has exerted considerable influence on youth ministry, first under the leadership of Thomas Downs and now under Father Edward McCarthy. Thomas Downs has described elsewhere his vision of youth ministry and the models he and his staff developed to implement it in Orlando, before he assumed his new duties for adult education. Edward McCarthy has now carried these developments another step: the development of what he calls "Peer Catechetical ministry" among young people themselves.

McCarthy's report, excerpted from a longer, more theoretical essay on youth ministry, examines the relationship between ministry and spirituality. An understanding of both realities and of how they relate provides background for his account of the specific training program used in Orlando. The training phases outlined here provide a good example of how one diocese took the key step of moving from ministering to youth to inviting youth themselves to engage in ministry. This program in Orlando is one of the newer ones in the United States, and readers will want to follow its progress.

▲

The following report is an account of some aspects of our efforts in the Orlando Diocese to enable young people to engage in a ministry of their own. As in other dioceses where similar programs are being developed, we in Orlando are operating out of a broader theory about the nature of human personhood and of the religious dimension of human nature. An explicit understanding of these matters has been important to us in Orlando for understanding just what we are attempting to accomplish. Because of the limits of space, however, I will treat only the matters of spirituality and ministry, two issues that logically come after an examination of personhood and its religious thrust. Within the framework of ministry and spirituality, I will be better able to set forth our actual formation program.

Henri Nouwen explains the concept of ministry in this way: "Ministry means the ongoing attempt to put one's search for God, with all the moments of pain and joy, despair and hope, at the disposal of those who want to join the search, but do not know how. . . . We lay down our life to give new life. . . . We realize that young people call for Christians who are willing to develop their sensitivity to God's presence in their own lives, as well as the life of others, and to offer their experience as a way of recognition and liberation to their fellow people."[1] Elsewhere he also states: "Ministry is a very confronting surface. It does not allow people to live with illusions of immortality and boldness. It keeps reminding others that they are mortal and broken, but also that with this recognition of that condition, liberation starts."[2] From this the question seems to be: How do persons develop their sensitivity to the presence of God in their searching and sometimes burdened minds? I would like to suggest that the presence of God can best be discerned when I am aware of the mystery of Christ in my life.

As a general rule, both spiritual and psychological growth occurs best in the atmosphere of a caring community, where warm relationships with one's peers and those who are in authority manifest a certain fullness of life. In such a style of life, love becomes the root and foundation from which walls are gently broken down, and each person is allowed to be him or herself. The spiritual life consists in the circle of love. The interaction takes its origin and power from the love of God, "poured into our hearts by the Holy Spirit who is given to us" (Romans 5:5). But it manifests itself in the ever-rising spirit of loving and being loved on the human level. The basis of this circle of care is the inter- and intrarelationships characterized in part:

- by a genuineness and a transparency in which I am my real feelings;

- by a warm acceptance and prizing of other persons as separate individuals;
- by a sensitive ability to see his world and himself as he sees them;
- then the other individual in the relationship—will experience and understand aspects of himself which previously he has repressed; will find himself becoming better integrated, more able to function effectively; will become more familiar to the persons he would like to be; will be more self-directive and self-confident; will become more person, more unique, and more self-expressive; will be more understanding, more accepting of others; will be able to cope with the problems of life more adequately and more comfortably.[3]

In this type of community, one can have the support necessary to begin his or her spiritual journey in search of the Lord. I would like to suggest that the beacon, the lighthouse, for that journey is the Christ and His Paschal Mystery. Now when I heard the words "Paschal Mystery" presented in the context of spirituality, my gut level reaction was, "Unreal; not based in my experience." I wondered how much more jargon was going to follow. I would ask the reader to bear with me because, as I discovered, it was not just jargon.

If I am to be a disciple of Christ, I must be willing to consider and imitate the Lord in the one thing He spoke about most often, and the one thing He wished to do during His life. That one thing was the will of the Father. This was the burden and conviction in the Lord's life. In the concrete, the acting out of the will of the Father was the Paschal Mystery. The Mystery first and foremost refers to the physical and psychological experience of Jesus in passing from life to death to a risen life. His physical "passover" from one way of life to death to a better way of life was an externalization of His internal passover from living to dying to rising. The external act of Christ in His Passion, Death and Resurrection was an acting out of an internal conviction of doing the will of the Father. Jesus' experience of dying and rising thus becomes the prime analogy for the true and ultimate meaning for our Christian life. We are not just merely to imitate, but in fact to appropriate the mystery of His dying and rising into our own lives. Just as the

Father called Jesus to life to death to risen life, so also He calls us, who are followers of the Lord. I can be most assured that I am following the way of the Lord when I can discern and live out the rhythm of the Father's invitation to me to follow Christ in my own daily deaths and resurrections.

Christian spirituality, then, for me, consists in living out and experiencing throughout the whole course of one's life the death and resurrection of Christ that we have been invited to participate in by our baptism. It consists in living out, in our day-in and day-out lives, the passage from sin and darkness to the light and warmth of God's free love. It is the *process* whereby one rejects the tempting but illusory destructive force that separates persons from their environment, their brothers and sisters, their God, in favor of accepting the free gift of love and the gentle yet powerful translation that takes place because of that acceptance.

Where is this experience of the Paschal Mystery to be found? I would like to suggest it is to be discovered in the interfacing of the Christian and his culture; in one's ministry or service to the Church and all persons; in one's exercise of vulnerability in significant personal relationships; in one's relationships with self; and, finally, in one's relationships with the Lord. It is in life that the Father calls us to imitate the Lord. In all of these circumstances the Christian is to be challenged to learn the art of discernment whereby he or she responds to the call of the Father to life and death.

This art of discernment can best be learned in a caring community that has the spirit of prayer and the spirit of reconciliation as two of its main functions. Reconciliation must be part because we are "wounded healers." We are not perfect. We seek and search for wholeness in the petitioning and granting of forgiveness, one to the other. Redemption begins when we are willing to admit to our confreres our limitations; when we are willing to let go; when we are willing to die to the proud illusion of our own independence. Prayer must also be a part; for, without continual communication with the Lord, we sometimes lose sight of what it means to be a disciple, a follower. Father Edward Farrell can truly write, "The Father is fond of me"; however, without prayer, one loses sight of just how much the Father loves us. Not only the prayer of words and of the head, but even more primarily the prayer of feeling and of the heart must be practiced.

I would like to share briefly some convictions that seemingly one must have before one can enter into the prayer of the heart, by describing briefly what seems to be necessary for those who wish to begin the journey toward the prayer of the heart, or the prayer of quiet. First of all, those beginning the journey must believe in the spiritual life, must believe in the interior life. Secondly, they must then, based upon that belief, set the climate for entering into that life. The climate is usually set by fasting and almsgiving. Thirdly, they must provide themselves with a sacred time and a sacred place where they go to engage in this type of prayer. And, fourthly, they must be willing to listen. In listening to the sounds of silence, in listening to the quiet music, we become aware of the presence of the Lord in our lives. By sitting quietly but comfortably, becoming relaxed, slowing down our breathing, we can, in fact, get in tune with this listening process.[4]

In this type of forgiving and prayerful community, the Paschal Mystery is lived out in the members' lives. The Paschal Mystery takes hold of me, and the Lord brings me into unity with Himself. Our spiritual life becomes life itself. The Lord is in our life and death experiences of our daily life. Father Jerry Brocollo from the Archdiocese of Chicago, in giving a retreat to the priests of the Diocese of Orlando, summed it up best when he said:

In genuine dying and in genuine rising, the motif of prayer is praise, rather than petition. Dying in Christ only occurs when there is a focus on the saving, loving Lord, independent self-surrender. It does not occur when we stubbornly fight in self-righteous "clinging" to the deception of being able to save ourselves. Unless a man loses his life, he cannot really find it. Similarly, "rising in Christ" occurs only when there is a focus on others and on mediating to them the healing love of Jesus; it does not occur when we incessantly look out for ourselves and our desire for resurrection. In being able to lose our life, we truly find it. In both cases there is not an emphasis on begging God to be delivered from death, or pleading for new life.

Young persons can be empowered to discern the Paschal Mystery in their lives. Through their own efforts and the assistance of their spiritual leaders, young persons can be challenged to the invitation of allowing the death and resurrection theme of the Lord to become experientially known and integrated into their lives. They can discover the Father's call to death in the dying to self that it takes to listen empathetically, not judgmentally, to the burdens of another. They can also discover the Father's call to life when someone affirms them to who they are, or when in service to another. They, in fact, can "see the goodness of the Lord," It can be thus if they but decide to become aware and participate in the redemptive process that occurs within themselves, in their culture, in their interpersonal relationships, in all that they do, say and feel.

PILOT CURRICULUM: ENABLING YOUTH MINISTRY VOLUNTEERS

In attempting to begin a formulation of a curriculum, I have utilized the goal statement of the NCEA National Conference Directors of Religious Education.[5] I would concur with them that the end product of Christian Education is the person.

1. Who is aware of his/her own
   worth including an
   understanding of his/her
   identity and integrity as a
   human person with thoughts,
   feelings, desires, and
   actions ....and including an understanding
   of his/her relationship with the
   Father, through the Son and in
   the Spirit.

2. Who is conscious of the social
   dimensions of his/her life
   through a deepening of his/her
   relationships to
     family,
     friends,
     the larger communities,
     and ....through a special deepening of
   his/her relationships to God in
   the social context of the Church
   and with a vision of the wider
   Kingdom of God.

3. Who is open to all of human
   experience, taking part in the
   communication process that
   reveals and promotes truth
                    beauty
                    goodness
   and responding with a healthy
   sense of celebration ....and open to the gift of faith taking
                                     part in the communication
                                     process wherein God reveals
                                     Himself in
                                        Jesus
                                        Church
                                        Creation
                                     and responding with love and
                                     worship.

4. Who is growing in his/her
   consciousness of vlaues and in
   his/her ability
           to choose
           to prize
           to act
   according to that which is
   good ....and who is growing in his/her
                                     consciousness of the redemptive
                                     meaning of Christian values,
                                     especially the invitation of the
                                     Gospel, and in his/her ability
                                     — to live by these values,
                                     — to respond to human need
                                        with faith and concern,
                                     — to share in the transformation
                                        of the world,
                                     — to witness to the ultimate
                                        destiny of man and his world
                                        in God.

5. Who is maturing as a
responsible person who freely
exercises choices on life's
options and who realizes
he/she is accountable for the
choices he/she has made ......and who is maturing as a
Christian person who is
continually open to God's will
and His Spirit, who freely
chooses and assumes
responsibilty for his/her
choices—a person in whose life
faith really makes a difference.

Tom Downs, Director of Adult Education for the Orlando Diocese, has aptly organized this material using a five-point star. The inside of each point of the star describes five psychological processes leading toward psychological wholeness. These processes are:

1. Individuation: A Jungian term describing the process of rounding out and integrating the many facets of personhood; e.g., masculinity, feminity, consciousness, unconsciousness, etc.

2. Relationship: Upon finding one's self, one must begin the search for human contact with others through listening, self-revelation, etc.

3. Ritual: Discovering and celebrating the many "myths" that influence our lives.

4. Valuing: Exploring within one's self the type of decisionality we choose or do not choose to live out.

5. Living: Discerning the possibility as well as reality of self-actualized life.

The outside areas of the star suggest the five corresponding spiritual processes: prayer, scripturing, worship, virtuing, and living out the message and the mission of the good news. The reader is encouraged to explore in even more detail these ten processes in Down's book.[6] I would like to place the star within the backdrop of the Paschal Mystery.

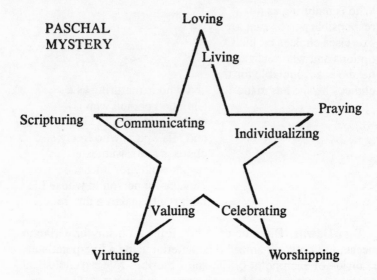

PASCHAL MYSTERY

Loving
Living
Scripturing
Communicating
Praying
Individualizing
Valuing
Celebrating
Virtuing
Worshipping

One can discern the call of the Father to die and rise in each of these areas. The Father indeed may call one to "let go" as one proceeds to the inner journey toward wholeness—holiness. Obviously, in the actual living out of the Christian life, the ten areas of the star will constantly and continually overlap; but for the purpose of reflection we consider them as separate processes. The catechetical Peer Ministry Program is an attempt to integrate these ten dimensions. The program began after wide consultation of both lay and clergy. Our diocese did an extensive study of the eighteen-to-thirty age group. It came up with findings similar to a pamphlet entitled "Religion and the American Youth."[7] In our consultation it became obvious that the needs of the young person were centered more on being and becoming, rather than on doing or acting. The latter, ideally, should be an outpouring of the former. It also became quite apparent that the local pastors' involvement was pivotal in the potential success of any program. Therefore the pastors, in consultation with the religious education coordinators or other appropriate persons, chose and sponsored candidates for the program.

The fee for the program was paid for by both the candidate and the pastor. This was done to foster involvement and ownership in some way by the candidate. It has been my experience that if you ask nothing, you will get nothing. Yet I wanted the candidates to feel truly that they were being sponsored by their parish because of the importance of the work.

The program itself is divided into four phases. Time required for the entire program is about five months. The first phase begins with a concelebrated Mass to which all the pastors and the candidates are invited on a Friday evening. After the Mass, the candidates assemble at a designated place for the weekend experience we call "Alpha." During this weekend, it is hoped that the future youth ministers will experience Christian living. The aspects of Christian living focused upon are: (1) discovery of self through personal appreciation of gifts; (2) the Sacrament of Reconciliation; and (3) what we call strength support.

The candidates on the weekend come into contact with many who are more mature in the faith. Men and women of the Cursillo movement witness to both the staff and the candidates by their service. They take care of all the physical needs of the candidates. It is hoped that through the use of sign and symbol and ritual the candidates experience the dignity of being a gifted child of God.

The second phase involves eight three-hour sessions, during which eight to twelve candidates gather in groups and attempt to learn basic life skills. The groups are facilitated by one or two group leaders who aid the members in living out the Egan model of a contract group.[8] Each member strives to form a real relationship with every member and/or explore why such a relationship is or is not taking place. The types of interaction that put people into human contact with each other are modeled and encouraged. Some of these types of interaction include: appropriate self-disclosure; appropriate expression of feelings; empathy; confrontation; response to confrontation; etc. Each meeting begins with the group sharing about their lives with the Lord. They then move into the skill-learning aspect. The third phase involves four three-hour sessions where the stress is more didactic than experiential. The four sessions are devoted to the further exploration of issues like prayer, human liberation, Eucharist.

The final phase takes place after the Commissioning Mass by

the Bishop (see next page). It includes advanced education sessions. These meetings involve prayer, common sharing, and teaching. The teaching aspect of the meetings is facilitated by a number of the priests of the Diocese, the men and women and couples of the Cursillo and Marriage Encounter movements, and by the Office of Education Staff. Specialty training is also given based on apostolic needs. For example, at part of the meeting there may be four or five different groups, based on work that is being done, e.g., liturgy groups, retreat groups, CCD groups, etc. Let us now return to the star and see which phases of the Peer Ministry Program attempt to respond to the five aspects of the star. It is hoped that during the first phase (Alpha) the candidates will touch upon every aspect of the star briefly. In Phase 2 (Encounter Group), the candidate has a chance to look more perceptively at the five psychological processes. In Phase 3 (adult catechesis) the youth minister takes a more perceptive look at the five spiritual processes. In Phase 4 (continued education) the candidates are given the opportunity, under supervision, to further explore any of the dimensions of the star.

The entire program gives the candidates the chance to become more and more convinced of their self-worth as sons and daughters of the Father. They are given the opportunity both to practice and improve the art of discernment.

They are given time to increase their intra- as well as inter-personal skills. Within this type of caring community,[9] the seed of the Christian life can, if they decide, blossom into their own story, their own gospel. Throughout all the phases of the program, self-evaluation is done by both the staff and candidates in order that it might be an ongoing, improving program. It is hoped that during the training, as well as during the year of apostolic work that follows, each and every candidate will become more aware of the spiritual journey, more attuned to the Paschal Mystery that exists in each life, and that, finally, because of this, all will be able to grow into true, Christian maturity.

The present youth culture has all the characteristics of a religion.[10] Young people are groping for meaning and spirituality, while reacting to both rugged individualism and the dogmatic materialism of the state with its systematic power enforcement.[11] This particular natural desire that many find in our youth must be translated by them. It is hoped that the Catechetical Peer Ministry Program is an attempt to recognize this larval faith of many of our youth, and with God's help bring it into the process of development and fruition.

PEER MINISTRY COMMISSIONING MASS

Introduction: Michael Quoist: *Prayers* 121-123 (two readers, background flute and recorder)

Entrance: Trumpet Fanfare—Mauret

Entrance Hymn: People and Choir—All People That on Earth Do Dwell

All people that on earth do dwell,
Sing to the Lord with Cheerful voice;
Him serve with mirth, his praise forthtell,
Come ye before him, and rejoice.

Know that the Lord is God indeed;
Without our aid he did us make;
We are his folk, he doth us feed,
And for his sheep he doth us take.

O enter then his gates with praise;
Approach with joy his courts unto;
Praise, laud, and bless his Name always,
For it is seemly so to do.

For why? the Lord our God is good:
His mercy is forever sure;
His truth at all times firmly stood,
And shall from age to age endure.

To Father, Son and Holy Ghost,
The God whom heaven and earth adore,
From men and from the angel host
Be praise and glory ever more. Amen.

Greeting: B. In the name of the Father and of the Son and of the Holy Spirit

A. Amen.

B. Send forth your Spirit.

A. And renew the face of the earth.

B. No one can say Jesus is Lord

A. Except in the Holy Spirit

B. There are different gifts

A. But the same Spirit.

B. There are different ministries

A. But the same Lord

B. The body is one and has many members

A. But all the members are one body.

B. May the grace of Our Lord and the fellowship of the Holy Spirit be with you all

A. And also with you.

Penetential Rite: You have called us to service from our baptism—and we have at times failed to respond—Lord Have Mercy.

You have showered your grace upon us—and we have faintly acknowledged your presence in our lives—Christ Have Mercy.

You have been with us in your Spirit—and we have been slow to receive him into our hearts—Lord Have Mercy.

Gloria

First Reading: Hebrews 10:19-25

Response: Father, I adore you, lay my life before you, How I love you.

> Jesus, I adore you, lay my life before you,
> How I love you.
> Spirit, I adore you, lay my life before you,
> How I love you.

Second Reading: Ephesians 3:7-21

Alleluia: Sung, repeat after Cantor

Gospel: Luke 9: 23-36, 57-62

Homily: Bishop

Commissioning Rite: Bishop is seated.

The Call:	Commentator—Let those who are called to be youth ministers in the Church come forward.
Bishop:	You have been called to serve the Church and its youth with your gifts and talents; and you have generously responded to our Call. We are grateful for your willingness to collaborate in the ministry of the Church.
	(To Congregation) I ask all of you here present: Do you as the community of faith accept these servants, the candidates for youth ministry, and do you authorize them to serve the Lord and us in the ways?
People:	Signify approval by applause.

Candidates kneel

Bishop stretches his hands over them (with priests) and says:

> We who celebrate your everliving, everpresent Spirit, God, and who desire nothing more than to be led by your Spirit and to talk in your Spirit ask your grace and loving kindness for

these servants, and for the communities whose life they pledge to serve. Help us to make the faith life of these communities true experiences of refreshment and strength, of inspiration and sharing, for all your people, that we may better serve you in the service of the world. Through Christ our Lord.

All: Amen.

Candidates stand

Bishop: Sisters and brothers, the community calls you to its service, to teach and instruct in faith and prayer and example, and to announce the good news of Jesus Christ to its youth. Will you accept this ministry and responsibility?

Candidates: We will accept it. (Candidates two by two wash their hands and dry them before entering sanctuary.) At the washing each candidate says, "Wash me from my iniquity, and cleanse me from my sin."

Music: Spirit of God by Deiss

The Spirit of God rests upon me,
The Spirit of God consecrates me,
The Spirit of God bids me go forth to
Proclaim his peace, his joy.

Song by Life Unlimited

Candidates then move to kneel, one by one, before the bishop who is seated. The bishop presents each candidate with a lit candle and says.

Bishop: Receive again the light of Christ, may He strengthen you inwardly through the working of his Spirit. Amen.

Placing cross over head of candidate says, May Christ dwell in your heart through faith, and may love be the root and foundation of your life.

Candidate: Amen.

Bishop: Peace be with you.

Candidate: Shakes hands with Bishop and says: And also with you.

Offertory: Instrumental

Bring up on procession Altar covering, Corporal, Basket of filberts, Basket of flowers, Candles, Bread and wine.

NOTES

1. Henry Nouwen, *Creative Ministry* (New York: Doubleday, 1971), p. 116.

2. Henry Nouwen, *The Wounded Healer* (New York: Doubleday, 1971), p. 92.

3. Carl Rogers, *On Becoming a Person* (Boston: Houghton Mifflin Co., 1961).

4. Thomas A. Downs, *Journey to Self Through Dialogue* (West Mystic, Connecticut: Twenty-third Publications); Herbert Benson, "Your Innate Asset for Combatting Stress," *Harvard Business Review,* (July-August 1974), pp. 58, 59; Morton Kelsey, *Encounter with God* (Minneapolis, Minnesota: Bethany Fellowship, Inc., 1972).

5. *A Curriculum Guide for Continuous Progress in Religious Education* (Washington, D.C.: NCEA, 1972).

6. Downs, *op. cit.,* pp. 1-15.

7. Raymond Potvin, Dean Hodge, Hart M. Nelson, "Religion and the American Youth with an Empahsis on Catholic Adolescents and Young People." Commissioned by the Office of Research, Policy and Program Development, Department of Education, USCC. Done by Boystown Center for the Study of Youth Development, Catholic University of America, Washington, D.C., 1976.

8. Gerard Egan, *Encounter: Group Processes for Interpersonal Growth* (Belmont, California: Brooks/Cole Publishing Co., 1970).

9. Milton Maycroff, *On Caring* (New York: Harper & Row, 1971).

10. Andrew Greeley, Presented at the American Sociological Association meeting in Washington, D.C., August 31, 1970; see the *Mental Health Digest,* Vol. 3, No. 6, June 1971, pp. 40-42.

11. Charles S. Reich, *The Greening of America* (New York: Random House, 1970).

Developing Youth Ministers in the Southwest

Thomas Cahalane

In surveying the dioceses of the United States for developments in youth work in 1973-75, I quickly became aware that special attention to training young people in youth ministry was being given in the Diocese of Tucson. That program, growing still, was developed by Father Tom Cahalane. One of the special characteristics of the Tucson effort is that it has evolved a step at a time, out of particular local needs and out of firm action in meeting those needs. There was no initial master plan for developing youth ministers in the Southwest. What has evolved has come from intelligent people engaging in the experiment called ministry.

When Father Cahalane first explained his program to me, I became eager for him to put it in writing for others. I felt that its gradual evolution would give hope to persons in other dioceses who see problems all too clearly but who do not see results as quickly as they would like. Tucson seems to say, "Make haste slowly; start small well and then watch things grow."

Readers will note the stress on evaluation, on taking a second look, and on remapping the route that seems to characterize this program. In the future these characteristics are going to be more and more central to all efforts in ministry.

▲

This article encompasses the sharing of a six-year journey and the experiences and efforts of many who providentially joined me on the way. It deals with efforts and experiences spanning the years 1970-1976 in the field of ministry to youth. In being appointed CYO Director for the Diocese of Tucson, in May of 1970, my overwhelming feeling was one of not wanting the job and telling the Personnel Board of the Diocese: "If you can find someone else for this job, give it to him." However, the next communication from the board was a letter of appointment by the bishop. In hindsight, my not wanting the job sprang basically from personal lack of conviction that CYO was a viable approach in meeting the real needs of young people. Prior to this time, I had been director of CCD high school programs and CYO programs in three different parishes over a seven-year period of time.

My basic resource in becoming diocesan CYO director was a lot of frustration with the two basic approaches of the Church to young people. In too many instances, both these approaches resulted in groups expending much of their energies in maintaining themselves against each other, and at best they survived in a cold-war atmosphere of coexistence. This reality is unfortunately still to be found in too many parts of the country today. In personnel staffing, I found a vast amoung of goodwill on the part of the youth population and on the part of the adults functioning in these groups. Most frequently adults were present in the capacity of volunteers serving in the varied functions of teacher, moderator, chaperone, adult advisor—in many instances with very little training. Again through the window of hindsight, the basic emphasis of both these program directions was heavily adult-centered in leadership style. For the youth, it was better to receive (from the adult world) than to give to each other and the adults. For the adult, it was better to be givers than receivers from youth. Gradually, however, in our diocese the adult leaders of CYO and CCD began to work together in an entirely new way on Weekends of Christian Living. Using as they do some of the insights and techniques of humanistic psychology, these weekends helped the adults encounter one another and helped them in turn meet the young people in a new way. Through these weekends, the discovery that young people could minister to young people in significant ways was a rediscovery of the pearl of great price.

Young people sincerely desiring to commit themselves to these weekend community encounter groupings became a feeble whispering sign of a hopeful vision, which in turn has given birth to the more fully developing youth ministry vision emerging today in the Catholic Church. Ministry to young people had suddenly in this rediscovery process changed focus from the ministry's being heavily adult oriented, to a youth orientation, properly described as youth ministry. Youth ministry is a calling to minister *by, with, from, to* and *for* youth.

The challenging task confronting us at this point in youth ministry in Tucson is training and forming three basic categories of people who are being called into ministry: 1) Youth to be peer ministers to youth, 2) Young adults to be full-time or part-time ministers to youth, 3) Adults (lay, priests, religious) to be effective ministering persons to youth, to the degree that they are called now in full-time, part-time, volunteer, or paid categories. The key words for all these categories are "called into ministry," training and formation. Unless there is sustained effort on all these levels, the dangers of shortsightedness will become very real. A developmental movement, from peer ministry to young adult ministry to adult ministry, calling forth gradual commitment, in the individual ministering person, is to be supported as the ideal, with sensitive flexibility. Our efforts in the Diocese of Tucson are presently so directed.

Leaders from the peer ministry efforts of the Search weekends, as they move into their young adult years, often express their need for a more prolonged involvement by asking the question; "What is there for me now?" It was somewhat on the basis of this question that two of our young adults volunteered themselves as Diocesan staff in a ten-month "Project Y.E.S." (Youth Extends Service), as full-time Youth Ministers among four parishes of the diocese from August 1974 to May 1975. They did so for a nominal salary, but especially in response to their call into fuller ministry.

Mike Berger, one of the Y.E.S. staff, saw a two-fold purpose for the project: "To respond creatively to the needs of young people and to motivate the adults of each community to take a greater interest in the lives of their kids." As young people search for identity, self-esteem, and the reality of God, Berger claimed, there is a tremendous skepticism whether or not institutions such as the Church can help them in that discovery process. In explaining the program, Sharon Komadina, the other Y.E.S. person said, "To create any lasting youth programs, a team of adults and parents working with the parish staff and the Project Y.E.S. staff is necessary. Too often priests or nuns are transferred and then the youth program falls apart. We want to work with adults, share insights on youth ministry, and build a program together, so that when the ten-month project ends, there will be confident, prepared adults to continue working with the kids." Berger added, "We hope to be in a position, after ten months, to make a more definite statement of what really is needed in youth ministry to make it effective. We are also obviously experimenting with a new form of lay ministry in the Church." Both are presently Associate Diocesan Youth Ministry Directors and their conclusions of Project Y.E.S. are documented in a twenty-page written report available from our Diocesan Youth Ministry Department. One of their conclusions reads: "Pastors must become more committed to supporting financially the training experiences for selected adults in youth ministry, for it is in encountering spiritually alive adults that youth will come to experience the true Church."

In communicating this to the leadership of the fifty-six parishes of the diocese, through priests, vicariate meetings, and *Esperanza,* our diocesan newspaper, we refocused our diocesan youth ministry direction. Our budget rationale for 1975-1976 noted: "The concept involved here successfully illustrated in Y.E.S. is that of tapping a real part-time commitment from college-age kids, for a definite period of time and directing it to benefit the total believing community. The fruits of the pilot Project Y.E.S. should become a reality for some of the other vicariates and will hopefully invite them and challenge them to do something more for youth. Matching funds, from a core group of parishes in the vicariate, would be the main source of funding, while the Youth Ministry Office would offer $1000.00 towards each vicariate. Individual parishes must participate with support and matching funds." Further budget rationale indicated: "Youth ministry is a full-time endeavor and it requires more direct contact with youth and adults on a sustained basis—but especially in outlying areas. The Youth Ministry Office will put $1000.00 towards the salary of the Project Y.E.S. college person for each vicariate requesting such a person, provided that the requesting parishes, working as a unit, will come up with matching funds." At the moment the desire and request for such a person is strong from many areas of the Diocese. There is likewise a strong interest on the part of five or six college graduates for such a personal investment and commitment. The need exists all over the diocese and will be answered only by extended services on a full-time, live-in basis. The extension of this project will initiate "new ministries" for young people and will hopefully bring more commitments to the people of God—the Church.

In appealing to the leadership of the parishes to seriously consider placement of full-time people willing to serve as youth ministers, we pledged ourselves, as diocesan youth ministry staff, to be a support unit in training and forming them. During that year (1974-1975) we sponsored and placed four full-time people to serve among sixteen parishes. Yet our training and formation on an in-service basis was less than satisfactory because of the lack of a consistent comprehensive approach.

From this experience grew our present Certification Program for developing youth ministers. In the process of the 1974-1975 year, other points become clearly evident and gradually formed essential components of our certification program. Nobody is accepted into the program unless willing to make at least a two-year, full-time commitment to serve as a youth minister. On the assumption that the heart of ministry is a calling into special relationship with God through persons, it became evident that a lesser period of time diminishes or totally destroys consistent fidelity, so central to effective ministering presence. Again we communicated our clarified direction to parish leadership through priests, vicariate meetings, *Esperanza*, and a poster publicity drive, inviting young adults, twenty years of age or older, to consider a two-year commitment to youth ministry. Between twenty and thirty people responded for more information and six of those now belong to Track I of the program. Two of those are serving out of the Youth Ministry Office in the Diocese of Phoenix, while the other four minister to youth in eight parish situations in the Diocese of Tucson. As part of the admittance process, each applicant had a personal interview with a staff person, had to have three favorable recommendations, and had to undertake an evaluation of their commitment desire in a four-day orientation Certification Program process. During these orientation days, two of the prospective participants decided they were not ready for this kind of two-year full-time commitment.

In designing the two-year program for these six participants (Track I) we discovered nine other people who wanted to grow into fuller commitment in youth ministry, but who because of time conflicts could not meet the requirements of Track I; so Track II was begun out of necessity. The overall requirements of Track I and Track II are outlined as follows:

YOUTH MINISTRY CERTIFICATION PROGRAM DESIGN

First Year

Two categories of people are accepted into the program:
1. Beginners in Youth Ministry—Track I
2. People already in the field with at least one full year's experience in full-time Youth Ministry—Track II

Time Involved: First Year (September to May)

At the end of this period of time diocesan youth ministry will certify qualifying participants as knowledgeable and competent in youth ministry. Competency will be measured on the attainment of the following requirements by participants, plus one full year thereafter or its equivalency. Certification as a youth minister happens after two full years.

I. (a) *Develop a core group of adults,* at least four in each parish, who have grown in responsiveness and shown a sensitivity and understanding of the vision of youth ministry. So that isolation between adult and youth leadership does not happen, have developed a youth ministry planning team (board) that includes the core group of adults and at least two teen leaders who together will plan and carry out parish youth activities.

(b) Work on at least two retreats a year—1) in an observer-helper capacity, 2) in significant witnessing capacity as part of the team.

(c) Conduct and facilitate two or three youth ministry meetings during the year.

II. (a) Design three different retreat models (at least 24-hour duration) and execute at least two of them with the youth communities with whom you share ministry.

(b) Design a calendar of activities by May outlining goals, needs, resources, by which the activities calendar will be attained during the forthcoming year.

III. Report by mid-term evaluation of places where youth come together in your area, and what efforts, if any, are being made to minister to them in their community.

IV. Chart noticeable change, if any, in responses and participation of young people from September and during the existing year's program.

V. A performance evaluation will be sought on each participant in program from parish staff (priest, religious education coordinator).

VI. Time investment and requirements in the program will be specifically as follows:

Track I	*Track II*
a. Two weeks in residency orientation at Regina Cleri Center (Sept 7-21)	Four weekends in residency orientation at Regina Cleri Center
b. One full day/overnight in-service training and formation for each of the following months:	October 29,30,31 December 10,11,12 March 4, 5, 6 May 6, 7, 8

October 19-20
November 16-17
December 14-15
January 25-26
February 18-19
March 8-9
April 12-13
May 3-4

VII. A required reading course will be part of ongoing certification program, with a reading report required from each participant at regular get-togethers, as well as the critique of a tape of a youth ministry meeting conducted by participant since the preceding meeting. During the two-week orientation, and at each succeeding one-day meeting (Track I) and each of the succeeding weekends (Track II), shared process presentations touching on desired areas of growth and need in participant life will be a regular feature of the certification program.

Second Year
   Requirements for the second-year certification program:
   I. Develop a two-year position statement on youth ministry based on ministry experience.
   a. Personal philosophy of youth ministry
   b. Levels of youth ministry
   c. Settings for youth ministry
   d. Needs of kids
   e. Whom do you get to work with youth—What do you look for?
   f. Two case studies (preferably for a longer duration than one year).
   g. Resources—references—at least sixteen, six scriptural.
   First draft due January of second year.
   II. (a) Report on perceived change in oneself for the two-year period of time.
      (b) Keep a personal journal of experience in ministry.
   III. Evaluation of program by key personnel in the area.
   IV. Personal growth experience
      a. Twenty hours of workshop participation—where—what did you learn? How have you used it?
      b. Seven day retreat experience—where—when?
   V. A tape of how you have done Number 1 in a youth ministry setting. Tape must exemplify twenty focal points from your position statement. Your explanation and exposé of at least ten of them will be part of the final evaluation.
   The basic schedule of the monthly overnight (Track I) and the weekend group (Track II) have the following common components: Each participant: 1) gives a basic update of his/her ministry experience of the past month, 2) identifies at least one problem, for shared brainstorming, 3) brings a tape of a meeting conducted since the last get-together to be critiqued by the group, 4) submits a

written book report and gives a verbal report of insights gained from reading. Beyond these points a major presentation is made by diocesan youth ministry staff, or an outside competent person, on a topic previously requested by the group or decided by the staff. Morning and night prayers and Eucharistic liturgy and meals in common are a regular feature of these scheduled get-togethers.

The following evaluation comments, from both groups, measure in some way the success of our efforts in developing youth ministers in the Southwest:

Two-Week Evaluation Track I

"I'm really glad I came, have learned a lot and grown a lot and I know it will help me when I leave, thanks."

"This has been one of the best experiences for me. In this short two-week period, many questions and hangups on community were answered, Thank you Jesus."

"I thank God everyday for leading me into this special ministry and for all in our youth ministry family. Blessed be God forever, Amen."

Track II Comments

"I appreciated the presentation outlines on 'Styles of Leadership,' they will be of great help to me."

"This was a great time together, it was neat, I learned so much."

Evaluations of Monthly Overnights

"The overnights are a wonderful learning process for me. It's very helpful to the extent that all youth ministry 'trainees' are able to share the good, as well as the bad, with each other and to share problems. It seems that most of us are normally experiencing the same things but in different ways. By talking things out, we gain support in a beautiful way. Every month I've experienced life in different ways and sometimes I need space and time to think and talk and sort things out. Whatever it was I needed, I received either from my fellow ministers and from the sessions by the staff. I find these overnights highly beneficial to the spiritual development of the youth minister trainee. The knowledge and guidance of the staff is fantastic. I always look forward to our monthly overnight! I treasure this time spent together in prayer, study, meals shared, discussions, planning, and play. Very special place in my life right now."

"The overnight is a time for me to get away from my area and be with people who understand and support me. The atmosphere is non-threatening, so I feel relaxed from a lot of pressure of the job (sort of, a time of little risk). I need time to evaluate things that have happened (meetings, retreats). It is time to talk about some problems that have come up—not to solve them—but to look at the way I have handled them. It is difficult to look at the large picture, when you are in the middle of it and much easier when looking back from a distance. I don't feel quite as alone either, when I see the other people, struggling with similar situations. The overnight also serves as an enforcer of goals (reading, tapes, core group), I would be very inclined to just say 'I didn't have time to read' but the team is there to 'answer to' (in a positive way)."

These comments gleaned from a few evaluation forms, at the end of each get-together, measure at this point God's blessing on us in our risk-taking into the revelation of His ministry vision.

The basic focus of our certification program could be summarized as follows: It is to help the person 1) grow into his/her fullest potential, 2) into the doing of ministry, 3) to take a look at "how" am I doing ministry, with real emphasis on the ongoing evaluation of "how," 4) share with peer ministry people "my how of doing it."

From the hit-and-miss approach during the early seventies, with basically nontrained volunteers in ministry, to youth in our parishes, we are moving slowly as a diocese to meet the larger need of trained ministers. Presently twenty-eight parishes of the Diocese of Tucson are being touched by youth ministry full-time personnel, in an area-wide or parish-wide approach.

Part IV

Special Issues

Career Counseling
Weekends/Days

Thomas Cahalane

Father Thomas Cahalane, Vicar for Educational Ministry in Tucson, reports here on an innovative program in career counseling he developed for younger teens. As with the issue of sexuality, career guidance is an appropriate issue for youth ministry. At a particular time in adolescent growth the question "What do I want to do in later life?" is an acute one needing some attention. Father Cahalane's program uses this "teachable moment" skillfully. It is included here especially as an example of an effort to meet one of the neglected needs of teens.

In the course of my graduate studies at the University of Arizona a few years ago I had the good fortune to take a course entitled "Materials For Career Guidance." I designed a group career counseling program for high school students entitled "Exploration". The program is for any young adult who has a need and desire to explore the following questions:

Who Am I?

Where Am I Going?

What Do I Do Now?

What's My Future?

The "Exploration" program, born out of a term paper, is basically a method of assisting the high school student:

1. To make career choices.
2. To make life plans.
3. To explore the world of work.

My intentions in developing "Exploration" as a term project went far beyond the immediate task of a course requirement. As I reflected on my own journey through high school, I found the Church's major concern in my career was almost exclusively a "vocation concern." While I remain deeply grateful for the guidance provided me by the Church in my career choice, I have often wondered about the lack of career guidance opportunities for those who did not so choose. My feeling and experience indicate that the career needs of young people in Church settings are poorly served, if at all. In my ministry as a priest, I found a complete lack in our parish programs of any effort directed at the career needs of young people. The "vocation concern" still holds a secret preeminence. In doing research for the program design in trying to generate my own concept of a group career counseling program, I was startled to discover the mass of materials available under the category of "occupational material" in comparison to the handful of materials catalogued under "career development."

Career development in the context of this program format refers broadly to self-development, career planning, decision making, and exploring the world of work. In investigating what was being done in many of the public high schools in the city of Tucson, Arizona, I discovered that counselors function more as occupationalists who merely interpret job requirements to individuals. They function either in this capacity or as deep-seated therapists who can't be bothered with surface manifestations such as; where, how, and what does one look for in oneself by way of preparing for the who, how, and what of career choice.

The traditional high school counseling model has for too long been the one-and-one counselor/client relationship approach, with very little emphasis on career guidance.

The program entitled "Exploration" is designed to touch career guidance needs in the peer-group setting. The specific focus of the one-day program is to help the individual participants get in touch with their own lives through a series of appropriate exercises and discussion-feedback techniques. The program is designed to help the young participant deal with and focus on the need to build a strong sense of self. The importance of self-knowledge as a prerequisite for decisive commitment in career choice is a basic assumption of this "Exploration" career guidance approach. For many young people, choosing a career is the first really complex adult decision they are called upon to face. First of all, they have to learn more about themselves—their abilities, interests, aptitudes, and personality. Getting them in touch with these aspects of self through exercises on self-values, self-abilities, self-interests, self-limitations, personal decision-making processes and implementation of these self-discoveries into a practical and flexible goal schedule are the specifics of the program process. The following fundamental personal questions of career development are explored: "Who am I? Where am I going? What do I do now? What's my future?" The entire program process assumes that developing a strong awareness of self is a necessary and essential prerequisite to exploring the complex world of work. Occupational choice is not a matter of blindly taking a job or choosing a career like a prize from a grab bag. Mistakes are frequently far too costly in terms of personal fulfillmet as well as time, energy, and dollars.

Any person of high school age who is open to and seeking direction in career development will benefit greatly from exposure to the program process. Evaluation comments of two participants who went through the day-program process recently indicated its general and specific purpose. This program is "for the person who is looking for a career in the near future, but I think anyone with an open mind would get a lot out of it." The program is "for anyone in high school because they will help themselves."

The process of the program offers opportunity to the participant

1. To affirm and clarify choices already made.

2. To confront and clarify indecisiveness where no clear choice has yet been made.

The final part of the program leads participants to a personal commitment to explore three possible job situations "I am contemplating as possible career choice." The following skeleton model of the program is time-framed over the period of one day.

FULL-DAY SCHEDULE

9:15 Arrival/Registration/Introduction/Orientation Session
10:00 Self-Awareness Exercises

10:10 One-and-One Feedback
10:15 Eulogy Exercise
10:30 Group Sharing
10:45 Eight Worst Things
10:50 Group Sharing
11:00 Work Values and Activities Exercise
11:20 Role/Behavior/Feelings Exercise
11:30 Self-Abilities Exercise
11:40 One-and-One Feedback
11:50 Self-Interests Exercise
12:10 "Events in My Best Interest" Exercise
12:25 Feedback in Each Group on What Has Happened So Far
12:45 Lunch
 1:30 Implementation/Constraint Exercise
 1:40 One-and-One Feedback
 2:00 Self-Limiting Beliefs Exercise
 2:05 Self-Limiting Beliefs/Corrective Exercise
 2:15 Group Sharing (Each one shared first two S/L Beliefs)
 2:30 Big Decision Identification Exercise
 2:35 Analysis of a Past Decision
 3:00 Flexible Planning Exercise
 3:20 God and My Goals
 3:45 One-and-One Sharing
 4:00 Job Exploration Exercise
 4:15 "Putting Me Together" Exercise
 4:30 Break
 4:45 Celebrating the Liturgy
 5:00 Evaluation
 5:30 Go and Explore Life Through Your New Self-Discoveries

The schedule can be extended over the period of a weekend, if peer-group team facilitators are involved in the process of the program. This extended community dimension of the program adds greatly to the effectiveness of the experience.

The following summarizations of the program are taken from a fuller presentation of the program currently being readied for publication under the title "Exploration."

WHAT EXPLORATION OFFERS

Exploration utilizes group interaction techniques for the world of self-exploration and the much-needed study of person-job relationships. It's a process designed to help participants make better use of their own personal resources and skills.

Exploration offers the participant opportunity for broad exploratory self-study, with the immediate goal of sampling work experiences in three job areas of interest.

The chance to explore self and know self is the real opportunity presented in this program. With widened horizons of self-awareness the student is helped to make choices of courses in college and clarify from the many options a career choice in which the participant chooses the job rather than the job choosing the participant.

OVERVIEW OF OBJECTIVES

The underlying purposes of the day's activities are:

1. to look at one's self, goals, and objectives for the future and examine where God fits in with them;

2. to look at one's own behavior and evaluate it;

3. to figure out what obstacles must be overcome in striving for one's goals, and to identify positive influences;

4. to determine where God fits into one's future and how to utilize one's religious convictions;

5. throughout, to determine realistically whether one's goals and behavior are consistent;

6. to achieve a formation of community through the general interactions of the whole day.

GENERAL GOOD OF EXPLORATION

The general purpose of the program is to help each participant to a deep personal awareness of self through a three step process that will include (1) understanding of self and situation, (2) integration of self-discoveries into (a) setting goals, and (b) making plans, and (3) implementation.

INSTRUCTIONS TO PARTICIPANTS

From the start, participants are told they will be doing a lot of writing and some sharing in small groups. They are encouraged to respond as honestly as possible to each of the exercises since otherwise the experience will have little or no value for them. A folder is provided for each participant with the idea that each will develop a personal file from the materials used in the program process.

By way of getting started, each completes a life-planning questionnaire designed to help discover where each person now is in relation to career choice.

PROGRAM METHODS AND MATERIALS

The methodology of the program is basically inductive, experiential—small groups beginning with one-and-one sharing. Each is to find another person who is not too well known and share with the other (1) family background/number of brothers and sisters, etc. and (2) what one's expectations are today.

Then each couple is to find another couple and introduce each other and share what each has learned about his/her partner. At various points in the program participants will be sharing reactions with their partners and also in groups of four.

ARRANGEMENTS

The Process

The Exploration lasts on the average about eight hours; however, this is open to variation. Team members staffing the exercise should be college students or high school seniors. The director, usually the group moderator or someone closely associated with the unit, takes an active role in the exercises and celebrates the Liturgy if one is scheduled at the end. To allow maximum participation, it is advisable when possible to have some youth representatives from the parish group serve on a joint committee for the promotion layout arrangements and actual presentation of the Exploration. Ideally there should be no more than thirty in the group. Small-group discussions, individuals pairing off, and total-group process sessions are used throughout the day.

Some game-type exercises are used or suggested in this program, but only with the serious realization that such exercises serve no purpose unless they can unite theory with reality, or teaching with practical experience. They are neither the "end-all"/nor "be-all," and when used without discussion and interpretation often are not understood by the participants.

As in any other group work situation, this program should be flexible enough to be changed if the group leader feels interjection of another exercise or introduction of some other topic would be more beneficial at a given time.

Pre-Program Planning

The Exploration team should set up a meeting with officers or teenage representatives of the parish or of two or three parishes if the program is being planned inter-parochially. At this meeting, the team should outline the program for the officers allowing for discussion. This discussion might bring to light the need to alter some of the originally scheduled exercises in order to make the program more relevant in meeting the needs of that parish most effectively.

Physical facilities should be checked out and the team leader should meet or arrange to meet with the pastor or parish priest. If time allows, the group's officers should send out invitations to members and include a reply form. Then, if insufficient interest is evidenced by these replies, the scheduled Exploration can be postponed, cancelled, or merged with another. Notification of cancellation should be one week prior to the scheduled dates.

Some of the activities for the day's program may be assigned or offered to the parish representatives. Maximum participation from the parish members of the core group at this initial meeting will both benefit involvement in the program and afford the representatives a chance to develop their leadership potential.

Equipment Needed
    Easel (or blackboard)
    Osterboard or newspring (or chalk and erasers)
    Magic markers or crayons
    Pencils or pens
    Name tags
    Workbooks or mimeographed sheets for the Exercises.

Facility

The Exploration can be held in a church hall, school hall, gym, community center, classroom, or even in a private home (depending on group size). One will need enough space for small groups to gather away from one another as well as sufficient room to assemble the entire group in one place for the processing sessions and Liturgy.

Time

Six to eight hours (approximately) depending upon the group, its progress, and lunch arrangements. Time is a flexible factor.

Refreshments

Cokes and other refreshments should be made available. If teenagers are bringing their own lunches, make sure that soft drinks are available.

Staff

1 (or 2)	Exploration Team Leader to coordinate whole program.
1	Priest for celebration of the Eucharist and to partake in whole program if time allows.
1 per group	Discussion Leader (workable groups are 4-8 members).

The program will be published in book form in the near future. Informational packets with all the exercises are available, at a nominal cost, from Youth Ministry Department, Diocese of Tucson, 8800 E. 22nd Street, Tucson, Arizona 85710

There seems to be a real need for this kind of program. Since a brief overview informational piece appeared in "Youth Program Services" and "NEXUS" a few months ago, our Diocesan Youth Ministry office has had requests from thirty Dioceses (including one from Hong Kong) for material and more specific information on the program.

Deciding for Oneself,
Not by Oneself

Nancy Hennessy Cooney

During a one-year period recently, when I was directing a series of workshops on youth ministry, I asked the adults present to list in order of importance the ten most important needs of teens. With rare exceptions, the matter of adolescent sexuality was omitted from these lists. Yet the task of pursuing a sexuality is one of the crucial tasks of adolescence. Issues related to sexuality are never far from center stage in the lives of teens themselves.

To a large extent, American Catholics have responded to the needs of adolescent sexuality with either silence or moralizing. To some pressure groups in the American Church, the matter of adolescent sexuality is one to be kept locked in a basement cupboard. Some parents also are rightfully anxious about possible harm that might be done to their youngsters by ill-planned and poorly implemented programs of sex education. As a result of these tensions, courageous educators like the late Brother Hugo Hurst, CFX, have suffered much for their efforts to make a contribution to education for adolescent sexual development. Other educators and catechists possessing both the interest and ability to make a contribution to this area have taken the safer route of silence and inaction.

One who has not taken that route is Nancy Hennessy Cooney, specialist for adolescent catechesis in the Milwaukee Archdiocesan catechetical office. She has been examining the available information and current programs of sex education for adolescents, especially those developed by religious groups. What she has found is the existence of a few excellent programs that involve parents and teens in dialogue on matters of sexuality and genitality. She is currently engaged in sharing this information with Catholics in youth ministry in hopes that they themselves will develop new

179

programs suitable in different contexts for different age groups. Certainly this is an area deserving of much more attention by those ministering to youth.

Have you ever seen someone pull a tablecloth out from under a set of good china? A friend of the family once did that trick just as we were about to sit down to her beautifully prepared meal. I forget what we ate that night but I will never forget the sense of awe and relief I felt after I heard the cloth snap and saw all the dishes standing upright on the polished wood.

That experience has been a help in explaining to myself and others the possibilities within a certain program in sex education for junior high youth and their parents. It succeeds in pulling away the invisible barriers between young people and parents surrounding discussion about questions of sexuality. Questions like:

How do you get VD?

What is a rubber?

Do boys like girls who are easy?

Is it a sin to have sex before marriage?

How do you know if you are queer?

Many parents wait for their youngsters' questions although, when they reflect upon their own experience at puberty, they remember how difficult it was to confront an adult with them. In the "Deciding" program, parents and youth are given the structure of a weekend workshop and the stimulus of its content to share a new experience and allow it to be the occasion for getting conversation going.

Such conversation is the goal of a weekend program conducted by a trained leader and a small group of local adult parishioners. They lead large and small-group sessions primarily for the youth but include additional sessions for parents. Ultimately, it is the adult volunteers from the parish who act as catalysts for better parent/youth communication in the home.

On another level, the tablecloth is pulled from the problem of "doing sex education in a parish setting." Many parish leaders realize the limitations of an approach that brings a doctor, priest and parent in for a couple of hours to lecture a group of youth. This structure makes it difficult for youth to raise their questions or to be challenged to look deeply into their attitudes. In the weekend program young people meet much of the time in small mixed groups of eight that are led by a man and a woman parishioner who have been trained the previous weekend. Sexuality through them is witnessed as something that is normal and can be talked about with nonexperts who are interested in them as persons and who believe in their capacity to make their own decisions.

On still another level—that of the wish, the not-yet-realized event—the tablecloth can be pulled from a vision of the Church that is concerned about sexuality only as a series of "Thou shalt nots." If young people and adults begin to share and grow in their appreciation that sex is good through this program, perhaps ventures like this can multiply and show what is underneath the admonitions and accretions of history—a desire that the beauty and power of sexuality can be an expression and a concrete sign of God's creative love.

The program "Deciding for Oneself—Not by Oneself" was first developed by the United Methodist Church and is being reworked for use in Catholic settings. My first acquaintance with this program was in a Methodist parish in Fond du Lac, Wisconsin, as I was trained in the first stage of the five-step process. Following that, I became co-leader of a small group as part of a parent/youth program. After describing this experience, I will share some of the changes that have taken place in the model as it has been piloted in the Milwaukee Archdiocese. Finally, I will offer some observations and suggest implications for Catholics who wish to develop sound programs in sex education.

The Program

This program touched the lives of youth, their parents, and a small group of adult parishioners who were the discussion leaders. When he had gained approval from the parish leadership, one of the pastors sent a letter to the parents of the junior high youth. These young people were invited to participate in five hour-and-a-half sessions on Christian Sexuality over a weekend on the condition that the parents agree to attend two sessions of their own. Parents and young people were told that the course was designed to "open up a channel of communication within the home about sex." The letter explained that the course leader, Rev. Wayne Banks, Director of Academic Procedures and Associate Professor of Education at Perkins School of Theology, Dallas, Texas, had been on the planning team for the course in 1968 and has since led many courses throughout the country. Rev. Banks intended to give twelve hours of preliminary training for parish religious educators and youth leaders familiar with the young people. He also invited others around the state who had expressed interest in the program. I was one of the eight local people selected from the total training group to co-lead the small group discussions. These discussions are at the heart of the youth program.

Most of the twenty-eight young people who signed up had done so at the urging of their parents. On the first evening, the attitudes of the participants ranged from hostile to uneasy. These young peole were concerned that they might be embarrassed in the presence of their friends or be given a lot of moral exhortations about how to behave sexually.

Youth Session 1: Friday night's meeting was designed to break down hostilities and begin to create a climate of trust between the young people and their adult leaders. This was accomplished by introducing the course in an enjoyable manner. We broke the ice by playing a famous-person guessing game when the participants came in. Then at supper, provided by parishioners, my partner, Bob, and I met our group of four girls and three boys. All of us moved into a large meeting hall decorated with pictures and symbols about love and sex, where we participated in an introductory values-clarification exercise. This exercise focused on the folly of making decisions that are not based on correct information. The whole group then viewed a filmstrip called *Learning about Sex.* It shows the importance of learning more about sexuality in the junior high years and was also used to introduce some of the topics to be covered. Small-group discussion of the filmstrip was followed by an Agree/Disagree sheet. The purpose of the sheet was to surface some of the course topics and to indicate something about the level of student maturity. A question box was an opportunity for the leaders to communicate their belief that any question brought up by a group member confidentially would receive an honest answer. Central to the course is a climate of openness and ease in which students can raise questions that are important to them and have these questions discussed. Finally a short paperback, *Love and Sex in Plain Language* by Eric Johnson was given to each person. This book contains both factual information on biological functioning and an emphasis on forming values that respect other persons. This session closed with all groups forming a large circle and giving thanks to God for making sexual persons.

Youth Sessions 2 and 3: As in the first session, these two meetings moved quickly and contained mini-lectures, discussions, games and questions. The purpose on Saturday afternoon was to help develop correct vocabulary and ease in discussing the male and female reproductive systems. There was much to do and the participants were free to linger over subjects of interest in the small groups. I had presumed that students who had had courses in hygiene would find these sessions repetitious. However, they quickly moved from the factual presentation to questions about the Christian perspective on sexual conduct.

Youth Session 4: The first topic discussed on Sunday afternoon was sex roles. Opinion sheets, a filmstrip and a value-ranking experience were used to aid in the process of discovering what authentic masculinity and femininity mean. Through this process, the group began to see the conflicts between the culture's narrow view of sexuality and a Christian view in which preference, experience and the acceptance of oneself as loved by Jesus Christ play a large part in the decision about the kind of person one wants to be.

Youth Session 5: Late Sunday afternoon was spent discussing relationships with parents. Three skits involving issues of pornography, influence of the gang and exclusive dating gave a humorous portrayal of how young people and parents listen to one another. We stressed the responsibility young people have to initiate conversation with their parents and, if that failed, with adults from the church. Our discussion ended with a spontaneous prayer in which we thanked God for His love, for our capacity to love and for His forgiveness when we fail to respect ourselves or others.

Parents' Sessions

Parent Session 1: On Saturday morning, parents were presented materials that had been taught the night before. A telescopic introduction to the next few sessions was also given to the parents. They had a chance to meet with their child's discussion leaders and talk about how he or she was responding to the program. The aim of this meeting was to give parents the opportunity to talk about whether they felt their child reacted positively to the experience and to discuss any difficulties they foresaw. The leaders had been instructed not to betray the confidentiality of their talks with the young people. It was a time to create feelings of trust among the leaders and the parents and to give the parents the positive reassurance that they were being supported in their role, not superseded.

Parent Session 2: In the final session, the content of the youth sessions was summarized and Rev. Banks answered questions from the parents. Small groups provided the opportunity for further discussion and the chance for parents to sample the evaluation of the program by their child's group, e.g., "I see that sex is beautiful, not dirty." "I talked to my father about these things for the first time last night." Most of the evaluations were positive and the students expressed hope about continuing this communication with their parents. Our discussion with parents included ideas about how they might keep the door open for further communication and how the local church would be available to serve them on a formal or informal basis.

Adult Training Sessions

The initial twelve-hour training classes included interested persons from around the state, and after this training the group of eight prepared for each session with the youth and evaluated the sessions afterwards. This schedule produced pressure but helped forge us into a strong community. The group also found satisfaction in accomplishing our limited objectives. One leader said: "Sometimes I get tired of working through a process at church. Real progress often seems so far away. It was good to be trained this time and be in a structure in which I knew what was happening and could concentrate on getting to know the kids and respond to them."

Rev. Banks's training erased whatever doubts I had about my own performance in the program. Our sessions included practicing short, clear ways to answer questions. We reviewed our plans and reflected on the responses of the young people. Working with a partner assured me that I did not have to know everything, and this reassurance gave me the freedom to relax and enjoy myself. I felt that I had come a long way in my ability to communicate about sex with youth. Parish leaders had the added satisfaction of being able to offer themselves as resources to youth and parents in the future.

Some Observations and Implications for Catholics

1. The Certified Leader: The position of a certified leader in a program of Christian sexuality in the Methodist Church is not taken lightly. A person like Wayne Banks, who has great humility, charm and a sense of humor, used a five-step process to pass on his expertise to others. A person wishing to become a certified leader in the church must:

—act as a group discussion leader,
—be responsible for organizing a program in a local parish,
—assist the trained leader in giving a course,
—design a program on his or her own,
—lead a program under observation.

The leader must be able to make the many hours of adult preparation and evaluation challenging and productive. He or she needs to be a living example of a Christian who has integrated his or her sexuality, and must also be a serious educator able to operate within a behavioristic mode. Sessions are tightly structured, and clear directions of how and what to do next are provided to ease leaders and students in awkward moments and help them overcome feelings of insecurity. Rev. Banks once said to the adult leaders: "My concern is primarily for the young people. If I disagree with one of you in front of them it is because I believe you are wrong. I count on you to be willing to accept such correction for their sakes."

2. Parent-Youth-Pastoral Support: Both parent and youth groups were encouraged to keep communication going. Going home at night was essential to the program because much informal conversation was carried on in the home environment. The adult leaders from the parish were presented to the young people as normal people who were willing and able to talk openly.

3. Religious Content: The religious content per se came predominantly from answers to questions raised by the young people. For example, when they asked about the sinfulness of intercourse outside marriage, we gave a full and positive Christian perspective. But the real religious content came from adults witnessing to their belief that sex is a joyful gift from God. For Catholics, a natural conclusion of this conviction would be to end the course with a celebration of the Eucharist. This liturgy could be a strong demonstration of the unity formed over the weekend.

4. Adult Education: Catholics have had a great deal of theological background accompanying any change or new development in the Church. In the area of sexuality, too, it would be well for parents and adult leaders to study some of the current writing on the Church's teaching about sex in order to update their knowledge and review their own understanding of the subject. They might also seek opportunities to explore their attitudes on the subject.

5. The Text: Catholics need to search out a different student book instead of the one by Eric Johnson. Official Catholic thought on topics such as abortion, birth control and homosexuality differs from Johnson's and would need to be presented along with, or in place of, the more secular view.

Subsequent Developments

1. Pilot Program in a Catholic Parish: Since that initial experience of the program I have worked with a team in Milwaukee and we have successfully conducted a pilot at St. Rita's Catholic Church, Racine. A certified Methodist leader, Rev. Bob Hays, worked with Mrs. Raejean Kanter and me on the presentation of the adapted model. Full support from the parish education committee and pastoral team helped make the weekend important in the parish. Senior high youth volunteered to baby-sit so parishioners could be free for training and program weekends. (They had one condition—that a program be created for them, also!) Parishioners responsible for food, recreation and organization also attended some of the training sessions and increased the number of parish people willing to be available for future conversations with parents and youth. A liturgy celebrating the beauty of creation and sexuality ended the youth program and brought parents, youth, leaders and support team around the Lord's table. The joy and enthusiasm with which people celebrated the liturgy was a reminder to me that once the questions of young people are met openly, they are free to enter into other dimensions of Church life without reservation.

2. Expert Critique: Last fall Raejean and I presented the model to a group of eighteen persons with backgrounds in sex education, theology, education and parenting. They made a number of recommendations that helped shape the training process of Catholic leaders. They also recommended that every parish interested in our program have three evening sessions of adult education before the youth weekend. If the parish community is to be a resource in this area, they reasoned, then the adults must first meet on the level of their own needs, then concentrate on the youth. The format recommended for this a shortened version of the process that will be described below as the *Awareness* weekend for program leaders.

3. Training Program Leaders: In March 1977 we completed the first stage in a process that will culminate in certification of leaders for the Christian sexuality program. It was called the Awareness weekend. Here is the outline sent to the fifteen invited participants:

The aim of the weekend is to evaluate our own attitudes toward sexuality including the Church's tradition on it. Participants will have a chance to come to grips with whether or not they feel ready to continue with practical training in the weekend model.

SATURDAY

9:00 a.m.-12:30: *Sexuality, American Style: Decisions and Consequences.* This session aims to help participants situate themselves along a continuum of values held in our pluralistic society. We will review some major elements shaping American consciousness in sexuality. We will have an opportunity to experience "desensitizing" and also ask whether it is a useful tool for coming to a deeper understanding of attitudes.

12:45-1:45: Lunch

2:00-4:30: *Understanding the Catholic Tradition Concerning Sexuality.* The reality of human sexuality is often isolated from the totality of human, Christian life. What is our relationship to our Catholic Christian tradition regarding sexuality?

5:00-600: *Liturgy* planned by three group members and introduced by the film about prenatal development "The First Days of Life."

6:00-8:00: Social hour and dinner

8:00-10:00: *The Future of Sexuality and Sex Education.* A time to loosen imaginations and freely explore: Where is it all going? What are the limits? Who sets the limits? What are our hopes and fears for our children, grandchildren, ourselves?

SUNDAY

9:00-11:00: *Catholic Guidelines for Sexuality.* A chance to reflect upon an approach taken by a committee from the Catholic Theological Society of America in their book *Human Sexuality: New Directions in American Catholic Thought* (Paulist Press). We will also test the usefulness of the principles and values outlined there by applying them to a concrete dilemma.

11:30: Evaluation of the weekend

12:00: Close

We encouraged people to get to know one another through the small-group sessions, the work projects (preparing food and liturgy) and the social times so that they could decide whom they would like to work with on the program weekends. We decided that a team of two or three (married, single and celibate) would better image the diversity of life-styles in the Catholic Church. This was also a practical decision. Since the "first generation" leaders do not have as much experience as we will eventually require, we want them to have as much support as they need. Further, we believe that young people and adults need to be exposed to team ministry—a role they can and must play in the Church of the present and future.

Although the full training process is not yet complete, we have a good idea of the steps that are necessary:

a. Private conversation with Raejean or me about the person's interests and abilities.

b. Participation in an Awareness weekend to refresh ideas and attitudes and meet possible teammates.

c. Specific preparation in how to use the model, how to train parish leaders, how to run the youth/parent program, how to deal with specific questions, how to share leadership.

d. Experience as a small-group leader on a weekend.

e. Experience as a team member for the program leadership.

f. An interview with the coordinators (Raejean and me) to discuss our evaluation of the person's progress and explore further background that might be needed.

g. Experience as a team member who initiates new persons into sharing the leadership for the program.

h. After observation and conversation, written recognition by the Office of Religious Education that the person is qualified to be on a team for the Sexuality Program.

As we experience the process with the "first generation" we will revise this outline. There is much opportunity to learn the best way of training in the coming year. There is a waiting list of parishes that wish to have the program, although we did no formal publicity. The fifteen leaders will begin to function as program leaders and discussion leaders for the small groups. Meantime, we will conduct other Awareness weekends to surface others willing to serve youth in this special way.

Some say one weekend for a junior high youth is not much. This is true in the light of the many needs Christians have concerning sexuality. But it is a beginning—the kind that elicits joy and gratitude from those involved. Perhaps the people who are touched by this program can be witnesses of the special presence and insights that Christians bring when they accept, share and celebrate their belief in the totality of the human person. Perhaps these young people and adults will strike observers today with the same amazement as did the early Christians when outsiders remarked "See how these Christians love one another."

Ministry to Hispano Mexicano/Chicano Youth

Teresita Basso, P.V.B.M.

In preparing this book, I searched for persons working with various segments of miniority youth. This search made me aware of innovative work being done in several areas; yet it has been difficult to get these busy, creative persons to write of their efforts. One who agreed to do so is Sister Teresita Basso, a member of USCC's Working Board on Young Adult Ministry, who works with Spanish-speaking youth in California.

Her report on the cultural situation and needs of these young people is an interesting contrast with that of Jeffrey Johnson, dealing with midwestern youth, in an earlier section of this book. In addition to the obvious differences of Johnson's report being of a specific program and Basso's being a statement of a cultural situation, there is a more important difference. Basso's program for marginalized Spanish-speaking youth centers on social justice and social identity questions. Johnson is summoning youth into Christian community, especially through friendship. Basso is first concerned that her youth have a place in the *human* community. Both, however, are calling youth to wholeness.

Sister Basso's reflections here are cast in somewhat academic language. Careful reading will show, however, that she does offer definite programmatic directives for those who would serve these marginalized young people. Her article deserves close study.

In attempting to identify ministry to Hispano youth, it is essential to incorporate the cultural-ethnic setting of this group as a basis for a better understanding of current developments and needs in this area of ministry. This article will deal essentially with that

Hispano group known as Mexicano, Mexican American, or Chicano, mainly because this is the group with whom I identify culturally and with whom I have been in ministry. The term Chicano/Mexican refers to any person of Mexican heritage living in the United States. Mexicano refers to the more recently arrived and less acculturated person of Mexican descent. However, much of what is presented here with reference to Mexicano/Chicano youth, is to a great extent, also applicable to other Hispano youth.

I am aware and realistic enough to know that my efforts and insights in this area of ministry are my existential response to a given situation and, therefore, not necessarily descriptive of the total reality. Nonetheless, this article will hopefully give exposure to a field of ministry that should be of concern to the Church and to our society. Each of us can begin a process of "concientization" —questioning and reflecting on the dilemma and plight in which Hispano youth find themselves.

According to the 1970 U.S. Census, there were 9 million persons of Spanish origin in this country. Because the Census took only a 5 percent sampling, many feel it has undercounted the Spanish-origin group. By 1975 the U.S. Census Bureau with improved sampling and counting methods estimated the group to be 11.2 million.[2] The major subgroups are identified as Mexican origin (6.7 million), Puerto Rican (1.7 million not including the Island of Puerto Rico), Cuban (743,000), Central or South American (671,000), and "other Spanish" (1.4 million). However, Latino spokespersons estimate the figure to be nearer to 16 million, since the U.S. Census Bureau does not include undocumented aliens from these countries.[3]

Contrary to popular belief, 80 percent of the total Hispano population is United States native born and 52 percent speak Spanish primarily in the home.[4] The median age of this group is 20.1 years, as compared to the total United States population which is 28.5 years. About 70 to 90 percent of the Hispano population is Roman Catholic,[5] constituting at least 25 percent of the total Catholic population in the United States.[6]

Of what importance are these statistics? At some point in the Church's ministerial life it will be necessary for many of its personnel to deal with this particular segment of the Church's membership, especially its young adults 16 to 35 years of age. Hence, as minister, it is important to face one's inner perceptions of this group now, so that one's evolving ministry among Hispanos will concretely relate the Hispano reality to the pastoral practices and theological beliefs that frequently are based on theory alone. A relationship exists between attitudes and ministry. The effectiveness or noneffectiveness of one's ministry with this group depends greatly on one's willingness to honestly seek to discover and evaluate one's attitudes toward Hispanos.

Chicano/Mexicano youth share the same basic human needs and undergo similar crises as other youth groups—mainly the need to be affirmed as a human person in order to develop self-love and a positive self-image. As a member of a family, there develops the need to experience freedom and independence outside that family sphere; there exists peer pressure on one's conduct; there is an awakening and development of one's sexuality, as well as one's affective life. Chicanos/Mexicanos, like everyone else, are also confronted by a personal identity crisis. But the Chicano/ Mexicano personal identity crisis is shaped and compounded by a *cultural* identity crisis. This cultural identity crisis, consciously or subconsciously, influences all aspects of their personal development. This struggle for self-identity is sought within the context of a cultural setting. The Chicano/Mexicano is confronted with the monumental challenge of searching and maintaining the self, while at the same time being an agent of change.[7]

The person of the Chicano/Mexicano has at some point been exposed to two cultures: Mexican and Anglo-American.[8] Each culture offers its learned and shared experiences, artifacts, and beliefs. Every Chicano/Mexicano can be placed on a continuum. At one end exists the minimally acculturated "Mexican" Chicano and at the other extreme the very acculturated "Anglo" Chicano. All Chicanos/Mexicanos are at various points on this continuum, depending on their degree of acculturation. Some Chicanos as members of a minority group in the United States will according to their degree of or lack of acculturation:

a. Accept the learned and shared experiences and beliefs of the minority culture and reject that of the dominant.

b. Accept the learned and shared beliefs of the dominant

culture and reject that of the minority.

  c. Be in a state of confusion as to which learned and shared experiences and beliefs to accept and/or reject.

  d. Question the learned and shared experiences and beliefs of both the dominant and the minority culture and decide to choose from either or from both.

This setting creates an internal struggle in the process of cultural identity. Chicanos/Mexicanos in groups *a* and *b,* by the fact that they have chosen to accept one culture and reject the other, are viewing one cultural set as desirable and the other as undesirable. Even though these groups, in a sense, are limiting their choices and therefore minimizing their internal struggle they are, nonetheless, caught in the process of a cultural identity crisis. Chicanos/Mexicanos in group *c* are in a state of anomie. They have not decided for themselves, either socially or psychologically, with which cultural group they will identify. The Chicanos/Mexicanos in group *d* are constantly questioning the learned and shared experiences and beliefs of both cultural groups, dominant and minority. Their internal struggle is greater since they are attempting to choose for themselves from two cultures that they know influence their lives. Such greater awareness of influencing cultures creates a greater struggle in choosing one's priorities among two desirable cultural universes.

Chicanos/Mexicanos find themselves in the midst of cultural forces that necessitate constant preferences that do not necessarily constitute "now and forever" decisions that are mutually exclusive. Their personal and group responses are varied. In some aspects of their lives, they might prefer to identify with the dominant cultural values; while in others, they might prefer to identify with the minority cultural values. It is also conceivable that the option might not necessarily be an "either/or" choice among dominant and minority values but can be a creative, bicultural response to this pulling cultural tension.

As can be noted, Chicanos/Mexicanos are a heterogeneous group whose degree of assimilation and/or acculturation to Mexican or Anglo technological values is affected by their total human environment: whether they live in a rural or urban setting; whether geographically they are in the Southwest, Midwest, or East Coast; whether they are first, second, or third generation Chicano/

Mexicano. Their economic and social status, their level of education, their degree of fluency in Spanish, and, where applicable, their condition of immigrant, that is, their documented or undocumented status in the United States also affect their degree of assimilation and/or acculturation.

In their attempt to assimilate into a technological society, where difference is often equated with uniformity and distinctiveness, the Chicano/Mexicano, especially in his/her formative years of young adulthood, has been and is in a state of confusion. Many experience within themselves, at various times, both extremes of the continuum—denial of their "Mexicanness" or denial of the influence the United States culture has had on them.

One important aspect of cultural conflict relates to the very different value systems between Mexicans and Anglo-Americans. The conflict of values systems is intensified among Chicanos/Mexicanos because historically, as a colonized mestizo people of a traditionalist Catholic and mainly agrarian society, they have been confronted with a "progressive" Anglo-Saxon Protestant technological society.[9] Survival in the midst of these cultural forces has required acculturation and paradoxially the maintenance of a distinctive language, religion, and cultural value system.[10]

The clash of these two value systems between that which is Mexican and that which is U.S.-Anglo technological is better understood when the following generalizations about these cultures are reviewed. Mexico's tragic sense of life explains human existence as a series of choices that are ultimately mystery, involving a force greater than oneself. The importance of an individual inserted within a family is secondary to the good of the family. A sense of community and sisterhood/brotherhood is a possible by-product of this reality. The various set role-expectations and behaviors of man-woman, elder-youth, wife-husband, brother-sister are deeply rooted in an established *hierarchical* order, whereas the United States epic sense of life explains life as a struggle between good and evil waged by equals. Hence the *eglitarian* ideal of United States society. Life is a problem and to live is to succeed, that is, to solve the problem. Reason and science can answer life's questions for the Anglo.[11] Definite values, then, proceed from this technological society: individualism, competition, progress, striving, thrift, and profit. Interestingly enough, most of the words that express these values have a pejorative connotation in the Spanish language.

The Chicano/Mexicano depending on his/her own cultural background and awareness will be able to distinguish which cultural values are essential and inalienable and which can be sacrificed in the process of acculturation.

Like other youths the Chicanos/Mexicanos also face a personal identity crisis. Their search for a personal identity is a threefold struggle. On the level of race, the Chicano/Mexicano young adult like the rest of La Raza must face pressures, prejudices, and discrimination as a member of a minority group living in a predominantely white society. On the level of sex, if the Chicana/Mexicana is a young adult woman, she shares with all women experiences of oppressive forces that cut across ethnic lines. On the level of culture, the Chicano/Mexicano young adult experiences a cultural struggle to become within the very rootedness of his/her own "Mexicanness" and to choose to "be different" or "nonconformist". This can cause an inner struggle of extraordinary magnitude.

As can be seen in the following diagram, the Chicano/Mexicano has influenced and been influenced by the two cultural groups' sets of expectations and behavior patterns. The expectations are applied to him/her in his/her given position as young adult, daughter, son, wife, husband, student, mother, father, and single person. The social-psychological processes of looking-glass image, self-fulfilling prophecy, role, and status influence and reinforce one's development.

Looking-glass image process: process by which an individual perceives him/herself as others perceive him/her. →	←INFLUENCES ←	*Role:* Set of behavior patterns and expectations appropriate to a given class, position, rank. →
↓ ↑		
Self-fulfilling prophecy: acting out perceptions of others in regard to one's person thus becoming "it" ←	→ REINFORCES →	*Status:* standardized criteria by which people are evaluated and ranked according to income, education, etc. ←

The search for and maintenance of the self takes place in the context of this cyclical social interaction. Chicanos/Mexicanos have internalized many norms, values, beliefs, and customs of their cultural groups, a culture they have helped to create. A break from this set of expectations and behavior patterns creates an internal struggle in the process of establishing one's personal identity. If the Chicana/Mexicana chooses to place greater emphasis on her evolving self-concept than on her "role" performance she will have to face the consequences of her choices and similarly for the Chicano.

Very often the actions of Chicano/Mexicano young adults will be questioned and perceived by others, Chicanos/Mexicanos included, as contrary to his/her role and status. Again the Chicano/Mexicano is caught in a personal identity struggle through these external pressures toward conformity.

From their earliest years Chicanos/Mexicanos are constantly being bombarded through the media, the educational system, and society as a whole, with negative images and stereotypes of themselves. Chicanos/Mexicanos have incorporated many of these images into themselves; these stereotypes have, in turn, influenced the development of their personal identities. Very often, the individual Chicano/Mexicano, as well as the total ethnic group, has perpetuated these stereotypes. The Chicano/Mexicano has been and is currently viewed both by "scholars" and "novelists" as emotional, spontaneous, sensuous, earthy, fatalistic, present-oriented, lazy, greasers, "machistic," primitive, superstitious, cruel, drug dependent, traditional/backward, woman beaters, submissive, culturally deprived, outsiders, uninvolved, and dirty.

At some point in personal development the Chicano/Mexicano has to question these objectionable descriptive qualities ascribed to him/her simply because he/she is a member of this particular ethnic group. These stereotypes based on prejudice, emotion, incomplete information, faulty judgment, fear of the unknown, or ignorance, nonetheless inflict tremendous damage. The Chicano/Mexicano is left with the task of raising his/her own consciousness positively in order to get personal alternatives to these ethnic stereotypes. Prejudice and discrimination toward this particular group go hand in hand with stereotyping on the part of many in the dominant society.

Personal Reflections

Upon reflection of this reality as it affects the lives of Chicano/Mexicano youth, I ask the question, what special efforts are needed in ministering to them? We, the ministers, will have to deal with the results of societal and personal prejudice in the lives of these people. Before us stand young adults who because they belong to this particular ethnic cultural group called Chicano/Mexicano have experienced, to a greater or lesser degree, economic, educational, linguistic, legal, cultural, housing, medical, and, yes, Church discrimination.

Such stifled and imposed restrictions upon a person or a group of people often hinder their total development and ability to contribute in our society. This discrimination coupled, very often, with a low economic status often results in frustration and, at times, behavior and actions that are incomprehensible to others, in this case the minister.

A low self-image or loss of self-esteem on the part of the Chicano/Mexicano will frequently emerge. Will we in ministry to them be able to provide a positive alternative to this seeming loss of human dignity? Can we as ministers, because we are familiar with Chicano/Mexicanos' cultural setting, encourage them to take pride in their cultural distinctiveness? Can we as ministers foster, within the Chicano/Mexicano, an appreciation of intercultural diversity that can provide the Chicano/Mexicano with a distinct ability to, personally and professionally, relate to different ethnic groups? A sense of powerlessness that can be a cause of apathy, isolation, and resignation also often emerges. Can we as ministers initiate a process of critical analysis with Chicanos/Mexicanos so that they can better understand their place in society? Subsequently the Chicano/Mexicano might feel the need to reach out and build a communal power base for change. This sense of powerlessness can also lead to a sense of hope—hope in God, a power greater than oneself who, through each of them, has the power to affect their lives. In this way, God is not merely seen as the attributive Cause of their existential condition, nor is the total Christian response understood solely as the unquestioning acceptance of life as "God's will."

We who are ministering to the Chicano/Mexicano will often

encounter the "give-up syndrome," that is, that feeling of "why bother about one's overpowering dehumanizing situation since protest might lead to even worse situations? Isn't this God's will and if it is, who are we to protest?" However, this "give-up syndrome" might be the occasion that produces an urgent force compelling Chicanos/Mexicanos to call attention to and attempt to create alternatives to these dehumanizing situations. Creativity frequently emerges in the face of overwhelming forces: If Chicanos/Mexicanos have little now they have less to lose.

As the Chicano/Mexicano youth encounters personal and group oppressive situations and unjust structures in the world, in society, and in the Church, a sense of low self-esteem, a sense of powerlessness, and the "give-up syndrome" emerge. However, this reality can provide us who are ministering among Chicanos/Mexicanos with opportunities for consciousness-raising—an alternate way of viewing history and God and man's action in it. An opportunity for Chicanos/Mexicanos to acknowledge within themselves and sensitize society to their potentialities, not just their problems as bicultural and very often bilingual persons.

The feelings of anger-hate resulting very often from injustice create an inability within Chicanos/Mexicanos to rise above hurt and depression, an inability to love and to critically analyze their surrounding situations and circumstances. Hopefully, however, acknowledgment of the existence of these feelings of anger and hate can also occasion direct protest against institutions and public policies that do not facilitate the process of justice and self-determination as proclaimed in the Gospel.

Not infrequently, alcohol, drugs, and physical abuse will be used as a means of escaping the oftentimes insurmountable circumstances of their lives. Frequently Chicanos/Mexicanos have come to question, through our ministerings, this negative type of behavior. The results of this questioning process can often evoke a personal and social commitment from them. At times this necessitates the Chicano/Mexicano's involvement with the poor and the powerless in their struggle for self-determination, rendering a respect for the human person both in its frailty and strength.

As a minister in the midst of the Chicano/Mexicano communities I look around me and I see the growing number of

Chicano/Mexicano youth estranged and disenfranchised with reference to the Church. I also witness with concern, and at times anger, the ignorance of my colleagues who are not even aware that this segment of the Church's traditional membership exists.

In turn I ask myself how can I encourage others to enter this type of ministry or even just call attention to its existence? What type of commitment does ministry to Chicano/Mexicano communities, especially its youth, exact from us who are meeting or you who desire to meet their ministerial and pastoral needs? It necessitates a commitment whereby we strive to meet the total needs of the person; not just the spiritual but also the social, cultural, economic, political, and educational.

These communities should not merely be tolerated, but their presence should be respected and welcomed as enriching to the Church. Do we as ministers believe not only that there is room for Chicano/Mexicano culture in the Church but also acknowledge that they have a right to maintain and develop their ethnic-cultural distinctiveness? Do we ministers really believe that "El Pueblo" (The People) can teach us something concerning the reality of Christ in their midst? Do we ministers really trust the worth of values afforded by a culture other than the dominant one? Do we ministers foster among Chicano/Mexicano youth cultural alternatives in their liturgy, educational methods, and social gatherings?

Are we who are ministering or wish to minister to Chicano/Mexicano youth willing to examine their own view with reference to assimilation? Is assimilation rather than integration our goal? If so why? In ministering to the Chicano/Mexicano are we capable of going beyond value judgments that are based on a Western European mentality and are we capable of encompassing a different world view of life?

Is our role as minister so defined that an evolving creative response to the felt needs and aspirations of Chicano/Mexicano youth would lead to an unbearable insecurity within the person of the minister?

We must envision our commitment to this ethnic group in "non-missionary" terms. Our ministrial calling is not only to understand the rejection of Church and societal institutions by the Chicano/Mexicano, "nor only to minister to their needs but to grow in the wisdom they have accumulated in their unique attempt to strike out on their own, to discover from them their realization of selfless love, as experienced through their oppression."[12]

Presently there exist a few successful programs ministering to Chicano/Mexicano youth. Search. Encuentro Juvenil (Youth Encounter), and youth clubs stemming from parish programs are a few church-based programs meeting the more traditional, less alienated needs of the Chicano/Mexicano youth. However, for the less traditional, more estranged, and alienated Chicano, both inside and outside Church structures, the Church, through the heightened awareness of its ministers to the Chicano/Mexicano reality, needs to seek them out.

Ethnic studies courses in community colleges and universities, especially in California, through its classes in Chicano/Mexicano history, culture, sociology, and psychology, as well as through its counseling departments, have been somewhat successful in ministering to the Chicano/Mexicano. We as ministers must be able to provide programs such as did the community colleges that responded to the felt needs of Chicano/Mexicano youth.

Family counseling, job placement, reidentification of the emerging roles of women and men, language programs, and basic human interaction are important areas of ministry for Chicano/Mexicano young adults

> Proclaiming the Gospel means putting our good names and security on the line by being with the disenfranchised in their struggle for liberation from those things which prohibit them from realizing their full potential as human persons, loved by God. In that way, we are called to be both advocates and facilitators . . . to confront both Church and secular decision-makers to enable the disenfranchised to speak for themselves.[13]

NOTES

1. The term "Hispano" refers to any person of Mexican, Chicano, Puerto Rican, and/or Latin American descent or origin in the United States. The term

"Spanish-speaking" refers to a sizable number of these but by no means to all.

2. U.S. Bureau of Census, *U.S. Census of Population: 1970 and 1975 Subject Reports. Persons of Spanish Origin.*

3. R.F.M., "'Hispanic Tide' Largest U.S. Minority in 2000 AD" *El Tiempo Bicentenario*, 3 (1976), p.1.

4. U.S. Bureau of the Census, *op. cit.*

5. Y. Arturo Cabrera, *Emerging Faces The Mexican Americans.* (San Jose: Wm. C. Brown Co., 1971), p.50.

6. Archives of the U.S. Catholic Conference, Division of Spanish-speaking, West Coast Office.

7. Samuel Ramos's *Profile of Man and Culture in Mexico* and Octavio Paz's *The Labyrinth of Solitude* refer to this historical phenomenon of the development of Mexican character.

8. The terms Anglo-American and Anglo technological values refer to the white Anglo-Saxon Protestant ethic. Though many "Anglos" take exception to this term it is not being used in a derogatory way but rather as descriptive of a national phenomenon.

9. Dr. Manuel Zapata, "Enfrentamiento Cultural" *El Tiempo Bicentenario*, 1 (June 1976), p.1.

10. "Chicanismo" exemplifies this phenomenon whereby members of this group take on the organizational and pragmatic patterns of the Anglo while emphasizing their ethnic-cultural distinctiveness.

11. Jorge Klor de Alva, *Introduction to Mexican Philosophy.* (California State University, San Jose, 1972), pp. 98-102.

12. Statement by the Working Board on *Ministry to Young Adults*, Department of Education, USCC (June 5, 1976), p.3.

13. *Loc. cit.*

Adolescent Identity
in Secondary Education

Samuel M. Natale, S.J.

Samuel Natale's essay on adolescent identity was originally a talk given to a group of Jesuits teaching in Catholic high schools. He has graciously rewritten it for this book. Researcher and clinician, Natale uses his erudition to show those working in high schools that the competitive climate of so much secondary education deserves more attention and some rethinking. Otherwise our way of doing things in high schools can foster values quite antithetical to our carefully written statements of philosophy.

Those working with youth outside of school structures will also find in Dr. Natale's reflections several important guiding principles for their own ministry to youth.

One of the primary goals of the secondary school experience should be to provide an educational framework that permits the student to establish a personal identity. Because this process of self-discovery includes both a perception of oneself and the application of this perception to the "other," it is quite natural that certain problems will arise for the adolescent and teacher alike. In the case of Catholic education, the picture becomes even more muddled. This is so precisely because this tension between self and other must be worked out in the context of an educational experience deeply involved with the achievement of a sort of Christian identity. But practically speaking, the striving for a Christian identity is only one of many important aims in Catholic secondary education. It is, of course, of unqualified importance that we foster a sense of self in our students that can be recognized by service, care, and hope; yet the question remains: How do we offer the possibility of Christian identity in the midst of all our other educational concerns? Do we, for example, naively encourage in our youngsters an ideal of cooperation with others, or do we foster a hard-nosed competitive spirit in order to prepare them for the "real" world? For the Catholic educator, this concern is of critical importance.

The balance between cooperation and competition in an educational experience is an extremely delicate one. At times many high school teachers must have been confronted with this problem's complexity, feeling that in their own experience they have failed to strike an intermediate chord between these two ideals. How often have we witnessed well-intentioned teachers attempting to create a totally cooperative classroom atmosphere and winding up with an educational environment akin to the chaos of a lunchtime playground? Yet, on the other hand, haven't we at least occasionally suspected that our tightly controlled and highly competitive classes have stifled in our students any sense of creative or cooperative self? Perhaps our approach to this delicate juggling act merely reveals something about our own personalities as Catholic educators. By virtue of their academic and social backgrounds, educators are by and large products of a competitive society, but they also form a cooperative group in which each faculty member willingly submerges his or her individuality in order to achieve a corporate goal. As Catholic educators, our personal confrontation with the dilemna posed by individualism versus the common good can serve as a valuable lesson for our treatment of the similar classroom problem of cooperation among students versus a spirit of competitiveness.

Having posed what one might consider the central philosophical concern of Catholic secondary education, perhaps we should further define exactly what we mean by the terms competition and cooperation. The dictionary defines competition as "a mutual contest or striving for the same object; a rivalry; a trial of skill proposed as a test of superiority or comparative fitness." Essentially, words such as "contest," "striving," and "rivalry" suggest an aggressive attitude, a struggling or a push toward the one available prize. Unfortunately, in any competition the individual winner leaves in his wake any number of disappointed losers. In the realm of athletics, this has come to be somewhat acceptable ("It's not whether you win or lose, it's how you play the game"), but in the academic world being a loser is generally a more traumatic event. Naturally, in both cases it is possible that the "losers" may return to the arena to compete strongly and successfully, but they may also despair of achievement and begin to view themselves as academic and social unfortunates.

However, some measure of competition is a necessity in our classrooms if we are to prepare our students to live in a very competitive (and not so cooperative) world. Indeed, there must be a middle ground here; for as Christian educators we cannot turn out unscrupulous competitors intent only on material success. When we raise this issue, we begin to see the importance of a positive distinction between aggression and assertion in the realm of competition. Assertion is a natural and healthful dimension of human growth. It involves a clear self-indication and presentation that requires some sort of response validation and promotion. Assertion is then the energetic presentation of self in a context of definite limits that appear tolerable to the adolescent. Aggression, on the other hand, is assertion plus hostility. The addition of this negative attribute that transforms healthy assertion into undesirable aggression appears to point out the crux of the problem. That is, we must attempt to establish a competitive criterion that directs individual students toward a successful life experience, while it simultaneously fosters the assertive, and not aggressive, nature of competitiveness.

Cooperation suggests a community of action and joint ventures. The word itself is defined as "a joint operation or action" and it implies that individual talents are more potent in unison than separately. Yet even in the most successful cooperative effort, individual talents must be cultivated in order to ensure maximum efficiency. Thus, in the classroom no cooperative effort can disregard the importance of encouraging both individuality and a qualified competitiveness. Our committed role is to educate the whole person and hence to facilitate the congruence of affectivity, behavior, cognition, and assertiveness. But to do so effectively and empathically, the teacher must be aware of at least some basic psychological considerations concerning the adolescent years. Thus, there appears to be really nowhere else to turn but to the adolescents themselves, their needs and their abilities. It may seem very strange to suggest a return to direct observation and discussion when the libraries are filled with research, but the fact is that the research is generally inconclusive and certainly does not concern itself with our commitment toward developing a Christian identity.

Perhaps we may best understand the problem of competition and cooperation in the context of Catholic education if we focus our discussion upon adolescence and adolescent development. Thus, by examining the student's developmental tasks (situations and problems that must be worked through in the course of a teenager's experience), his mode of relationship and relations, and his cognitive growth and development, we might be in a better position to specify the coordinates within which we must work.

The essential task of the adolescent involves the relinquishing of childhood dependency. This process is fraught with ambivalence because it means both experimentation with a new sense of self and the terrifying recognition that one is responsible for one's own behavior. Since this quest for independence is so ambivalent for adolescents, it is achieved only with considerable rebellion and confusion. It is important to note that this is a rebellion directed more frankly at a rigid superego than at any external authority represented by parents and teachers. There is simultaneously an enormous upsurge in sexual and aggressive energy and hence the adolescent period is characterized by an intensive search for various outlets and diverse activities. There is also the strong need to seek support in numbers and to be affirmed and approved by peers. For the young girl or boy, the "we" of the group is always less frightening than the unbearable "I" of responsibility. Finally, we should be aware that adolescents are beginning to establish a sexual or gender identity. Obviously, this in itself is a catalyst for confusion, exploratory behavior, and unconventional experiences that in an adult might be viewed as perverse.

It is not our concern here to elaborate on the implications of these developmental tasks, but their mere mention should suffice to indicate that the major adaptations of the adolescent have considerably more to do with intrapsychic and interpersonal experiences than with skill acquisition. Since the sense of self is so fragile at this age, it seems dangerous to associate the heightening of sexual and aggressive energies with win/lose polarities. Or in other words, extremely competitive situations with a high risk of failure for the majority could be very harmful given the fact that the adolescent will generally put a vast of amount of emotional energy into such a task. The thrust of our educational activity should be to disassociate failure in an exercise demanding a display of skills from a perceived failure in one's entire personality. We should take great pains to indicate to our high school students that no such equation exists. It is only with this appreciation of the complexity of adolescent developmental tasks that we can distinguish for ourselves and for our young wards between necessary personality self-assertion and the undesirable win/lose schema.

When adolescence begins, the child is subjected to a multidimensional attack on his sense of self-worth. There are unpredictable and uneven body changes, unacceptable needs and impulses, and the strong desire for independence that forces the adolescent to disdain parents and authority figures. Interestingly enough, this rejection of authority is actually directed at a vital part of the adolescent himself. Teenagers earnestly desire to merge themselves with someone who has a strongly defined workable self, yet they fear the loss of themselves in such a process. Thus, their relationships and attachments are primarily narcissistic. This is not to indicate that the child necessarily exploits others, but rather that his interpersonal activity is predominantly colored by his individual inner needs. The "other" in relationships with adolescents is not ignored but is important primarily as an orientation point around which they may weave their fantasies, hopes, needs, and desires. They otherwise demand from adults total solutions to problems and therefore when "grown-ups" are unable to provide them, the adolescents are regularly disillusioned by those to whom they have attached themselves.

This narcissistic mode of relationship poses educational problems because for adolescents losses in any sphere of activity are internalized as something essential to themselves. They have not lost; the *are* Losers. This is actually a productive dilemma in terms of our concern about cooperation and competition. For we must ask ourselves, is it possible to arrange competition tempered by support and praise that would extend over all aspects of the adolescent personality (sports, tests, social graces, identity), or must there be an all-or-nothing validation? I think that one may arrange competitions as a part of school life, but this must not be the focal point of the educational experience. No one of us would say that competition was the earmark of Catholic education, yet each of us has often equated competitive skill with success, integration, and maturity. In fostering a healthy competitive atmosphere in our schools, we must carefully attempt to evolve a comprehensive program that will neither ignore the importance of support and praise nor encourage normal adolescent confusion between failure in an event and shortcoming in personality.

But we are still not really clear in our perspective and we need to turn our attention to the actual target of much education— cognitive development. How does the adolescent think? What are his processes? In my opinion, there is some difficulty involved with making the focus of education cognitive development because it is simply too narrow and constricted a view. In short, it misses the response to the whole person. For the sake of clarity, this area of adolescent development demands considerable emphasis.

Adolescence is marked cognitively by the development of "Formal Operations" (Piaget, 1967). Formal Operations is the capacity to manipulate thought itself, the ability to think abstractly and to understand the interrelationships and complexities. It is characteristic of an age involved in metaphysic interest par excellence (Piaget, 1968). Since this faculty is so new and wonderous to adolescents, they tend to overuse, overemphasize, and overvalue its ability to change reality. This cognitive development unfortunately reinforces the emotional predisposition to narcissism during adolescence and lends itself to prophetic preoccupations and to a dangerous overinvolvement of personal identity with cognitive ability. Since all adolescents are also struggling toward a sense of commitment, they spend a great deal of time thinking about and talking about and observing closely various life-styles. They are essentially utopian thinkers and have only a limited sense of historical perspective. Hence, there is a tendency to see each event as a unique experience. It is quite natural then that competitive losses go deep, while victory is questioned because it reflects a potency and independence that is too intimidating to deal with at this time.

A win/loss situation thus raises questions about adolescents' independence on the one hand, and it confirms their fears of impotence and inadequacy on the other. This is a significant dynamic; for what we have is a narcissistic adolescent seeking protection from reality yet freedom to act. The tasks nature has imposed are overwhelming enough and further institutional pressure upon the adolescent seems simply unkind despite our well-intentioned desires to prepare our young boys and girls for life in a competitive world. We must be extremely careful, however, not to direct our students solely in terms of our own goals and needs, in light of our own personal world view. It is their individual personalities that we must consider and their developmental problems inherent in the adolescent period.

Despite all we have said above, we must not be too rash in our judgment; for although competition produces insidious side effects, it is nonetheless highly spoken of in the literature on adolescence. According to the psychological studies thus far undertaken, the successfully competitive individual is self-confident (Carmical, 1964), motivated and aggressive (Roth and Puri, 1967), independent and autonomous (Thompson, 1965; Ringness, 1967). He has high standards (Battle, 1965), and conservative values and a conservative work ethic (Thompson, 1965). Furthermore, such an individual is described as more thoughtful, mature, and able to postpone immediate gratification (Hummel and Sprinthall, 1965); he likewise tends to accept authority, be more socially mature and sensitive (Gawronski and Mathis, 1965). As we might expect, the underachiever or "loser" is the virtual antithesis. He is less able to adapt meaningfully to school and less aware of long-range goals (Hummel and Sprinthall, 1965). He has self-defeating attitudes about academics (Roth and Puri, 1967), is pessimistic about the future and tends to emphasize self-gain (Gawronski and Mathis, 1965). Relevant research also shows the underachiever opposing authority and seeking excitement in pursuit of immediate gratification (Carmical, 1964). Interestingly enough, the underachiever is also said to have fewer personal problems than either normal individuals or overachievers and to be more adventurous, rejecting customs when they interfere with goals (Gawronski and Mathis, 1965).

The successful competitor is easily defined because he has fulfilled certain role requirements and has consequently been rewarded. Poor achievement is usually correlated (when physical limitation and overt psychological morbidity are ruled out) with developmental anxiety and personality disorganization. For example, underachievement among brilliant adolescents is quite frequent when these students' goals, hopes, and expectations conflict with those of the the the teacher. The most frequent occurrence of this is with the gifted adolescent who has little opportunity to develop his talents, creativeness, and critical abilty within a rigidly controlled structure. The pressure for conformity may provide success in skill performance, but at the price of retarding individual creative and exploratory efforts that move knowledge forward. This was most glibly expressed in Oscar Wilde's comment to Gide: "Would you like to know the great drama of my life? It's that I've put my genius into my life; I've put only my talent into my works." And what about us as Catholic educators? Are we developing a life-style or a skill?

It would seem that the creation of men and women for others is the creation of a self first. And this acquisition of self emerges as the result of a number of variables that are provided by the teacher. The literature attests to this assertion. Education, like psychotherapy, requires the exploration of self-limits, developmental tasks, skills, and potential and these can be present only under certain nurturing preconditions. In 1943 Carol Rogers pointed to the need for empathy (understanding what another person feels), congruence (a sense of affective, behavioral, and cognitive harmony within the teacher), unconditional positive regard (the assumption of the worth regardless of performance; that is, behavior may be unacceptable but the individual is not), and support (a promotive quality toward the student) in the educative process. Quite obviously adherence to these principles would reduce the competitive atmosphere of the classroom while fostering a favorable developmental and cooperative spirit. But I am not talking here about a sandbox in a fantasy land of love and flowers, but of the day-to-day teaching world of *Up the Down Staircase* where these conditions are difficult to achieve but nonetheless necessary for the promotion of personality growth. These needs that I am suggesting be met in our schools are well established by psychologists and social scientists as the cornerstones that foster generosity, care, achievement, and a sense of morality.

Finally, we should focus on the person of the Catholic school teacher, both lay and religious, as the major facilitator of the compromise between competition and cooperation. Nowhere in the literature has it been shown that competition produces superior achievement or skill in an academic setting. But we have seen evidence of an overly competitive environment encouraging insidious side effects, such as extreme callousness toward others. It has been demonstrated, however, that the teacher and his attitudes rather than his educational training are the essential factors in an achievement of student satisfaction, skills, and a sense of worth. Over and over again, student success over a broad spectrum has correlated significantly with individual teachers. Furthermore, upon a closer and comparative examination, these teachers appear to have provided the highest levels of empathy, congruence, unconditional positive regard, and support. As we educators have always suspected, our role in the personal development of our adolescents is indeed critical and thus saddles us with great responsibility and perhaps even greater joy.

What then can we offer the Catholic secondary school teacher in the way of practical solutions to our thus far theoretical view? Basically, I would suggest that individual faculties attempt to apply creatively the above reflections on cooperation and competition to their own unique educational settings, but perhaps I can offer some generalized considerations. It would seem to me to be extremely advantageous to the entire Catholic school system should we begin to reexamine our hiring policies, placing a clear emphasis on the applicant's ability to understand at least the basic trends in adolescent development. Having assembled a faculty concerned with developmental as well as academic problems, the teachers and administration should undertake to examine their system of rewards and punishments and to specify what is assertive and what is aggressive in all aspects of its educational atmosphere. As we noted above, the teacher and his or her attributes seem to be an overriding factor in the establishment of the Christian environment toward which we strive. Thus, in order that the establishment of the preconditions for growth of the students be implemented, it is critical that the faculty examine its own interrelationships and begin to demonstrate on some levels at least this supportive and trusting attitude toward one another. This can be most easily done by the use of modeling behavioral techniques. Both the faculty and the students could facilitate the general goals of Catholic education by establishing ongoing evaluation, support, and discussion groups that might provide an arena for dealing with individual and collective confusions and concerns.

All in all, there is reason to believe that Catholic education may be embarking upon a relatively new adventure as teachers, students, and administrators begin to verbalize a strong commitment to alternative education. That is to say, we can be genuinely hopeful that our desire to create men and women for others, to foster healthy assertiveness and concern for the common good, is an ideal within our grasp so long as we appreciate the importance of the psychology of the adolescent.

Catholic Theology and the Secondary School

Avery Dulles, S.J.

Recently I stumbled onto the following article by Avery Dulles. Originally a talk given at Xavier High School in New York, it later appeared in the *Catholic Mind*. Largely, I fear, it has been overlooked. At a time when it is increasingly difficult to find good material on the teaching of religion and theology in Catholic high schools, I am happy to be able to include it here. Its guiding principles will continue to be valid and helpful to high school religion teachers for some time to come. Dulles treats the relationship of theology to *the school*, not just the relationship of theology to the religion department. Samuel Natale called attention to the same matter of the values embodied in an entire school. Both seem to be saying: What the school does is more important than what any single segment does. Dulles's ideas, similar to Natale's, deserve the attention also of those working with youth outside of formal school structures.

It is our fate and our privilege to live in a time of rapid change. Science and technology are not only bringing men to the moon and back, but they are rapidly changing the face of the earth on which we live. Human relations and human society are being progressively restructed. The physical and psychological makeup of man are being altered, with the result that the aims and methods of education must be continually readjusted. The Reverend Pedro Arrupe, Superior General of the Society of Jesus, in many letters and addresses during the past few years, has insistently called for a

212

serious reexamination of the aims and methods of Jesuit secondary schools. In a letter of 1967 he wrote:

> This is, however, the time to study how to improve our schools and to endeavor to make them more adapted to the world which is taking shape and being put together before our very eyes. There must be room for experimentation and innovation in our educational planning. Our schools must never confine themselves to past patterns. They must be with men in their struggles, helping them to respond creatively to the challenges of history. If our schools are to perform as they should, they will live in a continual tension betwen the old and the new, the comfortable past and the uneasy present. Our schools must be open to changes in the Church, so that the students can assimilate its vigor, the vitality of a Church in change.

In scanning some of the recent literature on Jesuit High School education, I have been struck by the courage and imagination with which the Jesuit Secondary Education Association, under the able direction of Father Edwin J. McDermott, S.J., has undertaken to set forth guidelines for the development of the Jesuit High School of the future. Your headmaster here at Xavier, Father Vincent J. Duminuco, S.J., in his capacity as chairman of the JSEA's Commission on Research and Development (CORD), has been one of the leaders of the adaptation for which Fr. Arrupe has been calling.

From my perspective as a teacher of theology on the seminary level, I was particularly struck by the pedagogical principles enunciated in the statement issued by CORD after its June, 1972, meeting at Georgetown Preparatory School. For the most part these principles are applicable not only to the high school and college level but to graduate schools and professional schools, including seminaries. As a basis for our reflections this morning, I should like to pick our five principles which I seem to find in the CORD statement, and indeed in much of the current educational literature.

1. *Future-Oriented Learning.* Whereas in the past teachers had a tendency to concentrate on transmitting to their students the

contents that were thought to have resulted from previous investigations, the new tendency is to look upon knowledge as a process and upon education as a matter of "learning how to learn." The aim is therefore to equip the student to contend with the new problems he will presumably meet in the future. It is assumed that the present stock of ideas will rapidly become obsolete, and that education is of little value unless it imparts the ability to gain new skills.

2. *Participatory Learning.* Closely connected with this shift in the concept of the educated man is a new understanding of how education is best acquired. In an earlier day it may have seemed sufficient to memorize and accept the solutions set forth by others. Today, however, it is considered crucial that the student should have a sense of participation in the process by which knowledge is generated. He must acquire the habit of reflecting deeply upon his own experience and of deciding responsibly in those areas in which he has competence. Rather than regard the student as a dependent, passive learner the current methodology would seek to give the student a greater sense of responsibility for his own education. He is encouraged to gain real rather than notional knowledge.

3. *Climate of Trust.* Too often in the past, learning has been carried on in a coercive and competitive atmosphere, in which the student was motivated primarily by fear of failure and of disapproval by authorities. The result was that too many of the best students became timid conformists, unequipped to deal with new and different situations. In the current program of studies an effort is made to achieve an atmosphere of freedom and trust, in which varying sets of ideas can be examined with openness, so that the student may be free to express his honest convictions and to develop these in open dialogue with others.

4. *Pluralism of Values.* According to the CORD statement, the present situation calls for a shift from emphasis on uniformity, centralization and order to an emphasis on pluralism, diversity and acceptance of ambiguity (p. 9). Instead of seeking to inculcate a single value system, the school should develop the capacity to analyze and evaluate divergent life styles, ideologies and values. The student should be encouraged to appreciate other cultures (p. 11) and other types of personality. Goals should be varied accord-

ing to the diverse potentialities and needs of different individuals.

5. *Orientation to Service*. Rather than look upon knowledge as an end in itself, the student should be helped to see it in its relation to the whole life. The CORD statement calls for emphasis on the element of service which is defined as "creative contribution to the ongoing development of man and his world," in the framework of global consciousness and a sense of world citizenship. A few pages later (p. 14) there is a call for "a deeper commitment to promoting human fulfillment for all men . . . because the 'signs of the times' demand it."

These five principles, which I have distilled from the CORD statement, are not specific to any one field or area, but are proposed as normative for the educational process as a whole. All five of them must however be viewed in relationship to still another fundamental principle, namely, a strong emphasis on religious studies as a major and important discipline (p. 12). Both the constitution of JSEA and Father Arrupe's letters return frequently to the idea that Jesuit schools aim to turn out Christian leaders, and that they should concentrate on the unique contribution that Catholic education can make to the larger human community (Nov. 10, 1972, p. 5). It is at this point that a difficulty sometimes arises. In seeking to impart Christian doctrine, in full loyalty to the Catholic religious establishment, many teachers find themselves unable to follow the educational principles I have just outlined.

1. With regard to the first principle, orientation to the future, it must be asked whether the Catholic Christian may look upon religious truth as something still to be discovered. As normally understood, Christianity is a religion revealed in the past, a body of doctrine that was closed with the apostles, and one that must be handed down in the Church without substantial change. In recent centuries, at least, the Church has constantly put the accent on the integral preservation of the revealed deposit. Vatican I, in fact, taught that "the doctrine of faith which God has revealed has not been proposed, like a philosophical invention, to be perfected by human intelligence, but has been delivered as a divine deposit to the Spouse of Christ, to be faithfully kept and infallibly declared. hence also the meaning of the sacred dogmans is perpetually to be retained which our Holy Mother Church has once declared; nor is

that meaning ever to be departed from under the pretence or pretext of a deeper comprehension of them" (*DS*, 3020, *NR* 48).

2. The idea that knowledge should be derived from personal experience and reflection is likewise at odds with the accepted view of theology. According to Vatican I, again, faith is an assent based not on the intrinsic evidence but on the authority of God and of the divinely accredited witnesses. Faith may even require one to believe what is contrary to the indications of experience or human science. Does not Ignatius of Loyola tell us that on the word of the hierarchical Church we must be prepared to hold that what seems white to our senses is in fact black? (*Sp. Ex.* no. 365). Vatican I forbade the faithful to defend "as legitimate conclusions of science, such opinions as are known to be contrary to the doctrines of the faith" (*DS* 3018, *NR* 45). The authentic teachers of the faith, according to the usual Catholic understanding are the Pope and the bishops, and to them the laity should meekly defer. If this be true, it would seem useless to talk about participation and personal responsibility on the part of the individual believer.

3. Whatever may be the case regarding other parts of the high school curriculum, it would seem, at first sight, that our third principle—calling for trust and freedom—could not be applicable to the teaching of Christian doctrine. Catholics have been long accustomed to hold in accordance with the teaching of Vatican I that "those who have received the faith under the magisterium of the Church can never have any just cause for changing or doubting that faith" (*DS* 3014, *NR* 40). The true faith is regarded as a treasure to be defended against all who might seek to diminish or adulterate it. Imbued with a salutary fear of error, the faithful are taught to avoid exposing themselves to books that might subject them to the danger of heresy. St. Ignatius, in his "Rules for Thinking with the Church," praises not only filial but even servile fear (*Sp. Ex.*, no. 370).

4. Our fourth principle, calling for pluralism, fares no better. In the standard Catholic religious curriculum, at least in the recent past, all attention was focused on the dogmas of the faith, which were understood as truths revealed by God and demanding assent by all the faithful under pain of eternal loss. It would be patently absurd to ask students to make up thier own dogmas proposed by

the magisterium. While cultures might laudably differ from each other, all men were thought to be obliged to accept the entire revelation of God. Hence religious education would seem to be exempt from the pedagogical principle calling for pluralism, diversity and the acceptance of ambiguity.

5. How about the last principle, calling for "a deeper commitment to promoting human fulfillment for all men?" Like the other four, it too is suspect to Catholics of the traditional mold. The purpose of faith, they belive, is individual personal salvation. Christ, they would say, did not come to make life on earth more pleasant, or to help man with his cultural or technical progress, but for a solely religious purpose—to make men holier so that they could save their souls in a life beyond the grave. Whether people are rich or poor, sick or healthy, makes little difference, according to these Christians, for in the end all earthly goods will perish. Those who have suffered may be more blessed than those who have found, as the phrase goes, "human fulfillment." Why then should the Church concern itself with the building of the city of man? St. Ignatius would seem to be correct in advocating indifference toward all created goods. (*Sp. Ex.* no. 23).

At this point, therefore, we may conclude that there is a genuine problem. If the Catholic faith is understood according to the outline I have just given—which corresponds in great part with the teaching of Ignatius of Loyola and of Vatican I—an increased emphasis on religious studies, as called for in the CORD statement and in the letters of Father General, can scarcely fail to come into collision with the pedagogical principles animating the high school program as a whole. Those students who respond most enthusiastically to the new trends and values would tend to become most alienated from the Church. Before we accept this unhappy result as inevitable, we should, I suggest, examine very closely whether the conflict is necessary. Is it possible that this understanding of the Catholic faith is a culturally conditioned and outdated one—the ecclesiastical counterpart of an obsolete philosophy?

My own excursions into the history of theology have convinced me that the conservative authoritarian understanding of Christian revelation, though it still prevails even in some high ecclesiastical places, is a distortion of the true genius of Catholicism. This view of the faith came into prominence in the era of decadent scholasticism; it was defended in polemics against the sixteenth century Reformers, and achieved its culmination in the decrees issued against the Modernists between 1907 and 1910. But this stage of Catholic theology has in principle been transcended. Under the genial leadership of Pope John XXIII, Vatican II set forth a more balanced presentation of the Catholic faith—more personalistic, more future-oriented and more amicable toward the modern world. If the program of the recent Council were consistently carried through, it would be possible to align the teaching of religion with the principles that are found acceptable in other parts of the secondary school curriculum. Let me illustrate this with regard to the five principles already mentioned.

1. *Future Orientation.* Contemporary Catholic theology is by no means inclined to deny that revelation was given in the past through prophets and apostles, and that it reached its fullness in the life, death and resurrection of Jesus Christ. Vatican II, however, balanced this by saying that God presently speaks to the faithful when the Scriptures are read and when the word of God is preached with power. He reveals Himself through the saints, who mirror the sanctity of Christ according to the possibilities and exigencies of their own situation. God's revealing voice continues to be heard through the signs of the times, and particularly through the great events of secular history. Revelation, as an ongoing process, tends unceasingly forward to its eschatological consummation. Thus the council can declare, in the Constitution on Divine Revelation, that "as the centuries succeed one another, the Church constantly moves forward toward the fullness of divine truth until the words of God reach their complete fulfillment in her" (*Dei Verbum,* §8). This does not mean that the Church is being invited to move beyond Christ into some post-Christian era, but rather to grasp the true meaning of Christ for us and for our age requires a continual effort at discernment. Thus religious education might very properly be expected to equip the student, not simply with information about how revelation has hitherto been understood, but with an aptitude to "interpret the many voices of our age, and to judge them in the light of the divine Word," for, as the Pastoral Constitution tells us, "in this way revealed truth can

always be more deeply penetrated, better understood, and set forth to greater advantage" *(Gandium et Spes,* §44).

2. *Participatory Learning.* It would be absurd to imagine that, for the sake of accomodating oneself to some new pedagogical method, high school students should be asked to construct their own brand of Christianity on the basis of their personal experience. But there is ample room for the student to involve himself in the commitment of faith. Faith is not understood by Vatican II or by contemporary Catholic theology as merely intellectual assent to propositions held forth by the Pope and bishops. Rather, faith is a full personal commitment to God—one that involves not only the intellect but the will, the emotions, the imagination, and, in sum, the whole man. Faith goes out not simply to doctrines but primarily to God himself. It is a real, not a notional assent, and one that presupposes in the believer an authentic experience of grace.

To impose articles of faith as if they were brute facts to be blindly accepted would be to falsify the true nature of Christian revelation. Faith, as the Pastoral Constitution tells us, "throws a new light on everything, manifests God's design for man's total vocation and thus directs the mind to solutions which are fully human" *(Gandium et Spes,* §11). As the Church "labors to decipher authentic signs of God's presence and purpose in the happenings, needs and desires" of this age *(ibid.),* the Church invokes the assistance of all its members.

No longer is the elaboration of Christian doctrine viewed as the work of an independent magisterium which would be supposed to be in direct telephonic communication with God. In discerning the signs of the times, the Church relies upon laymen who are versed in different specialties and have access to different types of experience *(Gandium et Spes,* §44). The laity are invited and encouraged to express themselves with courage about those matters in which they enjoy competence *(Gandium et Spes,* §62). It is frankly admitted that the pastors of the Church need help; they do not have concrete solutions at hand for every problem that arises *(Gandium et Spes,* §43). For all these reasons the Council opened up the Church to increased participation, or co-responsibility, on every level—whether episcopal, presbyteral or lay.

Catholics of the preconciliar period were inclined to think of the Holy Spirit as assisting the official teachers, and only through their mediation, the generality of the faithful. According to the present view, the Holy Spirit is given in the first instance to the Church as a whole, and only secondarily to certain particular officers, in order that they may properly discharge their responsibilities toward the whole people of God. Seeing each individual member of the Church as immediately related to the Holy Spirit, Vatican II attached great importance to the "sense of the faith" aroused and sustained in the whole Body of Christ by the Spirit of truth. Any educator who is convinced of this doctrine will treat with great respect the spontaneous inclinations, attractions and aversions that manifest themselves in large numbers of the faithful. It will not be sufficient to order them, in an authoritarian way, to submit to decrees handed down from ecclesiastical authorities. The possibility must always be reckoned with that God is trying to teach something to the hierarchy by means of the lay members of the Church. Often enough the younger members of the Church are most sensitive to the demands of the new age.

3. *Atmosphere of Trust.* In speaking of the second principle, participation, I have already anticipated certain observations that would be equally pertinent to the third. In the century preceding Vatican II, the Church became so obsessed with defending the faithful against false doctrines that it began to resemble the apostles before the resurrection, cowering behind locked doors "for fear of the Jews" (Jn. 20:19). Catholics reckoned too little with the power of grace and set too little store by the Holy Spirit. They appeared to live under a regime of law, no less rigid than that of the Old Covenant, and failed to present the appearance of persons enjoying the glorious freedom in the sons of God.

In the Church, as in any human community, discipline will always be needed. The principle, "Love and do what thou wilt," is an ideal that cannot be put literally into practice in the lives of most Christians. But among human societies the Church should be more than others a place of freedom. To rectify the exaggerations of the preceding centuries, Vatican II gave strong prominence to the principle of religious liberty. As the Pastoral Constitution noted, freedom is an exceptional sign of the image of God in man. Man's dignity, according to the Council, demands that he act according to a knowing and free choice *(Gandium et Spes,* §17). The declaration on Religious Freedom demanded that no coercion, whether physical or moral, should be used in order to bring converts into the Church *(Dignitatis Humanae,* § 17), and the Decree on Missionary Activity echoed the same teaching.

Every effort was made by the Council to transform the Church into an open society—one that did not define itself in opposition to those whom it excluded, but a society that willed to embrace whatever was true and excellent. The Decree on Ecumenism attempted to be fair and open in acknowledging the positive merits of Protestant and Orthodox Christianity, and the Declaration on the Non-Christian Religions sought to do likewise with regard to the nonbiblical faiths.

It would be unfaithful to the spirit of Vatican II, therefore, if religious education were to be carried on in an atmosphere in which fear rather than love and cowardice rather than conviction were the basis of belief. In a school situation it would not be possible to present every possible option, as though the student were in a position to choose among all the faiths that had ever been known to man. The teacher may properly invite his students to share in the beliefs that he himself professes. This is what he would be expected to do in other fields, whether history, or literature, or music, or philosophy. Without any detriment to the students' freedom, the teacher can share with them his own tastes, preferences and honest convictions. The student may be urged to fear that he might err through pride or passion or some other excess, but he should not be deterred from honestly and openly expressing his difficulties. It should not be assumed that every difficulty against current Church teaching arises out of some moral fault.

4. *Pluralism of Values.* The acceptance of pluralism, as called for by our fourth pedagogical principle, coincides with yet another of the main themes of the recent council. Since Vatican II it is no longer correct, if it ever was, to look upon the Catholic Church as a great monolith. In the Constitution on the Church, Catholic unity was portrayed as a vast concert in which each local and regional church was expected to make its own proper contribution *(Lumen Gentium,* §13). The Decree on Ecumenism pointed out that differing ways of understanding and proclaiming the revelation of

Christ, when they are complementary in nature, can bring out the depth and splendor of the faith (*Unitatis Redintegratio*, § 16f). The Pastoral Constitution on the Church in the Modern World (*Gaudium et Spes*, § 44) taught that every major cultural grouping of Christians should learn to express the Gospel in its own way. The Decree on Missionary Activity, finally, said that the Church must not uproot, but rather preserve and develop, the indigenous culture and wisdom of the various peoples to whom the Gospel is preached. If education in our day finds a need to emphasize the values of decentralization, diversity and pluriformity, this would seem to be in full harmony with the current thrust of Catholic theology. While legitimate pluralism has its limits in the Church, the same is true in every human discipline, not least in the exact sciences.

The new tolerance for diversity within the Church should make it easier to deal with the so-called youth culture that has made its appearance in our country during the past decade. In principle there is no reason why youth, if it becomes a cultural grouping, should not be permitted to express the Gospel in its own way—as indeed is occurring in the rock operas now playing on Broadway. The post-conciliar years have seen the beginnings of liturgical forms devised for young people, in which they themselves participate in ways far more creative than anything witnessed by preconciliar Catholicism. Without wishing to deny that excesses have been committed, we may, I think, regard this development as generally enriching and healthy.

5. *Orientation to Service.* Finally, there is the question whether the Church can accept a deeper commitment to promote the human fulfillment of all men. Here again, the council has given clear and welcome guidance. The Pastoral Constitution declared in unequivocal terms that the Church has no other aims than those of Christ, who came to serve and not to be served (*Gandium et Spes*, §3). Seeking to promote the human values of peace, love, brotherhood and justice—which are also the values of the Kingdom of God—the Church "believes that she can contribute greatly toward making the family of man and its history more human" (*Gandium et Spes*, §40).

Throughout the Conciliar documents, a strong accent is

placed on the need for Catholics to cooperate with the whole family of man. They are urged to remember that the aspirations and anxieties of the men of our age are likewise those of the Christian people *(Gandium et Spes,* §2). In the Decrees on Ecumenism and Missionary Activity the Council encouraged Catholics to cooperate to the maximum with non-Catholic Christians and with men not of the Christian faith in building the world of tomorrow. Vatican II urged Catholics to lay aside all particularism, whether national or religious, and to acquire a truly global consciousness. It laid a solid theological groundwork for Christians to denounce with prophetic vigor any social systems or structures that oppress and dehumanize portions of the family of man.

It is time for me to draw a conclusion. On the basis of the Council documents, not to mention many postconciliar pronouncements, I think it safe to say that there are themes enough in contemporary theology to align Catholic religious education with the general thrust that is foreseen for the Jesuit school of the near future. I would go yet further and maintain that the Catholic understanding of the Christian faith, properly presented, could provide the most powerful motivation for accepting and promoting the new pedagogy that is becoming prevalent in Jesuit secondary education. For these new Catholic emphases to come home to the student, however, a deep theological conversion is needed in the faculty and administration of the schools.

We live in a time of crises. For many reasons the new image of the Church proposed by Vatican II has not been getting across to the faithful. The Church still appears to many as a stiff, old-fashioned, defensive and irrelevant institution, imposing in an authoritarian way a vast network of ideas and obligations that contribute nothing to the quality of human life. Father General in his talk here in New York last month to the Board of Directors of the JSEA mentioned that in many countries problems of personal faith, "which a generation ago were widespread at the university level, are now quite common among secondary school students." He referred to an instance in which he was told that in one Jesuit school in another country, the better students were "atheists only in religion class." Defections from the Church are occurring on a vast scale among youth of school and college age, and many of those who leave are the ones most responsive to the educational thrust which our schools are now seeking to adopt. Our young people, generally speaking, are not turning against Jesus, or against prayer or against spiritual values. They are not hostile to the principles from Vatican II of which I have spoken this morning. Rather, I think, they are impatient with the slowness of the Church to implement in its practical life the new vision proposed by the Council.

As the Jesuit high school moves toward the future, there will be an increasing need for theological updating, not simply in the curriculum, but in all the manifestations of religion to which the students are exposed—in the liturgy, in preaching, in student counseling and in the moral and spiritual attitudes of any teachers who identify themselves as Catholic. Only if these attitudes harmonize with the general program of the school, as set forth in documents such as those of the Jesuit Secondary Education Association, is there any hope of bridging the gap between a modernized pedagogy and an antiquated vision of the Church.

Can the Liturgy Speak to Today's Teenagers?

Michael Warren

The liturgy and teens. This is a difficult topic. Parents anguish over the topic as they try alternately to cajole and threaten reluctant teens to go to Mass. Teachers in Catholic high schools express concern over the large number of teens who have dropped out of Sunday Eucharist. Pastors stepping out before their Sunday congregations are not slow to notice the absence of most parish teens from the assembly. And if one is put in the position, as this writer has often been, of speaking some sense and some hope to those who would assist young people to take their next steps in Christian faith, one regularly faces the anguished question, "What can we do to get our kids to go to Mass?" What that question is lacking in phrasing and nuance is made up for in its earnestness. The following article is this writer's attempt to talk common sense and the possible rather than over-blown theory and pious exhortations about the matter of liturgy and teens. Written in response to the question that forms its title, these reflections reveal a conviction that the very question itself is badly put and betrays a misconception about liturgy. In order to make sense of a complex question, then, the following ideas approach liturgy from the point of view of *expressive human activity,* hoping by that approach to show how it relates to young people.

▲

My thesis is that liturgy is expressive human activity. The original Greek word for liturgy means "the action of the people," a meaning that suggests strongly that the people are expressing something by their action, that their action is expressive action. In its Christian sense, then, liturgy is an action by which a community expresses its attitude about the way it is between God and man, but more specifically about the way it is between this group gathered in the Spirit of Jesus and the one Jesus called Father. Quite simply, liturgy is a way of saying something. We have all had experiences where we just had to say something, where what was inside us just had to be expressed. Well, liturgy comes out of a similar thrust. Vatican II's *Constitution on the Sacred Liturgy* explicitly adverts to this character of liturgy when it says: "The liturgy is thus the outstanding means by which the faithful can express in their lives, and manifest to others, the mystery of Christ and the real nature of the true Church" (n. 2). In my judgment, it is this expressive character of liturgy that more than anything else helps us understand the various initiatives we must take with regard to Christian worship in particular circumstances.

Now there is an expressive character to all human activity. In fact one could argue that all human interaction falls on an impressive/expressive continuum.[1] One can see this more clearly in the matter of education. A large part of educational activity involves impressing on others concepts, facts, and skills. This is the impressive side of education. People need input; they need to be taught. Realities have to be communicated to them. Educators, however, recognize that impressive activity is not enough in the educational process. It must be completed by expressive activity, that is, the learner must come to express in her/his own way the ideas, facts, or skills that she/he is learning.

In education there are two levels of expressivity. Level one is a low level of expressivity, the one I would call "repetition." A child, say, is taught the multiplication tables and then is expected to be able to express them, that is, to repeat them. Until that level of expressivity is attained, the child really has not learned the tables. However, the math teacher hopes the child will go a step further and be able to use the multiplication tables creatively in solving actual problems as they arise. In other words, there is a second stage of expressivity, which comes when the person is not just repeating what she/he has been told but is actually using the skill or idea in a unique, original, and creative way. This creative act is what I would call level-two expressivity. As an English teacher, I always felt that my students would have truly profited by

my impressive activity if some of them became themselves creative writers, expressing in original works their imaginative perception of human existence. I was happy when in their composi-
tions, which they *had* to write, they showed originality and creativity, but I hoped that some day some of them would begin creating
out of their own creative urge, not out of my assignment.

We can see the impressive/expressive continuum clearly in the
interaction between mother and child. The mother repeats words
endlessly to the child, impressing on the consciousness of the child
human speech. And the child responds at first with level-one
expressivity. The child repeats or makes efforts to repeat some of
the more simple words. Eventually the child has a small repertoire
of words she/he can repeat. But true growth or another stage of
human activity occurs on that day when the mother lovingly makes
a request or gives a command to the child and the child responds
with the single word: "No!" That response is not simply being
repeated but is expressing in an original way the child's own will.
The mother may be shocked or dismayed but we can rejoice that a
new level of human expressivity has been reached, and that the
child is now expressing her/his own self.[2]

One further example. There was a time, not too long removed,
when teaching religion to children was centered dominantly (not
exclusively, but dominantly) on impressive activities and level-one
expressive activities. We were taught the Baltimore Catechism,
and we had to know it word for word. So much did we focus on
level-one expressivity that our repetitions were encouraged by
means of "the tickler," a long slender stick more accurately called a
rattan—because it definitely did not tickle. I would say that an
accurate though simple explanation of the catechetical renewal
throughout the world would be that focus has moved from level-
one expressivity to level-two expressivity. Words that have been
impressed on people are to take root in the soil of their own lives
and flower as their own special word, expressing in an original and
creative way the special meaning of that person's life. Those parents who still ask, "What does *that* have to do with religion?" may
simply not be aware of the importance of level-two expressivity.

If it is clear that there is an expressive character to all of
human life and that liturgy is expressive human activity, then we
can move to the next point, namely, that adolescence is a highly

expressive period of one's life. Expressivity is central in all human life, in all stages of development; yet it has a special urgency in adolescence. There are reasons for the acute expressivity of adolescence but I do not have time to go into them here. Instead let us remind ourselves of the way young people are and of how important expressivity is to them.

Listen to their speech. It has its own adolescent character of exaggeration. If anything, it is overexpressive. Listen to the words they use, especially the adverbs. Most adjectives used by young people employ backup adverbs to give added punch. Thus things are not just good or bad but "really, really good," or "really, really bad." Superlatives abound. It was not a wonderful party; it was the greatest, wildest, craziest party. ("It really was. Was it ever! I mean, I never saw anything like it—really!") Just allow yourself to hear their speech patterns, especially the adjectives and adverbs, and you will soon hear what I mean.

In other senses also, the speech of adolescents shows their acute expressivity. They are constantly checking, at least verbally, to make sure you are understanding what they are expressing. In other words their expressivity is so important to them they are fearful that it is inadequate or not being done properly. Did you ever notice how often young people use terms like "Do you know what I mean?" Adolescent speech tends to use as spoken punctuation marks certain expressions like "you know" and "right." (New York teens use "you know" most; those from parts of the Boston area use "right" a great deal.) Listen:

> I was working out at Jones Beach, you know, right there in front of Bathhouse 3, you know, and this guy comes up with this girl on his arm, a nice-looking girl in a yellow bikini, know what I mean? And he says to me, he says—and like I say, I'm looking at the girl in the yellow, you know—but otherwise I'm minding my own business or trying to, you know, and. . . .

In speech like this, expressivity is not just being carried on by someone telling a story. Expressivity is an underlying *issue*. Underlying the very story is a way of telling it that suggests that being understood is of key importance for the teller.

Of course, in addition to verbal expressivity, there are other senses in which expressivity is central to young people. Bodily and emotional expressivity are also important, probably because they are just being discovered as means of expressing the self. Read the poetry and witness the body contact of young people to see what I mean. Talk to teenage athletes of both sexes about what sports mean to them to get an inkling of that one aspect of their bodily expressivity. Any issue of *Seventeen,* a popular magazine for girls, betrays how important it is for girls in our culture to exhibit in their dress and features their self-image.[4] Clothes and music are also aspects of the acute expressivity of adolescence.

How if this overview of expressivity in young people has any merit, then it explains why catechetical programs for young people are dominated by expressivity. It is the nature of young people to have to discover their own word of faith. The flower of faith cannot be transplanted, because it would then be one person's flower of faith, growing in another person's soil. The flower of faith has to grow from seed in each person's special soil and grow as one's own flower.[5] In my experience, catechetical programs that keep young people passive or that are centered on level-one expressivity are doomed to failure. That is why I would say that for every sixty minutes of catechetical activity, forty to fifty minutes should involve significant and free expressive speech on the part of the kids themselves. In fact I would say that the key organ for the catechist dealing with teens is not the big mouth but the big ear. There is an important catechetical task of listening, of evocative listening, the kind of listening that encourages others to come to speech.[6]

Expressivity and Liturgy

What does all this have to do with liturgy? There are many implications for liturgy in these previous remarks about expressivity. First there is a danger of tending to think of liturgy as impressive activity rather than as expressive activity. In fact the very question that forms the title of this article seems to me to betray this tendency. The question asks, "Can the liturgy speak to teenagers?" Can it say something significant to teens? Yet the liturgy is not so much saying something *to* somebody as it is allowing people to express something of their lives and values by means of it. Liturgy is a vehicle for expression. There is a sense in which the liturgy is not making any statement to anybody outside of the liturgical assembly. The liturgy is itself a statement and is expressive activity of the assembly. The real question about young people and the liturgy is: How can the liturgy become a vehicle for young people to express in their lives the mystery of Christ and the real nature of the Christian community?

I am saying that liturgy, particularly Eucharistic liturgy, is an action expressing the faith of a believing community. Liturgy is an event in which faith comes to expression. It is also a mode of ritual expression in which faith becomes an event. Liturgy centers on faith coming to communal expression. Writing of the Eucharist in *Theological Studies,* liturgiologist John McKenna notes:

> It is normally, ideally, the faith of the Church here and now present, i.e., the local assembly, which shares in this realization [of the Eucharistic presence of Christ]. It may be true that, in the absence of a believing assembly here and now, the intention of the minister may supply the *minimum* required of a sacrament, *viz.,* the faith of the Church at large. This remains, however, the bare minimum, and one should build one's theology not on the minimum but on the ideal or normal. . . . Thus God freely and sovereignly effects a real presence in the Eucharist. He does so, however, through the faith of the Church, since this presence involves both Christ present and offering himself to his Church and the Church accepting and responding to this offer in faith. Moreover, involved in this mutual presence is an invitation to each individual in the assembly to personally share in this presence and thus have it attain the goal for which it was intended.[7]

Thus, for liturgy to become a vehicle for the young people or any people to express in their lives the mystery of Christ, the liturgy must be the prayer of a believing assembly. And there I suggest is a problem that is not just a problem of teenagers.

To avoid getting into a full critique of liturgical practice in our contemporary parish life, the following reflection must suffice. There was a time when we were all reminded of the dangers of servile work on Sunday. Servile work is that form of labor that has

its purpose apart from the enrichment of a person's inner life.[8]
Non-servile work is any kind of activity that has its end in the
activity itself. Artistic activity and even digging in one's yard is
non-servile since it is recognized as nourishing one's inner life. To
live a fully human life one needs non-servile activities; otherwise
one becomes a slave, a drudge. Based on this understanding of
servile work, then, I suggest that there is such a thing as servile
worship. This is worship that is engaged in out of obligation or
routine or out of cultural or family pressures. In worship that is
servile the purposes of the act of worship are not in the act itself.
Servile work is wrong only when it consumes all of one's life.
Servile worship is wrong all the time. In fact it is no worship at all.
It is pseudo worship. In some parishes young people's experience
of Sunday Mass is more like the scene depicted in the following
fantasy than like the coming together of a true worshipping assembly.

A Sunday Fantasy
(ideally to be choreographed and set to music)

It was a bright April Easter morning, with a cold blue sky sunning
itself waiting to be warmed. And they streamed down the sidewalks to
church. They streamed out of the sidestreets and out of neat houses and
down from tenements. And across the park they streamed, all decked in
finery. And they nodded and smiled to one another as they streamed.
Briskly they came from all directions. Hot coffee and warm buttered rolls
and the funnies were beckoning. There were no frogs in the gutters and the
locusts were nowhere to be seen.

It was to church they were coming. All knew what would happen:
Some would head for the front pews but most would head for the rear. And
the middle would be left for the latecomers trying to be casual. And they
would all wiggle out of their coats. And they would stuff parcels and purses
under the kneelers. Then they would prop themselves bum to knee in
prayer of hasty reverence, ending in the half-hidden, hasty sign of the
cross of a ball player on the free-throw line. No talk would be heard, just
heels clacking and shoes shuffling and coughing, the mindless silence.

But not this morning. For the prophet stood at the door, tall and thin,
like some lean male witch. And he shook the bony finger in their faces.
And his burning eyes pierced their stares and made the frogs and the
locusts hop out of nowhere. And this is what he said:

Servile worship is sin. Beware, beware lest you trespass in the Lord's
House.

Today is Sunday. Let there be no servile worship.

It is not allowed on the Lord's Day that you offer servile worship.

Except you be hungry for the Lord, you may not enter.

Except you be hurrying to the tomb to make sure he is not there, you must not enter.

Except you come to offer yourself, you must stay out.

Cease your Sunday sin of servile worship.

> Better to go to Seidmann's bakery before the rolls run out.
>
> Better to get an extra Sunday paper and linger over the real estate ads.
>
> Better hot coffee and a morning nap than to blaspheme the Lord's House and the Lord's Time and the Lord's Day.

For you are the Lord's and He wants more than your fifty minutes and your servile worship.

Put a young person with good Christian instincts in an assembly of servile worshippers, and she/he will not want her/his worship to be given in that servile context. Thus my first response to the question: How can liturgy become a vehicle for young people to express in their lives the mystery of Christ, is: Let them be part of a believing assembly gathered to express their love and gratitude to the Father for his deed in Jesus Christ. In some parishes, the problem might not be that young people do not want to go to Mass. It might instead be that they find that in fact they cannot worship in an assembly of servile obligation-fillers.

My second response to the question is: Remember that a crucial factor in all worship is what happens before worship. What life context does worship fit into? If worship is expressive activitiy, then it is expressing a perception of life based on a quality of reflectiveness. In worship we come in a sense to waste time on the Lord, to move from our servile world of pressure and work to a place where we can offer thanks to the Father for his many blessings, including the blessing of communion in the Spirit of Jesus. How does a person come to the point of wanting to offer this kind of worship, not out of servile compulsion but out of the thrust of one's inner life? I presume that such true worship does not occur automatically or mechanically. I have found myself that my Eucharistic prayer is as strong as my prayer outside the time of Eucharist. Only when the Sunday Eucharist (or daily Eucharist) is fitting into a context of prayer in my total life do I find that my own personal participation in Eucharistic liturgy has the quality of response it should have. This is my own experience, and from that experience I hypothesize that the need of most adults today is not so much for greater change in liturgical ritual as it is for a spirituality that will enrich daily prayer.

The same is true for young people. We need greater attention to their spirituality, that is, to the manner in which they attend to the presence of God in their total lives. A key contribution to the faith development and eventually to the liturgical development of young people is being made by informal prayer groups and by youth retreats. On a Christian experience weekend for teens they are coming to Eucharistic liturgy from a context of grappling with questions of faith, of sharing their own faith perceptions, and of prayer. Liturgy speaks powerfully in that context. Prayer programs are enriching the quality of reflectiveness of young people as well as their spirit of responsiveness to God. If we think about our own past history, who have been the people who have led us to a deeper spirituality? Who were the ones who helped us make progress in prayer? Were they not also the ones who helped us treasure our moments of more formal worship? The one affects the other.

I find lots of adults who would like to teach things to kids, to do a work of impression on them. I find many more who like to take kids on trips or supervise their sports programs. But I do not find enough adults who are willing to engage in spiritual direction of young people, that is, adults who are willing to own up to their own faith commitment as a means of helping young people begin to own up to or at least discover theirs.[9]

A third reflection has to do with the liturgy of the word. If it is true that adolescence is a special time of expressivity, then this insight must guide our approach to the liturgy of the word. Actually every homily should be highly expressive, in the sense that it should touch the hidden longings present but only dimly recognized in the assembled community. Human speech captivates us when it expresses and brings to the light what we had been feeling or suspecting but could not articulate for ourselves.[10] In that sense, every homily is expressive not just of the preacher but also of the community. To achieve this quality the preacher must know the lives of his people. He must have a feel for them. He has to have allowed the word of God to stir him up. He must have himself moved from darkness into light as regards this particular word. Unfortunately, instead of moving from darkness to light some homilists only move from silence to speech. Can we attend to the deeper needs, to the hurts and hopes, struggles and strivings of our young people? Can we be in touch with them in such a way that when we speak we do indeed speak not just to their lives but out of their lives? This is one aspect of the liturgy of the word.

There is another aspect, however. Young people need themselves to discover their own word. They need to listen to one another, to hear the gospel according to Matthew, Mark, Luke, John, as it has been discovered by Jane or John Doe. They need very much to dialogue about the gospel. They need to talk it over, talk it out in their own words. Unfortunately we still have not yet caught up with the articulateness of modern man. Even as a college theology teacher I must remind myself again and again of what I keep discovering about young people: "Your words, Mike, are of secondary importance; their words are of primary importance." In reviewing previous classes, what the students seem to remember best are not the things I said but rather the insights they themselves articulate in the class.

Finally, I wish to call your attention to a document published in 1974 by the Sacred Congregation for Divine Worship, a document I think has hidden in it much common sense about liturgy. The document is called *Directory for Masses with Children.* [11] It is a list of guidelines for liturgical expression suitable for children, but it contains many principles that could and I think *must* be applied to liturgical expression for many different age levels beyond childhood. Stress in the document is on leading persons according to their age, psychological condition, and social situation. This document, it seems to me, opens many doors with regard to introducing young people to a fuller liturgical life that is truly expressive of their relationship with God. Today we need many varieties of Eucharistic assemblies in which young people can express their faith: small groups of teens, large assemblies of young people, faith-filled adult communities that teens can affiliate with.

I realize that a myriad other questions have been ignored here: the proper use of para-Eucharistic forms of worship, training youth as leaders of song in worship, the role of youth as preachers of the word in many current settings such as youth retreats and programs to help younger persons prepare for confirmation. My thesis here has been that any attempt to assist young people to grow in faith through worship must take into account the specific kind of people they are. My conviction has also been that the Eucharist for us Christians is our special gift. In the act of handing it on to our youth, we receive it back with a new realization of its giftedness. Young people offer us that opportunity.

NOTES

1. The ideas contained in the following paragraphs, though not necessarily the terminology, are commonplace in many different works of education theory. See, especially, Paulo Freire, *Pedagogy of the Oppressed* (New York: Herder and Herder, 1970), pp. 75-118 and Freire's *Cultural Action for Freedom* (Cambridge: Harvard Educational Review Monograph Series, 1970), pp. 12-14. See also a provocative, brief section of Malcolm Knowles's *The Adult Learner: A Neglected Species* (Houston: Gulf, 1973), pp. 173-175, where he distinguishes between reactive and pro-active learning. The role of expressivity in religious functioning is also a commonplace theme in the sociology of religion. A good treatment with much potential application to Christian ritual can be found in Joachim Wach, *The Comparative Study of Religions* (New York: Columbia Univ. Press, 1961), pp. 59-143, esp. 97-120.

2. John Macmurray provides a useful analysis of the interaction between mother and child in *Persons in Relation*. Macmurray adverts to the character of delight and of play in the mother-child interaction, a character that suggests the unity and centrality of the *relationship* between mother and child. It is in affirming the centrality of that bond as a human relationship that the artificial distinctions made here between the impressive and expressive make most sense and are most useful. See John Macmurray, *Persons in Relation* (London: Faber and Faber, 1970), pp. 44-63 and *passim*.

3. Lonergan's analysis of religious experience and its outcomes hinges on the key role of expressivity. Although *Method in Theology* gives little specific attention to liturgy, Lonergan is speaking of the same reality in discussing the way community invites expression of the meanings that bind it together. The role of the community in expressing these meanings is a central issue in Lonergan's system. See Bernard Lonergan, *Method in Theology* (New York: Herder and Herder, 1972), pp. 108-119.

4. Any periodical targeted for various ages and segments of the youth population can be revealing as to the issues and tasks that are preoccupying their attention. The marketeers pay careful attention to the needs, dreams, and hopes of those they attempt to influence. Probably too little attention has been paid to this literature as a source of data about youth relevant to their growth in faith.

5. Gabe Huck in a recent discussion of children's liturgies called forceful attention to the dangers of speaking of "adapting liturgy" as if liturgy were something rigid and alien from life, that had to be artificially tailored to a person's experience. Actually liturgy is an expression of the life of the people. When that function is obstructed, then attention must be paid to correcting the situation. What some might call "adaptation" of the liturgy is actually an intelligent clearing away of obstacles hindering persons of any age or culture from coming to ritual expression of Christian faith. In this sense, then, adaptation is a process of letting liturgy be liturgy. See Gabe Huck, "Review" of Edward Matthews's *Celebrating Mass with Children, Worship,* 51:2 (March, 1977), 196-197.

6. What is said here of youth is just as applicable to adults. Adults need, and in the writer's experience welcome, channels for expressing their experience of God as much as do teens. Possibly this is one reason why so many middle-aged and older adults attend Sunday liturgies specifically designed for children and teens.

7. John H. McKenna, "Eucharistic Epiclesis: Myopia or Microcoms? *Theological Studies,* 36:2 (1975), 271.

8. Josef Pieper has a provocative section on servile activity in his fine little essay *Leisure: The Basis of Culture* (New York: Mentor-Omega, 1963), pp. 46-55. Rich resources for foundational reflection on liturgy can be found both here and in Pieper's later, *In Turn with the World: A Theory of Festivity* (Chicago: Franciscan Herald Press, 1973).

9. In this writer's opinion, far too little writing has been done on the theory and practice of spirituality and spiritual direction for young people. Though some Catholics working in Catholic high schools, colleges, and on youth retreats are in fact developing programs, few have written of these efforts. Two Catholics working and writing on this matter are: Mark Link, S.J., *You* (Chicago: Argus, 1977), and Richard Costello, Director of the Youth Ministry Office in Norwhich, Conn. At the 1977 Youth Ministry Workshop at St. John's University, Jamica, N.Y., Costello gave a week-long series of lectures entitled, "Ministering to the Spritual Development of Teens." His article "Imaginative Prayer for Teens" will appear in the October 1977 issue of *Religion Teacher's Journal;* other material is in process.

10. A statement on this matter worth frequent rereading by those called to preach can be found in Henri Nouwen, *The Wounded Healer,* Chapter 2, "Ministry to a Rootless Generation" (New York: Doubleday, 1972), pp. 25-47. Some readers will be more familiar with this chapter in its earlier (article) form entitled "Generation Without Fathers," *Commonweal* (June 12, 1970). See also the chapter "Preaching: Beyond the Re-telling of the Story" in *Creative Ministry* (New York: Doubleday, 1971), pp. 22-40.

11. Sacred Congregation for Divine Worship, *Directory for Masses with Children* (Washington: USCC, 1974).

Radio:
A Ministry to Feelings

Don Kimball

Father Don Kimball's work of reaching out to youth through the medium of radio has attracted a good bit of attention among Catholics in youth ministry. Many have expressed admiration for his low-key yet moving broadcasts entitled "Music With a Message." Few, however, have considered the possibility of starting a radio ministry to youth in their area. They reason that they have neither Don Kimball's talent for spontaneity nor his contacts in the local radio industry.

In hopes of encouraging many more persons to use radio as a means of communicating with youth, Father Kimball has contributed a lively account of his own experience in radio, together with some practical how-to suggestions for those wishing to get started. His account suggests that getting into this ministry is easier and the opportunities more available than many would suspect.

▲

THE DISC JOCKEY

(From Bob Talbert's column, August 4, 1971, in the Detroit Free Press. Reprinted with permission of the author.)

Disc jockeys are the freaks of the media midway. They are also the single most influential, persuasive and powerful force in the vast world of communication.

237

Sorry, editorial writers. Sorry, network newsmen. Sorry, Johnny, Dick, David, and Merv. Sorry *Newsweek* and *Time*. Sorry, *New York Times*. Sorry, Madison Avenue. Sorry, record companies. Sorry, syndicated columnists. Sorry, A.P. and U.P.I. All of you may have the more important roles in communications, but that little pipsqueaky rock jock on some obscure 5,000 watter can move and shake his audience, baby, like you wouldn't believe.

The love relationship between disc jockeys and their audience is frightening to behold. Other communicators often . . . most of the time, really, have a certain love and hate relationship with their audience. "I stay half mad with Walter Cronkite all the time, but I watch him anyway." "Sure, I read the editorials . . . I don't agree with all of them, believe me . . . but I read 'em anyway." And so on and so forth.

But not disc jockeys. You love 'em or hate 'em, and listen only to the ones you like. No one listens to radio out of hate. Radio is a love object. It's a friend, an auditory security blanket, in the home and car. It's hard to be alone with the radio on.

And the objects of your affection come in a variety as wide as the range of their salaries . . . from $300 a month to $300,000 a year. All of them have an overriding characteristic . . . they need to be heard, based on the firm belief that you want to hear what they have to say. Newspaper columnists have this same strange belief. Everybody out there in Audience, U.S.A. wants to know how we think, feel, and react. Please don't tell us you don't!

Disc jockeys . . . be they record spinners, talk showers, rip and readers, etc., all seek a "thing". They seek their niche in their ego tripping, super competitive world that will set them apart from the other on-the-air personalities. Some find their "thing" is their voice. Some have a natural wit. Some get by on style. Some rely on production and gimmicks and scripted schtick. Some rely on phones and the audience. But all have a power that is unequalled in the world of communication!

I am a Catholic priest, working part time in a parish, plus the Youth Ministry Coordinator for the Diocese of Santa Rosa, California, and I am a disc jockey.

Ten years ago, these ministries would have rarely interlocked. There were occasional priests who "worked with youth" but youth ministry, as we know it today, has become a new model for a perennial need. I don't know why all these roles in one person should blow people's minds, but as I reflect on it, the whole thing blew *my* mind as I tried to adjust to the challenge each role offered.

Becoming a priest was a big role-change for me eight years ago. Spiritually, I became a "marked man" living my life in a fish bowl. Moving to a diocesan office has forced me to stop the criticism and start the action. However, the biggest change for me has been the disc jockey bit.

In one sense, I am not a disc jockey, that is, a paid, full-time employee of a radio station. In another sense, I am. I do a weekly rock-music show that requires the skills and awareness of a professional. But it didn't start that way.

It all began six years ago in Eureka, California, during my first assignment as an associate pastor. The local radio station, up for license renewal, needed to show the Federal Communications Commission that it was fulfilling its promised public service commitment and needed a locally produced show; so I was contacted through another priest ("You work with teenagers; you can do it"). Fortunately, the music format at the station was rock music, and, after some terrifying doubts, I agreed to do the show provided I could use their music. A week later, never having even seen the inside of a radio station before, I went on the air—"live"—with *REFLECTION: MUSIC WITH A MESSAGE,* a program that was to run several years on Sunday evenings at 9:00.

In the beginning, I didn't know a turntable from a cart-machine. I just designed a thirty-minute show from the available music each week, then went to the station and did it. The disc jockey on duty ran all the equipment while I was allowed to operate one switch: number 4, the microphone. Listening to tapes that copied my first broadcasts off the air was scary. (Listening *now* to those early tapes is *really* scary, beyond my coping ability.) I was projecting my voice, as in pulpit, instead of laying back, as in friendship. That needed work. On top of that, within three weeks I had exhausted my knowledge of rock music and had used up all the songs I really knew. So I started spending hours—late hours—at the station, listening to songs, making notes. I began preparing my show *at* the station, taking advantage of all the records there. Gradually, the disc jockeys and other employees started dropping into the production room where I was working to chat and tell jokes and stories. We came to discover each other as people, and then things really took off. The disc jockeys began to teach me some of their broadcast tricks; then I was invited to join their "D.J." basketball team; and then there were the Christmas parties, the office parties, the benefits, the remote broadcasts. I was making it in *their* world, and I knew it.

Within a year I was running all the controls on the air (having received my license from the FCC), and was picking my show-themes from relationships and feelings instead of abstract theology. I had learned by now that most music focuses on relationships: people coming together, people falling away from each other, people alone. These were the areas in which Jesus ministered; why not a priest? I had a hook into something important here and didn't want to let it go. People needed healing in their relationships, in their feelings. I could speak to that and the music would *be* the message.

Rock music, I discovered, is effective more for its beat and cadence than for its words. Not only could I give the listeners a message; I could give them *momentum*. Pacing the show became important: open fast, use fast-moving songs in the beginning of the show; locate the listener in the feeling area; don't put two slow-paced songs back-to-back (that loses momentum); keep the block-buster, big-message songs in the middle of the show, then pivot on the "problem" and move toward hopeful options; tie it together in the middle with a personal experience shared over instrumental music; play up-tempo, hopeful songs going out at the end of the show; and never let the music stop!

Compared to TV, radio is much more effective in reaching teenagers. Their radios are always on at home, in cars, at parks and beaches, at school, even in the classrooms (watch for those earplugs!).

Production of a radio show is ten times easier than a TV show. I've worked with TV too, and I know! In radio, the image is created *internally* by the listener, making the impact more personal. Most people listen to the radio while alone or with one other person; so I become an intimate friend, one side of a vital dialogue. If people's greatest need is to be cared for, then radio is a great place to do ministry. TV doesn't quite have the same credibility or the same intimacy.

I am no longer stationed in Eureka. A year ago I was transferred to Santa Rosa; so I needed a new base to broadcast. Through the San Francisco Archdiocesan Communications Center I entered the radio world at a whole new level: Radio Station KFRC, the biggest radio market in the Bay Area: huge reach, top ratings, and the best equipment, with engineers who really know how to operate the equipment. Live broadcasting is out of the question for this kind of a show in this kind of market. Also, only the engineers touch the equipment. And public service time is from 2:00 A.M. to 7:00 A.M., Sunday mornings. I was assigned to 6:15 A.M., and later the station decided also to run the show at 2:45 A.M.; so now it runs twice on Sunday mornings. When the operations manager at KFRC told me they were going to run the show a second time on Sunday, I thought, "Wow! Noon, or late evening". Then he told me: "2:45 in the morning" and I must have winced because he grinned and cracked, "Well, do you want to be popular or do you want to minister?" I felt like one of the sons of Zebedee.

So now this humble son journeys each week into San Francisco (fifty-five miles from Santa Rosa), coming into the station on Wednesday afternoon around 2:00. I work for two hours in the disc jockey office, listening to current songs, hot albums, and also "oldie-mouldie-goldie" hits from the past. As I plow through the music available to me (and there are tons!) I work up a list of "possible" songs, including the introduction ("intro") time and running-length of each. Within an hour and a half, I have twenty to thirty titles listed. Then I gaze over the list and look for relational "events." Songs start clicking together and I draw up a "lay-sheet," listing in sequence the songs I will play in the show. It is unreal how different songs snuggle up to one another according to a relational theme.

Did I say "theme"? Right! Because it is only at this point—as I'm walking my play-sheet to the Xerox machine to copy it for my engineer—that I select the title theme for the show. I don't start with a theme and then build a show around it. The theme comes from the music. The activity inside the music suggests the relational areas I will deal with that week. I've seen too many people do violence to a song by trying to bend it to say something it really isn't saying. The people listening *know* the songs, and they know when the meaning is twisted.

Since the format of the show is designed to minister to feelings, I move into those areas to do some healing. I'm no psychologist, and I don't pretend to be. Instead, I become a journeyman joining the listeners in *their* world, sharing some of my hurts and growth experiences, sending some care, understanding and hope. This vulnerable approach is somewhat hard to handle with my friendly engineer peering at me through the glass. I pray the Lord never gives me a "crowd-shot" apparition of my whole listening audience (about 100,000). The thought of whispering "soft-heavies" into the hearts of all those people is a little overwhelming for this music-minister.

Like a conversation with someone, "Reflection" has an integrated theme, but usually parts of the show hit the hardest. So it is important not to pour it on too heavily. The listener needs room to move and respond, some space to supply the real feelings inside. I become a sharing friend and a fellow-listener, not an expert. I am not telling my listener-friend how to correct or reform. Instead, I offer an ear; I become transparent myself, melting into the music, the mood, the struggle, the doubts, the healing. I am with that person because Jesus is. When people have a friend, there is hope. And when there is hope, there is always a solution: *their* solution, not mine.

That's why I don't use a script. I ad-lib the whole show and share only what is going on inside me. In the beginning, I wrote out what I wanted to say, then later, I just outlined what I wanted to talk about. Now, I pretty well know what I'm going to deal with and the rest happens when I open my mouth. I operate with the confidence that spontaneity is God's gift to me and with the security that, if I blow a talk-up, we can stop the tape and edit. So I become free to fall into the music and share what is going through me. I find now that while I am recording, I am praying. Feedback on the show tells me that the listeners are praying too, praying the music, praying the feelings, celebrating the healing.

I don't think most adults realize how powerful music and the media world are yet. Media have an unseen audience with unmeasurable results. Media are still generally regarded as "the enemy." I remember in my first years of the seminary that we were not allowed to listen to radio or watch TV. I agree that some of the music and messages of the media world are destructive. A lot of the content, though, is excellent. And most of it is at least neutral, waiting to be used by the right person. A weapon is simply a tool in the hands of the wrong person. Media are tools of communication that loving, Christian people can use for ministry. If we abdicate this opportunity, then we have no business blasting the media for the junk they have to broadcast. Who is responsible for the Good News in this world? We are! Not station managers.

Media people are first of all *people* themselves. They are looking for some meaning to their lives as well as the listeners, viewers, and readers they serve. If they see something good, they will offer their public service time to share it with others. I've listened to many a public service director *beg* for some quality programming. Only now does there seem to be some small interest here and there in getting into media with some solid ministry.

I share this article as a story because it happened as a story. It happened because of relationships. It happened because I responded to something that fell in my lap. I didn't seek it, but was called to it. I didn't discover my gifts for this until I needed those gifts.

If people ask me how to get into radio, I tell them to start in the small markets first: build relationships with media people, share your dream. Chances are they will be willing to help design formats and teach skills. There is more than one format; in fact, there are millions of designs and formats that could be used, as many as people's creative minds can invent. Teenagers themselves could design shows from their own awareness of their music and their perception of God, other people, and themselves. How about taping rap-sessions and then playing the best chunks back punctuated by appropriate music selections? Many stations are playing shows with just that format right now. Sometimes Catholic disc jockeys at radio stations will work with teenagers in producing a weekly show. Believe it or not, even non-Catholic disc jockeys and program directors are willing to help! Some might even become—gasp!—friends.

Once you are into radio, there are a lot of residual benefits. It is usually very easy to produce sound tracks for slide shows by using the same skills that go into producing a radio show. Then one can take instamatic slides of the youth group or retreats and create some wild happenings. One person I know records a sound track focusing on retreat growth experiences, then brings a camera to the retreat and shoots slides of everyone on the retreat on Friday night, rushing them to an overnight photo-developer. Sunday morning at the Mass of Celebration: zap, a slide show, customized to that group.

Good slide shows, especially in small media markets, can be produced for television. We did this several times in Eureka. In addition, I produced over twenty-five slide-meditations that a local TV station in Eureka broadcast for its Sign-on's, one every morning. I found that when I did favors like that for radio and TV stations, they did favors for me and the programs I was working with.

There is much more to the media world than I have discussed in this article. But no one can really understand fully what I have already shared until they open up to a call to ministry and realize that the Lord is working through each of us to renew His people. If the opportunity is there, then it is a call, an invitation.

All ministers are scared to death of what will happen next because we know how quickly God moves sometimes, and how our lives are changed by the way He moves. I know that fear and the excitement that has been in my life ever since that first Sunday night over six years ago when I went on the air with: "This is REFLECTION: MUSIC WITH A MESSAGE. I'm Father Don Kimball. And this week: PANIC BUTTON!"